The Ocean of Grace

Tributes to Amma's All-Embracing Love

Volume 4

The Ocean of Grace

Tributes to Amma's All-Embracing Love

Volume 4

Edited by Sarvaga Grace Antrobus
Co-edited by Julius Heyne

Mata Amritanandamayi Center
San Ramon, California, USA

The Ocean of Grace – Volume 4

Tributes to Amma's All-Embracing Love

Edited by Sarvaga Grace Antrobus
Co-edited by Julius Heyne

Published by:
Mata Amritanandamayi Center
P.O. Box 613
San Ramon, CA 94583
United States

International:
www.amma.org

In India:
www.amritapuri.org
inform@amritapuri.org

Contents

	Preface	**9**
	The Path of Knowledge *A Message from Amma*	**13**
1.	**Keep Coming Towards *This*** *Narendra - USA*	***15***
2.	**Love Has No Distance** *Chinmayi - Italy*	**27**
3.	**From Death to Immortality — Our Journey with Amma** *Prakash Bhaskaran - USA*	**37**
4.	**The Shedding of All Masks** *Dhanya - France*	**51**
5.	**The Search for the Satguru** *Rishi - Finland*	**63**
6.	**Guiding Seekers of All Traditions** *Nirupama Orona - USA*	**75**
7.	**"Find *You*! Find *That*!"** *Devapriyan - France*	**83**
8.	**Amma's Grace** *Anadi - Finland*	**94**
9.	**Nothing Greater than the Guru** *Surya - USA*	**105**
10.	**Happiness Is a Decision** *Praseeda - France*	**115**
11.	**Amma's Way to Wellness** *Dr. Shankar Logaraja - India*	**127**
12.	**Indescribable Longing** *Kavyakala - USA*	**138**

13. **Gratitude and Grace** 149
Devanath - Spain

14. **Amma's Inner Presence** 159
Hansa Bhaskar - USA

15. **Amma's Love —
Lessons on Pain & Surrender** 168
Uday Allendes - Chile

16. **Guru Vākyam** 180
Meera Venkatesh - India

17. **The Two Moon Eclipses** 189
Devanath - France

18. **Amma's Family** 201
Ahalya - France

19. **The Path of Love** 212
Raghu Mannam - India

20. **To Be Grateful Is to Flourish** 220
Vikasita - Spain

21. **The Strength of That Love** 229
Dr. Sirisha Chakravarthy - India

22. **The Essence of Motherhood Is Love** 241
Marieke Engelbregt - Netherlands

23. **Sākṣhī — The Witness** 250
Dr. Chakravarthy - India

24. **Love Letter to My Mother** 262
Kuvalaya Nayana - Chile

25. **"Everything Will Be Okay
Now That You've Come."** 273
Radhika Murali Mohan - USA

Glossary 284

Pronunciation Guide 300

Acknowledgements 302

"We are all beads strung together
on the same thread of love."

— *Amma*

Preface

"God doesn't call the qualified, he qualifies the called" — this is the first line of the first satsang in this book. God does not see whether we are worthy or not when he accepts and loves us. He can never isolate or keep anyone away from him. Can a mother point to one among her children who is disadvantaged somehow and keep that child away? A mother's heart can only have equal love for her children. Their qualities and characters may vary, but for a mother, they are all her own. If a child is less capable than the others, the mother will spend more time with that son or daughter and try to find a way to rectify those shortcomings. She will patiently try again and again to train him or her to overcome those limitations.

If this is the nature of an ordinary mother, we can see this quality multiplied abundantly in the Universal Mother. But is it possible for us to see such a mother? A Universal Mother who encompasses within her the love of all the mothers in this world...is she for real? The answer can be found in the book series *The Ocean of Grace*. Each writer's words escort us to the presence of the Universal Mother. We are filled with wonder as we read about how each person gets to know about Amma, comes to meet her, reaches her abode at Amritapuri, travels with her, and the various other incidents and experiences with her in their lives.

Amma's words and actions reveal the fundamental responsibilities of a mother. Amma leads her children not to a temporary abeyance of their sorrows but to eternal freedom from sorrow. For this, Amma does not ask anyone to come to her with advanced degrees or qualifications. She only hopes they will call her "mother" from the depths of their heart. Even if they are unable to do so, she is content to see the expressions that blossom spontaneously on their faces as their hearts yearn to call her mother. This is enough for her; she will hold her children close and embrace and kiss them with love. It is not a mere kiss; it is an assurance. An assurance that she will not let the child she holds slip away from her hands.

Each person has attempted to convey, using words, the indescribable experience of Amma's presence in their lives — both in joy and in sorrow. Each experience described in this volume acts as a guide for us as we go through various circumstances in life, both favorable and adverse. When they show us the path they have travelled, it becomes easier for us to move forward on our own life's path. Because it is Amma who has led them by the hand and taken them forward, the ones who travel on this path reach life's fulfillment.

Each person's experience described in this book will help illumine our life's course.

Swami Jnanamritananda Puri

The Path of Knowledge

A Message from Amma

Children, the root cause of all problems is ignorance of our true nature. How can a king who does not know that he is king discharge his duties as a ruler properly? How can he enjoy royal pleasures? We are presently trapped in such a state of self-forgetfulness.

The scriptural texts say that we are whole and perfect, and that our true nature is that of infinite peace and bliss. But gripped by the delusion that we are the body, we frantically search for happiness and comfort outside. This delusion is the cause of all sorrow. For this reason, the sole remedy for all our problems is right knowledge. Ask, "Who am I truly? What is my true nature?" Inquiring into the self and discovering our real essence is the path of knowledge.

Each second, thousands of cells in our body die and new ones are born. Similarly, our mind, thoughts, emotions and intellectual abilities are all constantly changing. Yet, the awareness of 'I' remains unchanged amidst all these changes. Therefore, in truth, we are not connected at all to the body, mind and intellect. We are eternally free and of the nature of bliss.

Once, the goddess of darkness abducted the prince from the land of light and imprisoned him in a dark cell. She stationed many guards there to make sure that the prince could not escape. Sunlight seeped in through a small crack in the wall of his prison cell and advised him, "Give your crown and royal garb to the guards. They are greedy for wealth and will set you free."

The prince bribed his prison guards with his ornaments, robes and crown. They unlocked the prison doors and set him free. The sun god then gave the prince a sword, with which he slayed the goddess of darkness. When he returned to the land of light, the king anointed him the next king.

In this story, the goddess of darkness is ignorance. The sun god is the guru. The ornaments and robes are emblems of desire. The sword gifted by the sun god represents knowledge. The inner meaning of this story is that the disciple who heeds the guru's advice and gives up his desires gains the light of knowledge, which dispels the darkness of ignorance.

In truth, the experience of the self is not something to be gained. It is always with us. We are of the nature of truth. But ignorance has hidden from us the experience of the self, just as clouds cover our eyes but cannot conceal the sun.

Once, a child fought with another over a toy. He cried and screamed. Finally, he cried himself to sleep. While he slept, the toy slipped from his fingers and fell to the ground. The other child took it and went away. The first child continued sleeping peacefully. Only the 'I' exists in sleep. Therefore, there is peace and joy. When he wakes up, the notion of duality—the sense of 'I' and 'mine'—and consequently, desire and sorrow, arise. Therefore, even while interacting with the world, we must gain the awareness of non-duality. Then, no matter what happens in the world, our inner peace will never be affected.

1

Keep Coming Towards *This*

Narendra – USA

I heard a statement recently that said,"*God doesn't call the qualified, he qualifies the called.*" While most others would have given up on me long ago, Amma never has. She patiently orchestrates a transformation and she endures my growing pains. After years of misguided seeking, it's finally under Amma's great wings of protection that I have found a place I call home. I can only bow down to Amma with utmost gratitude.

Nothing in life has given me a greater sense of purpose and belonging than knowing I am a tiny thread in this massive net of goodness that Amma has cast out across our world. Nothing can compare to the feeling of completeness and fulfillment I get from serving in this global movement of Amma's love and compassion.

Whenever people used to question my choice to live with Amma in Amritapuri, I would answer them rhetorically, "If you lived 2,000 years ago and had the chance to live with and serve Christ, or 2,500 years ago with the Buddha, would you do it?" Well, I believe that we are all actively living that same precious reality right now.

In fifteen years of living in Amritapuri, I had one opportunity to receive a private room darśhan. As always with Amma, the timing was perfect. There was conflict in my sēvā (selfless service), and I was feeling discouraged by the mess I was discovering within myself.

When I walked through Amma's door, her eyes lit up seeing a notebook I was carrying in my hand. It was my prayer book.

She instantly nodded her omniscient approval. It's been an important practice for me over the years to write a morning prayer and summarize the day of sādhanā (spiritual practices) and sēvā at night. But I've had the habit of starting prayer books, then failing to fill all their pages. This was a recurring theme throughout my life — good at starting things, but not so good at sustaining or finishing them.

In that darśhan (Amma's divine embrace), I broke down in Amma's arms. I confessed that I didn't think I could take it anymore and was secretly considering it best to leave the āśhram. Amma paused, smiled and said, "*Amma thinks you should stay.*"

Her response carried great meaning for me. I lacked confidence that I could overcome all the obstacles and progress on this path. So Amma instilled confidence in me — in just those few words, like a sūtra — "*Amma thinks you should stay.*"

After a life of running, Amma was telling me that she accepted me here in spite of my shortcomings, and that she would give me the strength to stay.

Amma speaks about the importance of lakṣhya bōdham, having the clear intention to reach a goal. It is very difficult to focus on the goal without wavering. I know that I do not have enough strength to walk alone on this path, but even if I fail one thousand times, I am sure that I will succeed because Amma is holding my hand.

Michael Jordan, the basketball legend said, "I've missed more than nine-thousand shots in my basketball career; I've lost almost three-hundred games. Twenty-six times I've been trusted to take the game winning shot and missed. I've failed over and over again in my life, but I still keep going out on the court. And that's why I succeed." When we have the correct perspective, our failures are seen as mere setbacks and our mistakes become the stepping stones to success.

***

Let me share a brief background of what ultimately brought me to Amma. I was an only child and my parents divorced when I was very young. I was raised primarily by my mother. She worked extremely hard to give me a good education. But I did not receive a spiritual or value-based education.

In my first year of university, love for music led me to take a job as the DJ at my university's discotheque. This developed into a ten-year career DJ-ing in one of America's most notorious underground nightclubs in the 1990s.

During my second year of university, my mother was diagnosed with a very aggressive disease similar to Parkinson's. She was the closest person in my life and I didn't have the tools to cope with her rapid demise. I took refuge in all the wrong things, because I didn't have a conscious contact with God in my life. After my mother died, I slipped into terrible darkness. When the pain was great enough and the consequences severe enough, I reached out for help. It was then that I was introduced to spiritual principles and the possibility of a better way of life. I failed to change my behavior at first; many times. But in exchange for all that failure, I received grace in disguise – the precious gift of desperation.

Amma says, "It is when you have tried and failed that you are truly able to surrender. Though you fail time and again, you continue to try until finally there comes a point when you accept your failure; you fully understand your incapacity to move forward. It is at this point that you surrender. So keep trying."

After admitting defeat, I think my first significant act of surrender was to quit the club scene and start an entirely new life – a new job and a new circle of friends. Doors started opening and I discovered a wonderful fellowship based in spirituality. It was around this time that I became tangibly aware of God's presence in my life.

One of my mentors from that time told me, "If you put as much effort into seeking God as you used to put into getting high, you would make fast progress in spiritual life."

He was pointing to a universal truth in our experience; that we harness tremendous power and unshakeable determination whenever we cherish a strong desire in our minds. Nothing stands in our way. So, the question is, where do we put our attention? Sri Ramakrishna Paramahamsa[1] said, "You get what you seek. Those who seek wealth and power get that. Those who seek God attain Him."

To illustrate this point, let me share a story from some time I spent with a Vietnam War veteran who was trying to recover from alcohol and drug addiction. He had been homeless and hustling on the streets for many years and was given admission into a substance abuse program at the VA Hospital in San Francisco. He was in his late sixties, absolutely broke and with no family. At night, I would pick him up from the VA and together we would attend a group for spiritual upliftment. I got him an inspiring book and he found so much hope and comfort in reading about God's love and compassion.

One night, driving home, he asked me to stop at a nearby store. He emptied his pockets to count the few coins he had left to his name, then ran into the store. Five minutes later, he came out grasping a little paper bag. I was shocked by what was inside. A highlighter pen. He used his last coins to buy a pen to highlight words that gave him solace. This man had reached a bottom in life that most of us can't even fathom, but he was still determined to come out of that bondage and get closer to God.

---

[1] Spiritual master (1836 – 1886) from West Bengal.

Around this time, I began learning yoga and meditation. In the beginning, I practiced like my hair was on fire. One of the most valuable lessons I learned from meditation was that I could actually be present with what was unpleasant and uncomfortable. I began to replace the habit of wanting to escape and run away with a new habit of staying still and observing. This was incredibly empowering and gave me a new sense of inner strength and self-esteem.

After attending a few meditation retreats and being inspired by Eastern teachings, I decided to make a pilgrimage to India. A friend of mine, who had been encouraging me to meet Amma for years, was here in the āśhram at that time. Though I wasn't really interested in meeting Amma, that night I started searching for flights. There happened to be one flight to Kochi for $300 cheaper than anywhere else in India. We all know that doesn't happen. So, I booked it. That night I had a dream. My mother, wrapped in a white sari, came towards me in the garden of my childhood home. She embraced me tightly. I woke up drenched in tears. I felt my mother's love for the first time in many years. Only later, when I saw Amma's gait, did I realize that it was, in fact, Amma who came in that dream, in a form that my heart would recognize.

Immediately, I fell in love with this place and was blown away by the sheer power of being in Amma's presence. I used to sit in front of our Kālī mūrti, the deity in the temple, every morning after ārati[2] and write poems. I was so inspired. Here's one of those early poems:

Whenever we touch our heads to the Feet of the Lord
A rainbow is born somewhere on earth.

---

[2] A traditional ritual involving the waving of a lighted lamp to the Guru or deity usually done towards the end of worship.

Whenever we forgive the pain caused by someone we love
A thunderstorm is added to the desert sky.

Whenever we strive to live by a few simple truths
A fresh stroke of color is painted on the wings of a bird.

Whenever we recognize the beauty inside our enemies
A new ray of light is sent down from the sun.

Haven't you wondered where inspiration comes from?
It is showered down on us at all times
Like a gentle rain from God's heart
And it is the grace we receive
After removing the ignorance that covers ours.

When compassion dawns
Inspiration becomes our pilot
And with a visa from the Lord,
We can go anywhere we want to go.

***

Lord Buddha described spiritual life as going 'against the stream.' We are constantly confronted with the deeply programmed tendencies of craving and aversion. We want solid ground under our feet and we resist change. After the initial enthusiasm wears off, it becomes difficult to find the strength to keep swimming upstream. I remember once during a break between bhajans, Amma imitated some of us sitting in the front with our lazy postures and our slouching shoulders. She said, "When you first came here there was intensity. Now look! It's like we got married."

I once asked Amma in a Q&A session, "What should we do when our faith is shaken and our devotion dries up?" Amma went on to give a beautiful answer. The very first thing Amma said was, "Don't worry son, just keep coming towards *this*." Amma was pointing to herself – her body is the physical manifestation of our goal.

I believe Amma's words are a profound promise for all of us. No matter what challenges we face, be it doubt, depression, or spiritual dryness – as long as we keep trying to orient our lives towards her, towards God, even if the best we can do is crawl, then we will be triumphant in the end.

Of course, this is easier said than done. Have you heard the story of a devotee who took a nine-hour rickshaw ride to escape a South India Tour? That was me. Imagine how fed up you'd have to be to travel nine hours in an auto-rickshaw. I was having a miserable tour and was irritated about everything. I was trying to be "spiritual," so I ignored the advice of others, and traveled without a mosquito net. One night, I was the only guy in my room without a net. As soon as the lights went out, hundreds of huge, kamikaze mosquitos swooped down on us for a feeding frenzy. But because they kept bouncing off the mosquito nets, they got frustrated – angry, hungry, hippopotamus-sized mosquitoes in a closed room, with me as their only prey.

Before the sun came up, my bag was packed. I was leaving the tour. And nothing was going to stop me. I went to a nearby taxi stand and began trying to find a way back to Kerala. I started trying to negotiate a good deal for a rickshaw. All the drivers had gathered around and were laughing at my absurd request. But when they realized I was serious about saving money and taking a rickshaw instead of a taxi, one ambitious driver agreed to take me. After a bumpy nine hours, we finally reached a beach town called Varkala. I was in bliss and happy I had saved 800 rupees.

I ate a delicious meal and then to celebrate my new freedom, I went for a beautiful swim in the ocean. The first wave picked me up and slammed me head first into the sand. I had a badly sprained shoulder and needed to return immediately to the āśhram to visit the hospital. From Varkala back to the āśhram, I took a taxi.

Days later, when the tour group returned, I was standing there like a fool greeting the buses with my arm in a sling. "Hey, what happened to you?" people asked. "Long story!" I mumbled.

***

I've always had an affinity for stories of great souls who have turned their lives around due to divine providence. One of my favorites is that of Aṅgulimāla. The well known story is that a serial murderer met the Buddha, repented, and eventually became one of Buddha's disciples. When Aṅgulimāla would go begging for alms with his fellow bhikkhus, monks, he would often be stoned and beaten by the villagers. One time when he returned, the Buddha saw him bruised and bloodied and asked, "What happened to you?" "The villagers have beaten me, Master." With great compassion the Buddha replied, "Yes, Aṅgulimāla, it is because of your past actions. Bear it with a wise and noble heart."

Like my story from the tour, we tend to be reactive when unfavorable things happen. If someone throws a stone at us, our instinctive response is to look for the nearest boulder and throw it back at them. But Amma keeps crafting situations so that we feel the consequence of such reactions. Then we get to choose the way of acceptance, compassion, and forbearance instead.

One of our senior swāmīs, when I complained to him once of a perceived injustice done to me, calmly replied, "Remember that we've come here to exhaust all our karmas." When unfavorable circumstances arise, I try to remind myself that whatever comes is simply the return flight of a boomerang released from my own hand, and I try, as best I can, to bear it.

I feel that it's through sēvā that I get to work it all out, slowly chiseling away at the Kailash-size mountain of karma that I've accumulated. Amma makes the climb less steep by simplifying our short-term goals. She outlines basic principles for us to live by, reminding us to bring the quality of love and the spirit of service into everything that we do.

While language points to a goal that lives in the future, Amma points to our goal as living in the present. This is the paradox of speaking of goals at all in spirituality. As the Zen poet Ryokan says, "The Way goes nowhere." We come full circle. We start to understand that our awakening does not belong to a time called tomorrow — that our freedom isn't found in some far-off region.

Look at how much Amma has accomplished in just the last forty years. She took birth with a gigantic goal and has faced every adversity imaginable. Yet, when we watch her giving darśhan, there isn't a trace of tension or anxiety in her. Chaos is going on all around Amma and yet she's absolutely present and relaxed with whatever and whoever is right in front of her. With Amma as our ideal, of course we're going to fall short every day. But it doesn't matter. The key is simply being invested in the process for what it is.

To encourage us, Amma occasionally gives a tiny glimpse of the ultimate goal that she is leading us to. Those brief moments of clarity are so compelling that everything else pales in comparison. My guess is that this is by design, because Amma doesn't want us to turn back. She knows how hard it is for us to keep going. That sneak preview of the destination that awaits us helps to put wind in our sails. Our mundane mind-driven existence is henceforth completely unsatisfactory. Sri Ramakrishna

Paramahamsa, when faced with temptation would cry out with disdain, "You cannot fool me Mother, for I have seen your crimson lotus feet." I suppose this will eventually apply to all of us. Things that satisfied us before won't work the way they once did. There's no successful U-turn on this path.

***

I once told Amma that I was consumed with guilt and shame from my previous lifestyle. She became stern with me and said, "Don't think like that! The past is a canceled check. You are with Amma now." Then she went on to say, "Just look at the life of Vālmīki."

We know the story of sage Vālmīki, that he wrote the *Rāmāyaṇa*. But earlier in his life, he was a dacoit or highway robber named Ratnākara. Anyone with a troubled past can take comfort in these words of Amma. If, through his sincere repentance, his effort, and the grace of the saptaṛiṣhis (the seven great sages), Ratnākara the dacoit could become sage Vālmīki, what to say about all of us who are with the all-compassionate Divine Mother herself. We get to turn over a new leaf and script a beautiful new chapter in our lives.

If I had to choose a single message to convey from my life and this journey with Amma, this is it: no matter what we have been through, the failures, the mistakes we made, the harm we've caused, the sorrow and darkness we lived through or are maybe even facing right now... this can all be transformed with Amma's grace and our dedicated effort.

To illustrate this type of effort and quality of perseverance, let me share the story of Shelley. Shelley was a minister in a church. She had heard about Amma as being a powerful female spiritual leader and decided to come to Amritapuri for one month. Shelley also wanted to give comfort to hundreds of suffering people in her congregation and felt that yōga could help them. She registered for a continuous month of Amrita Yoga retreats. Shelley had never done yōga before and though she often struggled, she never missed a class. One morning, I called out to her in the back row, "Shelley, are you ok?" She popped up out of the posture she was in and with great enthusiasm said, "I'm here!" This is lakṣhya bōdham — showing up, in spite of our limitations, especially when we don't feel like it.

One of my neighbors, a long-time devotee who lives on the same floor, had a stroke two years ago. He is learning to walk and speak again. Each day, I see him and his wife slowly walking back and forth in the corridor. The other day they were practicing on the stairs. I can't imagine being older and having to relearn how to walk and talk. But every day, he patiently practices one step at a time. He joins his palms in salutation whenever I walk by, and his wife is always by his side, supporting him and smiling.

Because of the inspiration we get from Amma's life and her teachings, there are countless other examples in this community of incredible persistence like this — the formidable will to keep moving forward in spite of the obstacles.

To conclude, I will share one final poem that I wrote about a devotee who I always used to see pacing back and forth behind the Kālī Temple:

For years you have seen the same lonely soul
Trudging a hapless line behind the temple
With disheveled hair, dirty whites
And a serious look on his face.
Be careful not to judge,
Appearances are very deceptive.

There could be desperation in his heart
A constant yearning for Kali.
Externals lost their meaning long ago.
And while Mother holds the rest of us
Together in the wind -
That lucky kite, She may be preparing
To set him free.

Perhaps my favorite image of Kālī is to visualize her holding millions of kite strings in her hand. That's us, of course. Struggling to be free. And every now and then she releases one string. And then jubilantly starts to clap and dance and sing as she watches that kite soar high up into the sky.

Praying that we may all point the compass of our hearts towards love, service and truth, no matter what. Praying that we may all receive the grace to stay on this glorious path, to persevere in our efforts just like my neighbor, taking one step forward at a time, until that blessed day when she releases the string and we soar high up into the sky.

2

Love Has No Distance

Chinmayi - Italy

Being in Amritapuri in Amma's presence is like being in heaven. The place where life blossoms and the flower of the self opens its petals in the light of Amma's divine presence. Amma says in *Awaken Children Volume 6*,

"A real master teaches you to accept everything that happens in life. He helps you to be thankful for both good and bad, right and wrong, enemy and friend, those who harm you and those who help you, those who cage you and those who release you from the cage. The master helps you forget about the dark past and the bright future full of a thousand promises. He helps you live life in the present moment with all its fullness. He helps you know that the whole of nature — everything, everybody, even your enemy — is helping you evolve and attain perfection."

Thinking in this way is not a given. Many people in the world do not have this perspective. Yet, it is this vision that makes life a miracle and gives us the opportunity to live it in fullness and bliss. We all share the priceless fortune of having Amma in our lives, and this allows us to face everything that life offers with a wonderful perspective. That is a true miracle! A miracle is not seeing a fish fly, but developing the ability to adapt to every circumstance of life, knowing that Amma is with us, and that everything she gives us is for the best. Isn't it wonderful to have this gift, this way of understanding life?

For me, Amma is the most compassionate guru because she has offered this perspective to millions of people in every corner of the earth and universe. We will never be able to quantify the profound changes she has brought into the lives of millions of people. This is extraordinary! Amma's greatness and compassion is endless.

I would like to share how this transformation began for me, and with Amma's grace, how I began to view life with this perspective. I have no doubt that Amma's compassion has always been present. It was her compassion that found me and my family many years ago in Assisi, Italy. Amma came into my life with absolute familiarity. I was seventeen years old when I went with my parents to meet Amma. My older brothers and sister had been there the year before, and they came back positively changed and deeply touched.

During that first meeting I had an experience of Amma's omniscience. As always, there were many people at the program. I was sitting in the middle of the crowd when my parents went for their first darśhan. Amma hugged them and, with her gaze, found me amongst all the people. She gave me a profound look, and in that moment, I knew that she knew everything. Who we are, where we came from, and what destiny we have. I can never forget this experience, as it continues to be a source of confidence and strength for me to this day.

At that point in my life, I had no notion of spirituality. I was simply a teenager facing the first challenges of the world. But Amma's compassion reaches people at every level and opens up a new vision for everyone. The annual meetings with Amma in Assisi instilled in me the strength to accept and face the aspects of the world that, with the eyes of a teenager, I did not like. At school and in my family, everyone noticed the changes that took place in me gradually after meeting Amma.

Thanks to Amma, I transformed from the rebellious and moody teenager I once was, into a serene, positive person, brimming with enthusiasm for the experiences that came my way. Amma came into my life, not as a tsunami that turns everything upside down, but as a subtle and gentle presence that illuminates the path. A presence that helped me to choose what brings peace and serenity in life.

With Amma's grace, after my studies, I was able to come live in Amritapuri for almost three years. I will be eternally grateful to Amma and to all the residents of Amritapuri for that time. Amritapuri is a great school of life, where everything helps one to grow and to stay focused on the ultimate purpose of life. All those who come to seek refuge and guidance are welcomed. Spending time in Amritapuri is like attending a specialized school. The main object of this school is to learn how to deal with every challenge that comes our way.

After I spent those three years in Amritapuri, I had a strong feeling I should go back to my country and do something good. With Amma's blessing, I returned to Italy and started doing social work. I am now involved in one of those projects which few people want to take on. I work in 'sheltered' apartments, which are places where people with disabilities live when, for various reasons, they can no longer stay with their families. I started working, and after a while I was asked to take charge of some shelter projects that were facing a lot of difficulties.

These projects are very challenging with very few economic resources, a lot of work to be done, daily emergencies, and zero recognition. But the purpose is beautiful: to give a home to people with disabilities and be at their side, offering them a life endowed with as much dignity as possible. As a daughter of Amma, how could I decline such an undertaking? Even though it seemed impossible, with Amma in my life, how could I say no?

At the same time, I was asked to take charge of coordinating Amma's activities in Italy. Basically, I was presented with two impossible challenges. In both situations, I took the liberty of asking the person who made these proposals to me, "Are you sure you haven't got the wrong person?" I doubted my boss at work, thinking that he was crazy for asking me to do this, or that he asked because he was simply understaffed. But I could not think the same thing about Amma's organization. I knew that everything that comes to us is for the best, so how could I decline this challenge? I had many doubts, and was not at all confident that I could do a proper job in either situation. But having Amma in my life, I felt I had to face the challenges, and remain confident that it was all for the best.

Over all these years, I have felt Amma's grace with me every step of the way, giving me the best experiences for my growth. In reality, it is only Amma's grace that enables us to accomplish anything, and if we remain open and engage sincerely in the task, Amma sends us all the help we need.

***

From my own experience, I can clearly say that Amma's teachings are the best guide to face all circumstances in life. In my job, I have to interact with various types of people, including those with aggression problems, psychiatric issues, and other significant hardships. I also engage with their families, doctors, social assistants, and politicians responsible for social affairs. Through my work, I can see that people in need are the people who need love, and that there is nothing better than treating them with love to improve their lives. Everyone responds positively with a love-based approach. In fact, the people who seem to be the most difficult, are also seeking love, just like everyone else. What Amma is teaching the world is the ultimate cure for all beings — love and compassion.

In my life, I have observed that an education for earning a living is not enough, rather, we need an 'education for life' — as

Amma teaches us. I have often observed people with excellent technical skills who cannot handle stress. This means that, while technical skills are certainly important, without facing life's circumstances with the right attitude, we may find ourselves lacking the real tools we need. Through her teachings, Amma gives us the basic tools needed to face life's situations.

I feel by doing sēvā, we learn a lot about 'education for life.' Amma teaches us to adapt to each person and circumstance, seeing the best in everything and pushing us to awaken the potential we all have within. That's why, for me, Amma is the supreme teacher, because she awakens our hidden qualities. Many centuries ago, Plato described Socrates's way of teaching with the word, 'maieutics,' which literally means, 'the art of the midwife.' Socrates' mother was a midwife. He said that his mother and the other midwives helped women deliver babies, while he, Socrates, helped people deliver their souls. So it was a spiritual process.

In my small experience, I can say that Amma's presence in our lives activates the same process. That's why we are all attracted to Amma, because she helps us bring out our soul — our true self. Her presence in our lives allows our true nature to blossom. Amma also gives us many tools to facilitate this process, including spiritual practices such as the IAM technique, white flower meditation, satsangs, bhajans, and so many opportunities to do sēvā. Amma's presence helps me to be careful in my decisions and actions. She helps me to accept the things that I cannot change.

***

Amma has helped me realize that what makes any undertaking possible is grace combined with sincere effort, an open heart, and faith that Amma is always with us, supporting us to face every challenge. I am sure my experience is among countless others that can show that physical distance is not a problem for Amma. We are the ones who feel that there is distance and separation, but Amma shows us that she is always with us, and that the growth process also takes place at a distance. Doesn't Amma tell us that lotus flowers bloom even when far from the sun?

On that note I would like to share with you about the lock-down period in Italy. As you all know, Italy was one of the first countries hit by the Corona virus in Europe. Especially the place where I live, Bergamo, where it all broke out. Do you remember the scenes of the coffins being taken away by military trucks because there was no more room for the innumerable coffins in the city? That was right near my house. The situation was devastating, and I found myself facing a series of emergencies that I could manage only because Amma teaches us to accept every challenge in life.

I was working all day until late in the evening. There was no staff for the shelters and people were scared. One day, we carried two disabled people to the hospital and the doctors cryingly told us they were helpless and unable to accept more people because the hospital was fully overcrowded. During this time, I used to get calls informing me about the deaths of various people, and I was really scared thinking who will be the next. I deeply feel that it was Amma's grace and teachings that prevented me from becoming discouraged and gave me the right perspective to try to help others.

In those dark days at the beginning of the pandemic, I remembered that Swami Shubhamritananda Puri, in one of his satsangs for Europe, had quoted Etty Hillesum. So I went to read some of Etty's writings. She was a writer who lived and died in the concentration camps during World War II. I will quote some of her aphorisms:

"I no longer believe that we can improve anything in the outside world without first doing our part within ourselves... If you claim to believe in God you must also be consistent, you must surrender yourself completely and you must trust. And you must also not worry about the next day... I believe that something positive can be derived from life in all circumstances."

Etty wrote very positive things and was able to see the beauty of life even in a concentration camp. I remember her writings in difficult times, and it is very helpful to me.

Sometimes to find strength, I wonder to myself, "I deeply love God in the fierce forms of Śhiva and Kālī. Yet, when God manifests in a destructive and fierce way in my life, do I still love him in his destructive form?" I remind myself that I must strive to remain consistent, and if I trust God when things are going well, I must also try to keep that faith even when things seem to be going wrong.

Amma is truly the guru who has shown infinite compassion and love for all of humanity, generously offering us the most precious gift, that is, the teachings that help us to know how to accept every circumstance of life. This gift that Amma gives us applies to all life situations, including death.

Recently, several people dear to me passed away. No school teaches us how to face death with acceptance. Once again, Amma is the supreme master in this as well. Amma teaches us that even death is a moment to be welcomed. It is not the end, but only a transformation. During the dark time of the pandemic, I could see how Amma's children embraced this teaching and found the strength to view death from this perspective. That is something truly extraordinary.

***

During the pandemic, there were some passages from *Awaken Children* that were very helpful to me.

"Children, Amma is always with you. Each time you think of her, Amma can clearly see your faces. Every night when Amma lies down to rest, Amma goes out to her children all over the world."[3]

In another passage, a devotee asks, "When I am not with you, Amma, do you ever remember me?" Amma replied, "How can Amma forget anyone, when the whole universe is within her? You are all parts of Amma. How can the whole forget the part? The part exists in the whole. The part may think it is different from the whole, but the whole, which is the soul of everything, knows that the part is not different from it. That supreme soul is pure and transcendent love; it cannot see the part as different from itself, so there can be no question of forgetting. Amma always remembers you, but your remembrance of Amma is equally important. When you remember that you are Amma's child, Amma's son or daughter, Amma's disciple or devotee, when you remember that she is always with you, that she sees all your actions and is your sole protector and guide, you are remembering the whole — you are recalling your real nature and true abode."[4]

"If you always remember Amma and you love her, that is sufficient. It is enough if you can remember her sincerely and intensely just once a day. Child, where there is love, there is no distance or separation. It is your love for Amma that keeps you close to her. Whether or not you love her, whether or not you're

[3] *Awaken Children 9*

[4] *Awaken Children 6*

able to feel her love, Amma loves you and she is with you. But you will feel her closeness or presence only when you love her."[5]

The motto we are all using during these difficult times is 'Love has no distance.' This is one of my favorite pearls of Amma's wisdom, and I am grateful to all those who believe deeply in this concept, and are committed to serving Amma and feeling her wherever they are. I am grateful to Amma, who, with her infinite compassion, reaches every nook and cranny of the earth; who offers each of us the opportunity to connect to her and receive all the guidance we need, even from a distance.

***

We, as Italians, were lucky to receive the new film on Amma, titled *Amma's Way*. For all of us, it was like meeting Amma again, in a new place — at the cinema! We went to see the film with the same enthusiasm as when we go to Amma's program.

Many of us feel that Amma has heard the cry of her children during these dark and challenging times, and wants to be even closer to us through the opening of the first Amma center in Italy. Amma's centers around the world are one of the many examples of her compassion. As Amma says, God's grace is present everywhere, like the breeze, but if we stand under a tree, we will be able to feel it better. For me, Amma's centers in the world are exactly that, places where we can concentrate and feel the presence of God — of Amma. I am extremely happy that Amma has blessed Italy with this opportunity.

In Amma's centers, we can recharge our spiritual batteries, take time to meditate and introspect, or engage in ecological and social projects. All of these opportunities allow us to stay focused on Amma, preventing our minds from wandering

---

[5] *Awaken Children 6*

and fixating on the things of the world, and thus, we remain immersed in her wonderful presence.

Once again I ask myself, "Isn't this all a miracle? That Amma's children have the opportunity to remain focused on her through different ways?" For me, all this should not be taken for granted. We need to put forward the necessary effort to maintain this perspective, and pray for Amma's grace.

May Amma's grace allow us to face all the challenges of life with awareness and acceptance. May we remain eternally grateful for receiving Amma's presence, teachings and compassion in our lives.

3

From Death to Immortality — Our Journey with Amma

Prakash Bhaskaran - USA

The Chinese philosopher Lao Tzu said, "A journey of a thousand miles begins with a single step." I feel my spiritual evolution is exactly that. Unbeknownst to me, Amma has invisibly guided my every step to bring me to her.

I physically saw Amma for the first time in San Ramon, California in June 2000. Upon reflection, the timing of my meeting Amma during this period was not coincidental. This was a tough period in my life during which I underwent a lot of changes and carried numerous responsibilities. I was in my early forties, raising a young family, in the process of building my profession, and at the same time caring for my aging parents. It was also during this time that I hit the bottom of my professional career.

Being an accountant, I had finally landed my first high-tech software job in the San Francisco Bay Area. Having worked there for four years as the head of their finance department, I had accumulated some stock options. In March of 2000, our company went public. The stock price took off. On the first day of trading, my stock options were worth $15 million. Wow! This is what people working in tech companies dream of, right? Well, not so fast! Amma had a different plan.

From March 2000 to early 2001, the U.S. economy and my company rapidly spiraled downward. Right after physically meeting Amma in November 2000, a month later, my company went bust along with my job. I was laid off. I had never been laid off in my life. My head was spinning with thoughts like, "How could this happen? I am so important in the company. I am the only one that can do the job." I was depressed and scared for my family's future.

This was the perfect entry point in my life for Amma. Through this experience, Amma could teach me a hard but very valuable lesson. Don't be attached to your title, position or fame. You are not any of that. I clearly realize that now. Even though I thought I had hit the jackpot, I did not benefit from any of the $15 million from my stock options, as they had become worthless!

Now, I realize that I had actually won the mega lottery of my lifetime — something priceless that very few people are blessed with — I got my Amma. It is as if she entered my life literally saying, "What is the point of all this name, fame and position when you have me?"

In order to put all of this in proper perspective, let me take you back to earlier in my life and bring you along on that journey.

I was born in India and spent my childhood days in Bhilai, a steel town in Chhattisgarh, East Central India. Unlike a lot of traditional South Indian families, my family was neither spiritual nor religious. Growing up, I don't remember going to any temples and I didn't know much about the spiritual significance of Hindu festivals. I simply enjoyed the yummy treats my mom made for the various festivals like *Gaṇeśh Chaturthī* and *Kṛiṣhṇa Jayantī*.

In 1970, my family immigrated to the U.S. and settled in the San Francisco Bay Area, California. I was a young teenager. My dad had heard about America being the land of opportunities and wanted to live and provide the American dream for his family. At that time, there were very few Indians or Hindus in the Bay Area, and almost no temples. I was very uncomfortable going to any temples. My parents would tell me, "*Namaskāram paṇṇu*," which means, prostrate to the idols — a gesture I felt very uncomfortable doing.

During my college days in the mid 70s, I frequented the Hare Krishna Temple in Berkeley, mainly for '*prīti bhōj*' — free food! However, I also enjoyed listening to and singing bhajans. This was a period in my life where I was spiritually searching for something to latch on to.

As a spiritual seeker, I was searching for something genuine to connect to. But at the same time, I feel I was at the beginning level of a seeker, much like the sentiment expressed in the bhajan *Nā Maiṅ Dharmī* :

Nā maiṅ dharmī, nā maiṅ dānī.
Nā maiṅ paṇḍit, nā maiṅ jñanī...

Neither am I spiritual nor a philanthropist.
Neither am I a scholar nor knowledgeable...

The bhajan goes on to express the seeker's longing for the Divine Mother. But I had not yet reached that stage.

***

My wife Jayanthi and I first heard of Amma in 1987 after we had just gotten married. My mother loved to meet any holy people that visited the Bay Area. One day, she brought the *India West* newspaper and showed me a small photo of an Indian lady saint who was visiting the Oakland area. This lady was dark looking, had a round face, and bore a strong resemblance to my mother. I agreed to go to see her, but my wife put her foot down saying,"Why would I want to see someone that looks like your mom?" Well, the wife is always right, so I had to give in. No choice there!

In 1996, with a growing family consisting of my wife and two small children, we were ready for a bigger place to live in, and started searching for homes in the San Ramon area. We identified several houses we liked, but our family astrologer in India kept shooting them all down for one reason or other. We finally found a house that we liked, but it was far beyond our budget. However, the astrologer insisted that we buy this house regardless of the price because it had "*Guru pārvai.*" This Tamil phrase can be loosely translated to 'the guru's sight or vision' on the house. I did not have a clue as to what this *guru pārvai* phrase meant. I was still not religious or spiritually inclined in any way, leave alone having a guru. In hindsight, I clearly know now what significance this had in our lives!

Now that we had moved to this area, different people came and told us that we should visit Amma's San Ramon āśhram since our home was literally only ten minutes away. However, we did nothing like that. We were caught up in our mundane lives with jam-packed days running from work to daycare and soccer games or karate classes on the weekends. My in-laws relocated from India and moved in with us as well. We did not go to the āśhram for several years, as at that time, our work and family life was all consuming with no room for anything else.

Finally, one evening in March 2000, we went to the āśhram. As I walked up the driveway leading to the temple, I heard the most beautiful voice singing the first notes of the bhajan *Adharam Madhuram*. I have always loved music and bhajans and this, to me, was the most divine singing I had ever heard. Walking into the temple, we saw Swami Amritaswarupananda singing bhajans in his powerful, booming voice. We stayed and listened, and I was simply hooked on the music. It was so melodious and captivating.

We started coming to the āśhram every Saturday for the programs. My spiritual thirst was quenched during my long work commute by listening to the talks on audiocassette tapes by Swami Paramatmananda. I was mesmerized by Swamiji's soothing voice and his down-to-earth talks, and became more and more drawn towards Amma and her teachings.

In June 2000, when Amma came to San Ramon for her summer tour, we attended an evening program. With kids in tow, we were late and the place was packed with people. We somehow managed to squeeze in and saw Amma as a small figure far away on the stage. We generally felt uncomfortable about the whole experience and left without getting darśhan. I guess Amma felt we were not ready yet!

We continued with our Saturday jaunts to the āśhram and finally in November 2000, we had our first darśhan with Amma. Our family's journey with Amma had begun! Our first darśhan, while pleasant, was certainly not earth-shattering or life-changing, or so we thought. After our hug, however, my ten-year-old son came running and very seriously told us, "Amma is God!" and then ran off to play and sneak in another darśhan. Those days there was no token system, so he got darśhan many times.

We started going to the āśhram regularly and attending programs, and my whole family got involved in various aspects of āśhram sēvā. In the summer of 2001, we had the good fortune to have Amma perform our son's Upanayanam, the sacred thread ceremony to initiate a child into studies. Amma was in Dēvī Bhāva, wearing an off-white sari representing Saraswatī — the goddess of knowledge and learning, and she imparted brahmōpadēśham[6] — the sacred Gāyatrī mantra, in my son's ear. All the while Swamiji was singing *Vāgadhīśhvarī*, a bhajan that glorifies Amma as goddess Saraswatī. Wow! Little did we know the significance of this then, but thinking back now, we feel it was such a great blessing for our son to have had Dēvī herself do his thread ceremony.

Over the next several years, our faith in Amma slowly continued to grow. Small incidents cemented our connection with her. For example, my mother had passed away on November 22, 1996, and in November 2001 during Amma's tour, I was feeling particularly sad thinking about my mom and missing her, as it happened to be the day of her death anniversary. I was sad and crying during darśhan, but I did not say anything to Amma. Amma immediately said, "Don't be sad. I am your mother now." How did she know? It blew me away.

***

Having been somewhat exposed to Vēdāntic teachings by Swami Chinmayananda and Swami Dayananda whose lectures I often attended in the 1970s and 80s, I used to wonder why Amma never gave talks on Vēdānta[7] but instead emphasized bhakti (devotion) and sēvā (selfless service). I found my answer one day while reading an article that appeared in *Matruvani*, the ashram's monthly flagship publication, in 2004. The article was detailing a very interesting conversation that Amma had with a

---

[6] 'Instruction about brahman.' Composed of 'brahma' — the absolute, and 'upadēśham' — instruction.

[7] The philosophy of the '*Upaniṣhads*,' the sacred texts found in the *Vēdas* which deal with the subject of brahman — the supreme reality — and the path to realize that truth. A follower or practitioner of Vēdānta is called a Vēdāntin.

couple of devotees in San Ramon in June 2003. I will share some of the statements that Amma made during that conversation.

Amma said, "Some people read a lot of scriptural books but they don't practice any sādhanā. They mouth Vēdāntic statements, but don't care a bit about cultivating virtues; they say, 'I am not the body, I am not the mind,' etc. but have no control over their senses. They lose their temper at the slightest provocation; yet they call themselves Vēdāntins."

Amma continued, "Even Ramana Maharshi, who is accepted as a great Vēdāntin, advocates pūjā (ritualistic worship) and japa (mantra repetition) in his work, *Upadēśha Sāram*. Ramana says that the seeker should start with pūjā, then go on to do japa and tapas (austerities). Only when the mind is in 'līnasthiti' (an absorbed state), is he ready for self-inquiry. Nowadays many people read Vēdāntic texts and decry bhakti. Yet they walk around Aruṇāchala like Sri Ramana did, not knowing the principle behind it. Circumambulating the Aruṇāchal mountain, beholding God in the stone mountain, is nothing but bhakti.

In the olden days, the guru would make the disciples study the scriptures, do sēvā, and practice meditation for twenty years. After twenty years, the guru would select a few worthy disciples and teach them the *Brahma Sūtras*[8]. But nowadays people just buy a copy of the *Brahma Sūtras* and read it without preparing themselves for it, or doing any spiritual practice whatsoever."

Amma then made a few startling comments on her own role. "In Ramana Maharshi's case, a few advanced disciples came to him and asked him spiritual questions. So, he was able to speak about Vēdānta to them. In Amma's case, thousands come and

---

[8] A central philosophic text authored by Sage Vyāsa synthesizing the teachings of the *Upaniṣhads*. It is regarded as a text for advanced students and is also known as the *Vēdānta Sūtras*.

they ask all sorts of questions: 'What kind of job should I do? Should I buy a house? Can I get a girlfriend?' and so on. How can Amma talk about Vēdānta to them? All kinds of people come to Amma; doctors, lawyers, engineers, clerks, prostitutes and thieves! Can Amma start talking about Vēdānta to all of them? Amma has to go down to their level and talk to them."

What profound statements!

***

During one of her U.S. retreats, Amma spoke about death. She said, "Death is not the end, rather, it is like a period at the end of a sentence. People are always afraid of death, but instead, one needs to think of death as a long-lost relative or friend. Just as you would eagerly await this relative every day and have a nice room prepared in anticipation of his visit, you need to prepare for death also and anticipate his visit."

On a cold February morning in 2011, death paid a visit to our home and we were woefully unprepared. God really tests our faith in many ways. For our family, it was a major test. Our twenty-year-old son, Akshay, did not wake up from his sleep that morning. It was like an unreal, nightmarish dream. We were all totally devastated. Only through Amma's love, grace and compassion, were we able to come out of it somewhat unscathed. Although Amma physically was not there, we really felt her love and compassion through Swami Dayamritananda and our entire Amma family in San Ramon. We were helped, supported and cared for by our Amma brothers and sisters for several months after the tragedy, for which we are eternally grateful.

> *ōṁ sāndra karuṇāyai namaḥ*
> I bow down to the one who has intense compassion.
> (*Lalitā Sahasranāma,* 197)

Ever the caring and compassionate Mother, Amma sent word through Swami Dayamritananda to not neglect our daughter Shreya while we were consumed by our grief. Shreya was just about to graduate high school in a few months. With this event now, she did not want to go to college. A few months later when we met Amma in San Ramon, she encouraged Shreya to go to college saying that it would make Akshay very happy.

Amma was our ādhāram — our support! She gave us the strength to accept and cope with Akshay's passing. She helped us understand that all of this happened due to our past karmas. Our family could have easily fractured and fallen apart, but Amma made sure it held strong with her "glue" and I feel our family emerged even stronger as a result of going through this difficult time with her support.

Strangely, hard as it was to lose Akshay, I feel that he catapulted our whole family more strongly towards Amma. In the months following our son's passing, I found a lot of solace listening to bhajans. That summer, one Tamil bhajan in particular caught my attention — *Jñāna Kaṭal Tannai.* This bhajan is pregnant with meaning, given what we had recently gone through. One of the verses is, "*Sōdanaigaḷ tandu āzham pārkinḍrai, padam pārttu nal bhakti nalkukinṭrāy.*" It means, by handing us problems and sorrows, God tests the depth of our faith in him and then grants us pure bhakti. In our case, all I can say is that our faith was severely tested to the breaking point, but our faith and devotion to Amma came back stronger than ever.

Amma turned this sorrowful time into the experience of learning to accept whatever happens in our lives with an attitude of prasāda buddhi — receiving everything as God's blessing. An experience like this is a great opportunity for spiritual growth and for developing detachment.

In *Bhaja Gōvindam*, Verse 8, Ādi Śhaṅkarāchārya says:

kātē kāntā kastē putraḥ
saṁsārō'yamatīva vichitraḥ
kasya tvaṁ kaḥ kuta āyātaḥ
tattvaṁ chintaya tadiha bhrātaḥ

Who is your wife? Who is your son?
Exceedingly wonderful, indeed, is this saṁsāra.
Of whom are you? Who are you?
Whence have you come?
O brother, think of that truth here.

This clearly tells us that the only attachment we should have is to the Lord. Everything else is fleeting and temporary.

***

In the *Mahābhārata*, there is an interesting story revealing the common man's attitude towards death. Nakula, the youngest of the five Pāṇḍava princes, goes in search of water for his exhausted brothers and comes across a lake. There, he sees a crane that is actually a yakṣha — a nature-spirit, in disguise. The crane tells Nakula that he needs to answer his questions before drinking the water or else he would drop dead. Nakula ignores the yakṣha, drinks the water, and falls dead. The same fate awaits Sahadēva, Bhīma, and Arjuna. Finally, Yudhiṣhṭhira goes in search of his brothers and finds them all dead by the lake. When he bends down to drink the water, the yakṣha appears and challenges him to answer his questions or else face the same consequences as his brothers. The yakṣha was none other than Yama or Dharma Rājā, the Lord of Death. In the end,

Lord Yama was so pleased with Yudhiṣhṭhira's answers that he blessed him by reviving all four of his brothers.

One of his questions to Yudhiṣhṭhira was, "What is the greatest wonder in this world?" To this Yudhiṣhṭhira replied, "The greatest wonder is that even though one witnesses countless people dying every day, the rest of humanity still acts and thinks as if they will live forever."

Amma always tells us that only this moment is ours. We are all like birds on a dry twig that may snap at any moment. So, we should not waste a single moment chasing after material possessions but rather spend our remaining life turning inward, doing good deeds and being of service to others.

To illustrate this, Amma tells the example of Alexander the Great, the powerful king that had conquered the world. As his death drew near, he called his ministers and asked them to make sure to place his empty hands outside his coffin when he died. This was to show the world that even a great king like him was not able to take anything with him when he left this earth.

This reminds me of a short story by the great Russian author Leo Tolstoy called, *How Much Land Does a Man Need?*

There was a poor man named Pakhom, who became fixated on the idea that his life would be perfect if only he owned more land. His obsession eventually consumes him and in his lust for land, he loses everything that matters in his life.

One day, Pakhom overhears his wife discussing the benefits of town-life versus farm-life. He thinks to himself that if he had plenty of land, he would have nothing to fear, not even the devil himself. However, unbeknownst to him, Satan, the devil, is watching him and overhears his thoughts. Satan decides that he will accept Pakhom's challenge and give him everything he wants, but then snatch everything from him.

A short time later, Pakhom scrapes together some money to purchase a small parcel of land. By working very hard, he is able to live a more comfortable existence. But he is not content and wants to build his fortune further.

He is soon introduced to the Bashkirs and learns that they are simple people who own a lot of land. He approaches them and negotiates to buy a large parcel of their land. However, the Bashkirs offer is unusual. They tell him that for 1,000 roubles he can walk around as large an area as he wants starting at daybreak and mark his route with a spade. If he returns to his starting point by sunset, he will get all the land he has marked. However, if he does not, he loses everything. Pakhom is delighted, thinking that this must be a very easy task. He sets off at daybreak and covers a large area of land. Suddenly, he realizes that it is almost sunset and frantically rushes back towards the starting point, making it just in time. The Bashkirs congratulate him saying that all the land he has marked is now his. Suddenly, totally exhausted from the run, his heart gives out and he drops dead right in front of the landowners. The story ends with his servant burying him in a simple grave, six-feet long. In the end, this was literally all the land he needed!

We too, have learned the hard way, that nothing is ours. Everything is a gift from God that we will have to return at any moment. Amma made us realize that our son was a precious gift given to us for only twenty years.

***

All these years, Amma clearly gave us glimpses of her presence in our life. With each passing day, more of her divinity is revealed to us. We are slowly seeing and realizing who Amma really is — Dēvī, the Divine Mother herself!

I am reminded now of another poignant statement Amma made during that same conversation from the *Matruvani* article. Amma said, "I have descended into the marketplace." Note the choice of word '*descended*.' This reminds me of what an avatār truly is. God, descending to our level, out of compassion. Amma continued, "I am not selling diamonds now. I have to sell trivial things, then give people diamonds when they are ready for it."

Then Amma drew a great comparison. "Kṛiṣhṇa was also like this. He had to talk to people about their dharma as a student, a teacher, a soldier... He too had to deal with the masses."

Someone then asked Amma, "We are seeing you now in front of us. What is the difference between seeing you and having a vision of God?"

Amma spontaneously replied,"That depends upon your mental attitude. At first, Arjuna saw Kṛiṣhṇa only as a friend. But later on, when he realized the truth, he saw Kṛiṣhṇa as God."

All were blown away by the utter simplicity of the reply, the comparison between Lord Kṛiṣhṇa and herself, and the reference to Arjuna's point of view.

A devotee then asked, "Amma, how does one develop the attitude of seeing you as God?"

Amma said, "Amma doesn't want anyone to see her as God. On the contrary, Amma sees all of you as God and worships you as such. Today, people call me God, but tomorrow, they may call me something else. Amma knows who has real faith and who is merely paying lip-service. When Amma tests them, the truth will come out, whether they really feel what they say. Amma is not interested in anyone calling her God."

May we all realize the truth and start seeing Amma for who she really is!

In 'Eternal Wisdom', Amma says, "A log that floats down the river moves with the flow of the river. Similarly, the disciple should move in accordance with the guru's wish, with an attitude of surrender that, '*You are everything.*' This is the only way to remove the ego."

We still have many miles to go on our spiritual journey. However, having taken that first step to board the Amma train, I feel that our thousand-mile journey is getting easier and easier.

So, now, I can complete the bhajan, *Nā Maiṅ Dharmī* :

Bas chāhūṅ maiṅ tujhē, mā bhavānī.
Maiṅ tērī hūṅ dīvānī!
Mujhē chhōḍ na dēnā, bhavānī!

O Mother Bhavānī, consort of Lord Śhiva, I am longing for your love and acceptance. O Mother, please do not forsake me.

Thank you Amma for your infinite compassion and patience towards us, your ignorant children! May your love lead us from death to immortality.

4

The Shedding of All Masks

Dhanya - France

Shyness, pride, and fear are some of the masks we wear throughout our lives. These masks make us feel separate from our true nature, from God.

Amma says, "Pure love wants nothing else but the emptying of your mind from all its fears and the shedding of all your masks. It exposes the self as it is."

The only time I spoke in public in Amma's physical presence, I was wearing a mask. It was a big Hanumān mask! I was around seven years old, and during Amma's visit to France, we were performing a drama based on the ancient Indian epic, *Rāmāyaṇa.* I had the role of Hanumān, my favorite character. I was happy because, being very shy, I could hide my face behind the Hanumān mask, believing that no one would recognize me.

At the end of the program, I removed my Hanumān mask and stood by Amma's path. Amma stopped right in front of me and exclaimed joyfully, "Śhrī Rām! Jai Rām!" Amma sees through all our masks!

For two years, I was not sure whether I should give a satsang (spiritual talk) in Amma's divine presence or not. Then, I came across a very innocent version of a story of Lord Hanumān that made me smile within. It inspired me to go ahead in spite of my inner obstacles.

One day, Sampati, an old eagle, noticed that the beach was crowded with monkeys deep in conversation. He asked the monkeys what had brought them to the seashore.

Amidst the monkeys was the old and wise bear Jāmbavān, who also belonged to their clan. Addressing the eagle, Jāmbavān spoke, "Rāma, the prince of Ayōdhyā, was living in the forest with his wife Sītā and brother Lakṣmaṇa. When the two brothers were away, Rāvaṇa, the evil king of Laṅka, carried Sītā away. Our king Sugrīva has sent us in search of Sītā."

After hearing this, Sampati told the monkeys that Sītā was indeed being held captive in Laṅka. So Jāmbavān and the monkeys started discussing how to get to Laṅka. At that point one of the monkeys suggested, "Let's jump across the sea."

"Wait!" said the monkey commander. "Tell me first, what is your potential?" The monkey blinked. "What do you mean by potential?" he asked.

The monkey commander said, "I mean, how far do you think you can jump?" The monkey answered, "Hmmm...20 feet."

"Then you will fall right into the sea!" shrieked a little monkey, and everybody laughed. "I can jump 100 feet!" said another monkey, "I can jump 200 feet!" said another one, and so on.

Then, wise Jāmbavān said, "There is one among us who can leap to Laṅka," pointing out a monkey who was sitting all alone.

"You mean Hanumān?" asked the commander. "But he is not even speaking up. He is staying so quiet."

"That is because Hanumān does not know his own potential," said Jāmbavān. "Let us surround him and chant a mantra, which will make him discover his capability."

So, all the monkeys surrounded Hanumān and started chanting the mantra, "Hanumān, you can do it! Hanumān, you can do it!" As the monkeys chanted louder, Hanumān started growing in size. He grew bigger and bigger. He stood up, stretched his hands and took one giant leap across the sea. Hanumān landed in Laṅka, where he eventually found Sītā, and gave her Rāma's message.

Amma keeps repeating that infinite potential is hidden within us. To awaken it, we need to develop real self-confidence – the conviction that a higher power is flowing through us. The world and all its experiences have been designed to help us surrender, sooner or later, to the universal self, to God, and to let go of our limited personality and ego.

***

Amma says that everything in this universe is God's creation, except our ego. We are the ones who have created it based on our likes and dislikes, as well as our expectations and preconceived notions, and we imagine that it is real. In fact, our ego-creation is keeping us constantly busy, going round and round in the cycle of births and deaths. Renouncing the sense of "I" and "mine" and surrendering to the Supreme, is a most difficult task, but the only way to everlasting peace.

Every time Amma holds a program in India or abroad, hundreds of devotees try to follow Amma's perfect example of serving others tirelessly and selflessly. For a few days, most of them forget food and sleep. Putting others first, they dedicate their whole energy to giving. I observed that whenever Amma has left at the end of a program, she leaves behind an indescribable, profound peace that permeates the whole atmosphere – a peace born of pure self-sacrifice; the sacrifice of personal comforts, preferences, likes and dislikes.

It is this same peace I was blessed to feel growing up in nature. The same feeling one gets when entering a green wood early in the morning or when surrounded by majestic mountains deeply rooted in the earth, yet eternally embracing the sky. Mother Nature and our Amma are the embodiments of self-sacrifice and pure love. Similarly, our actions done with a selfless attitude have the power to purify not only our hearts, but also people around us and the whole atmosphere.

I felt a similar peace when I visited Assisi, the native village of the Christian mystic Saint Francis. This saint wilfully embraced poverty and spent his whole life in prayer and selfless service. He was not yet forty-five years old when he started suffering from physical illness and blindness, forcing him to stay away from the light. His mind had gained so much purity from his selfless life that in extremely difficult conditions, and even when overcome by despair, he was able to constantly remember the divine. One day, he experienced God's presence filling the whole universe and a song sprang from deep within. It was a song of reverence for each element of creation. He sang in praise of Brother Sun, Sister Moon, Brother Wind, and even Sister Death. He had become established in peace.

Many of us have had a taste of this peace while resting in Amma's arms, close to her heart, and hearing her soothing words. Amma's touch or glance, emanating from absolute purity, has the power to transform our hearts. Through her darśhan she is giving us a glimpse of the state in which she is eternally established — the state of total freedom from the limited "I." This is the state we need to rediscover.

Amma says, "Children, it is doubt and fear that has torn us away from true joy and immortality. However, that lost and forgotten joy can be regained if we just make the effort to be selfless. Immortality, which is our true state, can be rediscovered through the attitude of selfless love and selfless action."

It is this same selflessness that Kṛiṣhṇa calls as yajña, or sacrifice, in the *Bhagavad Gītā*, Chapter 3, verse 9:

yajñārthāt karmaṇō 'nyatra lōkō 'yaṁ karma-bandhanaḥ
tad-arthaṁ karma kauntēya mukta-saṅgaḥ samāchara

> Except for actions performed for yajna, this world is in bondage to action.
> For the sake of yajña, engage in action free from attachment.

The *Gītā* teaches us that performing an action without any selfish expectations turns the same action into a yajña and thus helps maintain balance in the universe. Amma, the very embodiment of selfless love and motherhood, is feeding all her children with the nectar of love. Through her very life, she shows us how to turn each and every action into a celebration – an offering to the world.

Reaching that state of selflessness is not easy. As soon as a difficult situation arises, I realize how far away I am from this ideal. However, Amma says, "In Sanātana Dharma[9] everyone is eligible for self-realization." In my case, Amma knew that the flower bud would need a lot of time to slowly start opening, and that is probably why she decided to come into my life as early as possible.

***

Before I was born, my mother, who was very inspired by the lives of saints and mystics from different traditions, was praying intensely to meet a realized soul in this lifetime. When I was almost two years old, my father saw in a magazine that a saint from Kerala was coming to the South of France. In 1992, my parents, my two elder sisters, my twin sister, and I went to receive Amma's darśhan for the first time. Amma didn't need words to communicate her love, it simply flowed, and we all became like little pieces of iron attracted to the only real

[9] 'Eternal Way of Life,' the original and traditional name of Hinduism.

magnet — our Divine Mother. Our whole family life started revolving around Amma.

In the beginning, we could only see Amma three days a year. These three days were our biggest treasure. Seeing Amma coming in the morning, our hearts would bloom like flowers to the sun. We little children would grab Amma's hands and walk with her to the stage. She would then make us sit close to her for morning meditation. I still remember the magic of staring at Amma's shiny earrings, Amma's hair, Amma's sari... I didn't want to close my eyes, afraid of missing her enchanting form. Sometimes I would visualize that I was becoming very, very small and losing myself in her white sari, like a little wave in the ocean. Then darśhan would start, and I would sit as close as possible to Amma's chair, for as long as possible, watching her in silence. As I grew up, I also started tasting the joy of sēvā.

Every year towards the end of the program, the thought of being separated from Amma again was extremely painful. Watching Dēvī, the Divine Mother, showering her love and flower petals on all beings, visible and invisible, my heart and eyes were crying. The lines from the bhajan *Kaḍutta Śhōkamām*, would echo in my mind. "Oh Mother, do not walk away, simply casting an all-knowing smile at me." I was innocently hoping that Amma would take me with her.

Even though I had to stay physically away from Amma, throughout the year, my family and I were connecting to her subtle presence through satsang and bhajans, swāmī retreats, and through our childhood games! I feel eternally grateful to my biological mother who imparted the right values and noble thoughts to us. Through her self-disciplined life and deep yearning for the divine, she has been keeping our love and devotion to God alive, day after day.

***

One year, I was feeling very sad that Amma did not look at me when I went for darśhan. Then I thought, let me try to deserve her look. I had the tendency to be extremely sensitive and easily irritated. So I spent a whole year trying hard to overcome this weakness, hoping to make Amma happy with me the next time she would see me. During my first darśhan the following year, Amma held me close to her for a long time, and gave me the most beautiful smile! I clearly felt she was acknowledging my efforts.

This was my first lesson from Amma – forgetting my own frustrations, and trying to make others around me happy instead. Amma often says that her greatest happiness is to see her children develop divine qualities. She is creating a space in all of her children's hearts, so they understand that this life's purpose is not to take, but to give.

I was five years old when my three sisters and I received our names from Amma. My twin sister reminded me how Amma had stopped in front of us after a darśhan and lovingly repeated our names one by one: "Sudha, Janani, Manohari, Dhanya!"

My second lesson from Amma came through my name. Dhanya means blessed. When the meaning was first explained to me they told me, "One who gives wholeheartedly." As I was not the most generous at home, my new name helped me to slowly open my heart and become a little more giving. Every time I was being selfish, my sisters would tell me, "Are you not Dhanya, the one who is supposed to give wholeheartedly?" So, remembering Amma's love for me, I had no choice but to try and share more.

As a teenager, I was very eager to learn Amma's IAM meditation technique, but I was too young. So with one of my sisters, I went and asked Amma for permission to learn it. Amma's answer was vast and unexpected – it was taking into consideration all of the youth in the whole world! Instead of giving us the special permission we were asking for, Amma said she will make sure that all children can learn this meditation in the future. Amma heard the prayers of many of her children, who, like my sister and I, had the same desire. She clearly showed me that I was not an isolated island, and that I should not consider only my own needs. Soon after, Amma created shorter versions of the IAM technique for kids and teenagers.

Amma says, "Children, do you know what expectations Amma has of you? You should be like the sun, not like a firefly. Fireflies make light merely for their own needs. Don't be like that. Selflessness is all you should ever wish for. You should be the ones who raise your hands to help others, even at the moment of your death."

I have often asked myself, what does it really mean to help and serve others? As a child and teenager, wanting to change the world, my mind was filled with many dreams and aspirations: being a violinist and spreading peace through music in the world, being a painter and inspiring children through beautiful book illustrations, or being a gardener and protecting nature. In this way, the practice of music and arts, and my connection with nature, kept my young mind one-pointed and filled with positive thoughts. These goals were like stepping stones, helping me turn towards the real fulfillment of life.

Later, when I came to live in Amritapuri, I had a chance to ask Amma about these dreams for my future in a room darśhan. Amma answered, "Now that you have reached this sacred place, you need to go beyond your likes and dislikes. Use your time for your sādhana. Be like a horse with blinders." I realized the importance of offering my attachments to the feet of the Divine Mother, and surrendering to her divine will. Amma knows how to turn each of her children into a blessing for the world. Let us become like tiny seeds that bow down to Mother Earth in order to grow into beautiful trees.

***

The first time I came to Amritapuri, I was fourteen years old. Our family was going through a difficult time, and I stayed with my mother and three sisters for three months. Amma's āśhram immediately felt like home to us, and our hearts were fulfilled in Amma's presence. During our second visit in 2008, it was already clear for me that I wanted to stay in Amritapuri, but I knew I had to study first.

I asked for Amma's blessings to enroll in a school to study psychomotor-therapy. This was a degree for which there were very few places, and I had none of the qualifications. It was by Amma's grace alone that I got admitted to the only school I had applied to. Still, those three years at school were very challenging for me. I was not interested in mingling with other students, and I was missing Amma's presence terribly. Every year, Amma would inquire about my studies.

During that time, I used to have dreams of Amma almost every night. In one dream, Amma was dancing with her kaimaṇis (hand cymbals), and as I was getting closer to her, she stopped and said, "So, how are your studies going?" I answered with great difficulty, "I don't really know, we will see." I started crying, putting my head on Amma's shoulder. Then, with infinite tenderness, she said, "You will tell me when you come to the āśhram."

Amma found many ways to show me that she was with me every step of the way. At the end of my studies, I went to a printing press to get my final work printed. There, I was astonished to see a full display of beautiful photos of Amma! On enquiry I found out that a person working there had just returned from a journey to Kerala, and touched by her visit to Amritapuri, she decided to display Amma's pictures! I was overwhelmed with gratitude at the thought that Amma was always with me. This conviction alone helped me to successfully complete my studies.

When I started to work with children as well as elderly people, I realized how many difficulties people are facing in modern society. This made me very concerned and sad. At the same time, I was feeling helpless and unable to find the source of joy within. I was in a situation where, even though I had the possibility to help others to some extent, I could not make use of it due to my lack of inner strength and my inability to remain happy in any situation. I felt the urgent need to reach Amma's presence.

***

During Amma's visit to France in 2012, I asked her if I could join the āśhram as a renunciate. Amma smiled and said, "Yes." When I finally joined the āśhram a few years later, I had prepared special laḍḍūs, an Indian sweet, for Amma. Amma took the whole box and slowly gave all the laḍḍūs, one by one, to her devotees. Only then, she ate one and finally gave me the last crumb. Looking at me mischievously, she exclaimed, "*Tyāga*!" and burst into laughter.

'Tyāga' means renunciation — for me, this was a clear message. If I want to know what real renunciation is, I first have to give up all my small desires and sense of individuality, and consider others before myself. Amma's laughter indicated to me that I have a long way to go to reach the state of true renunciation.

However, Amma gives us the assurance that no effort, no matter how small, will ever go to waste on the spiritual path.

She says that, at present, the spark of fire inside each one of us is covered by ashes. We need to keep blowing on the ashes to rekindle the flame. In the same way, Kṛiṣhṇa says, "In this yōga, no effort is lost and no obstacle exists. Even a little of this dharma delivers one from great fear." (*Bhagavad Gītā*, 2.40)

I have noticed that as we develop a sincere desire to overcome our negative tendencies, Amma creates perfect situations for us to identify them. A few years ago in Amritapuri, I was blessed to participate in a five-day silent retreat. Throughout the retreat, out of habit, I couldn't help mentally judging others around me. For example, I felt that some people were proud of their meditation practice. At the end of the retreat, everyone was invited to share their feelings. To my great surprise, I realized that all the judgments I had conceived in my mind about others were totally wrong! This made me think a lot, and I resolved to always try my best to refrain from judging others, as most of the time our judgments turn out to be completely wrong. The next year, I was able to participate in another retreat. This time, I could see that because I had become more aware and watchful throughout the year, this tendency had reduced a lot. I am still working on it every day.

What greater gift can we offer to the world than the ability to stop hurting others, mentally, verbally and physically? Amma says that our thoughts and emotions each have their own vibration. Thoughts of love are different from thoughts of hatred. If we are able to watch and control our thoughts first, before they manifest as words and actions, then our inner being will become filled with the light of awareness. This light will spread around us, even without our knowledge.

***

In 2021, Amma asked all of us to develop more awareness in all our movements, like walking, brushing our teeth, taking a bath, and so on. The next day, I started practicing full awareness of my movements when I walk. I was quite satisfied with my effort. However, after a few minutes, I suddenly realized that I had reached a place opposite to where I was supposed to go! My focus was on my walking alone, but not on the destination. Sometimes, we proudly believe that we have developed awareness, but for awareness to become complete, it has to be practiced at all levels — it has to become our very nature.

Amma says that real awareness is awareness of our true nature. This is true spirituality, the essence of all religions. I pray to Amma, who is the very treasure of my life and the most precious gift to humanity, to remove my selfishness, and give me a heart that prays only for the happiness of others! May this life become a song of eternal gratitude to my mother, Amma. May we all realize how blessed we are to grow in Amma's presence, and never waste a second in our journey towards our real self.

5

The Search for the Satguru

Rishi – Finland

Let me tell you what made me look for a spiritual master. At the age of seven, when I attended school in Finland, I expected teachers to educate me about the real purpose of life. I found it a bit boring that they only taught subjects such as languages, mathematics and history.

In India, parents are considered as one's first guru. In my case, it was also true, since I learned film making from my father and yōga from my mother. I was about ten years old when I practiced yōga for the first time. Even at that age, a subtle memory arose of practicing yōga earlier, perhaps arising from a past life in India. I felt that my destiny was to continue on the yōgic path in this life too. As it is said in the *Bhagavad Gītā*, the power of yōga practice done in a former life, is sufficient to arouse his interest in yōga again.

Although my father was a famous film director, he also battled with an addiction to alcohol. Fortunately, he became sober with the help of the AA (Alcoholics Anonymous) movement, a program which integrates many spiritual principles to help individuals overcome alcoholism. From this, I learned that man can become free from his addictions. On the other hand, because of my father's alcoholism, my childhood was emotionally insecure. Even though my mother did her best to support us children, I was lacking love and security.

One day in our school, our teacher told us about Prince Siddhārtha, who sat under a tree for many days. I was wondering how he could sit there for such a long time! Our teacher explained that Siddhārtha attained *nirvāṇa* and became *Buddha*. "My God, what is nirvāṇa?" I asked. "It means that you are always happy!" my teacher explained.

I had not met anybody who was always happy. I started to wonder if there is anybody like Buddha in the world in our times. Some time later, another teacher told us about Jesus, how John baptized him and a white dove descended upon him. I was wondering if at that time, Jesus became the *Light of the World* — like Buddha had been. I thought, why didn't I live during Jesus's time? I wanted to be his disciple.

Socrates was another figure that made a great impact on me during my school years. Socrates said that he always followed his inner voice, which he termed as his 'daimonion.' When I heard that, I told my classmates and teachers that I would also always follow my inner voice in life. "What does your inner voice say that you are going to do?" they asked. "I am going to make films, write books, and teach yōga. I want to find someone who is like Buddha, Jesus, or Socrates, who can teach me the secrets of life." I replied. "You are unrealistic!" they said. "There is nobody like that in the world." However, my inner voice was telling me that such a person existed, and I was determined to find him.

***

In 1972, after graduating school at the age of eighteen, I started to look for a guru. Through divine guidance, I met an Indian yōgī named Karuṇānanda-jī in Copenhagen, Denmark. This yōgī taught me to meditate, which marked the starting point of my spiritual path.

Karuṇānanda was a young monk, not an enlightened master, so in 1974, I decided to travel to India to look for my guru. Unfortunately, I did not know that Amma had started giving darśhan at that time. I met many sannyāsins[10] in India, but not an enlightened one. I lost twelve kilos, but I did not lose hope.

Over the years, I met many spiritual teachers from Hindu, Buddhist, and Christian traditions. As I had become a filmmaker and TV reporter, I had an opportunity to interview many of them, including the Dalai Lama, J. Krishnamurti, Ramana Maharshi's disciple Annamalai Swami, Maharishi Mahesh Yogi, and others. But none of them felt like my guru.

Finally, I reached a point of crisis in my life. My marriage was about to end, I lost all my properties, and my plan to move to Hollywood to make spiritual movies crashed. I desperately felt that I must find my guru in order to discover a new direction for my life. One day, while I was visiting Mother Meera in Germany, I prayed fervently, "Please God, guide me to a spiritual master! One who accepts disciples, gives mantra initiation, has an āśhram, and for whom I can do selfless service." Almost immediately, I was told that an Indian lady saint, Amma, was going to visit Sweden that summer. I was amazed at this quick answer to my prayer. So, when Amma visited Stockholm in August 1993, I took my four-year-old daughter Oona with me and we sailed to Stockholm.

I was carrying my daughter and approaching the house where Amma's darśhan took place, when I experienced an enormous wave of pure love emanating towards me. I thought, "In that house there must be a perfect master of divine love." As we approached Amma, I strongly felt — this is the moment in my life when I am finally coming to my guru. I clearly sensed that I had been with Amma before. When Amma hugged me, I told her that I would like to write an article about her for a

---

[10] A person who has renounced the material world, including family, career, and other attachments, to pursue a life devoted to spiritual practice and the pursuit of enlightenment or liberation (mōkṣha).

spiritual magazine, and she agreed. I understood that she knew who I was and what I was doing. During those blessed few days, I also received mantra initiation. Thus, my lifelong dream to find a spiritual master finally came true after twenty years of searching.

When we returned to Finland, I felt I should travel to India and make a documentary film about Amma for Finnish Television. A channel agreed to my proposal, and I signed an agreement right away, trusting my 'daimonion' that Amma would agree — and indeed she did. So, I embarked on my first journey to Amritapuri with my camera man.

***

In Amritapuri, we got an opportunity to interview Amma's father, Sugunanandan, who told us many wonderful things about Amma's childhood. The most incredible story was when Sugunanandan went for Amma's darśhan and asked God to stop visiting his daughter's body — since he wanted to marry her off. Amma told him that only the body is his daughter, not the indwelling self. If he wanted it, the body would merge back to nature. Sugunanandan demanded his daughter back, and suddenly Amma dropped lifeless to the ground. There was no sign of life in her body. Amma's mother and sister fainted out of shock, and after some time, Sugunanandan also fainted. When her father regained consciousness, Amma was still lifeless. Sugunanandan prayed fervently that Amma would come back to life, and promised that he would never again try to dictate what she should do. After being lifeless for eight hours, Amma's body slowly showed signs of life again. It was then that Sugunandan understood who his daughter truly was.

When I was interviewing Sugunanandan, I felt like I was interviewing Jesus's father, Joseph. What an opportunity! I got an even bigger opportunity when I was allowed to interview Amma herself.

That was the most amazing moment for me as a filmmaker – to interview an avatār, a divine incarnation. I understood this clearly when I asked Amma, "Did you develop into who you are now because of doing spiritual practices and selfless service as a young girl?" Amma innocently replied, "Amma never felt that she was apart from God. Amma did spiritual practices and selfless service to set an example for the future devotees." I was in awe! I understood more and more clearly that I had indeed found what I had started to look for as a schoolboy.

During this precious interview, I asked, "What happens when Amma hugs her devotees?"

Amma said, "Amma is always in the highest state of consciousness, irrelevant of time and place. But when the devotee comes to Amma, she or he is like a baby drinking the breast milk from the mother. Near Amma, the child experiences the divine love, compassion, and grace which are constantly pouring out of her. Even though these qualities are always inherent in Amma, they manifest more strongly at the moment when she hugs the devotee."

Amma continued, "Human beings are always looking for happiness, this is the motive behind all of their actions. Still, man draws sorrow to himself. This is because of the wrong impression that lasting happiness can be found outside of himself. The outside circumstances are always changing, thus no outside thing can always give happiness. Only the divine inward being can give a human being lasting happiness. The purpose of life is to become aware of our true inner being. For those who realize this, life becomes an endless source of lasting happiness and joy."

This was exactly what I wanted to hear as a schoolboy and now I not only got to hear it, I was also able to film it! Incredible! My next question to Amma was, "Is a perfect master needed for this realization?"

Amma replied, "School children often forget the words of a song, but when the teacher reminds them about the first sentence, they remember the entire song. Likewise, a real master reminds us of our true being, so that the devotee becomes aware of the real self — the real goal of life. In order to attain the highest realization, you need to do spiritual practices. The mind of man is now like a jungle, full of the beasts of desires. The eternal divine energy is lying hidden inside of man, but he is not aware of it. The mission of Amma is to awaken this divine energy inside of man and lead mankind to the path of unselfish service and love."

By interviewing Amma, my life's dream was fulfilled in a way that was much greater than I could have ever imagined. I was allowed to interview an avatār! What a blessing it was!

When the interview was over, Amma looked at me and said, "People write thick books about spirituality, but the truth is simple — *sat-chit-ānanda*."

Amma must have known that I was going to be writing books one day. 'Sat' means absolute being, 'chit' means pure awareness, and 'ānanda' means perfect bliss.

***

A few days after the interview, I went for Amma's darśhan in the Kālī Temple. Since at that time, I had already been meditating for twenty-one years, I felt ready to ask her, "Can I also become enlightened?" Amma said, "Sit next to Amma." So I sat. As I watched people coming to Amma for relief from their suffering and spiritual upliftment, I realized that this was exactly what must have happened when people were coming to Jesus. I watched as an Indian woman came crying to Amma, maybe someone dear to her had died. My ego disappeared and I saw that I am that woman, but that woman does not know we are one. Whomever I watched, I saw that I am one with that person. I felt divine love towards everybody, free from likes and dislikes. Then I saw matter becoming energy and I could see through the energy. I saw the whole universe as an illusion, like a cosmic movie which is projected on God's consciousness. I saw that God is everywhere and that I am one with God. Tears of bliss were rolling down my cheeks. The bliss and divine love were so intense that I could not speak.

Afterwards, I understood that I had experienced nirvāṇa, samādhi, or heaven, and that Amma lives in this Advaitic state of oneness all the time. I became more and more convinced that Amma has the power to give that state whenever she wants to.

During the interview I had asked Amma, "How is the spiritual master able to help us?"

Amma said, "An incomplete being cannot remove the incompleteness of another — only he who has removed his or her own sorrow can conquer the sorrow of others."

So, there I was, I had found what I was looking for — a perfect spiritual master — and she had given me a glimpse of the final state of sat-chit-ānanda, the absolute bliss, and divine love. That blissful God-union vanished slowly, and I started the purification process of a sādhaka — a spiritual seeker with the aim of liberation.

The *Guru Gītā*, the 'Song of the Guru,' says, 'God is Guru and Guru is God.' So the divine teacher is everywhere and all life situations are teaching us. When the student is ready, the teacher will arrive and teaching will also happen through the body of the physical guru.

In my life, this meant that Amma began creating situations where my unconscious mind was spurred so that the vāsanās, latent tendencies gathered over many lifetimes, started to come to the surface. Amma has said that she will make a small spot of dirt so big that the devotee becomes aware of it and can work to overcome it. Sometimes, we might feel that this task is too enormous, that we can never overcome all the weaknesses that have been accumulated over hundreds of lifetimes. Because of this, I asked Amma during the interview, "Do the great spiritual teachers have the capacity to take the sins or the conditionings of their devotees?"

Amma replied, "All the sins can't be taken, but some can be taken. Sometimes, Amma suffers the sins of her devotees in her own being, but emphasizes that it is necessary that the devotee does his or her part. If necessary, Amma can burn all the conditionings away, but she only does this if the devotee is mature enough."

I asked Amma, "What must the devotee do to attain the goal as quickly as possible?"

Amma said, "Obedience to the words of the guru is very necessary. Conditionings will not be removed by themselves. That's why it is absolutely necessary to follow the instructions of the guru and to do the spiritual practices one has received from him. Intense longing for the goal is also very much needed."

***

After completing the filming I invited Amma to visit Finland. Amma said okay right away, even though there were only about six Finnish devotees at that time. However, when the film was shown twice on Finnish television, hundreds of thousands of people saw it.

When I told people about my experiences with Amma, I felt her divine energy coming through me. I saw people's hearts opening because of Amma's grace and some of them were shedding tears. So, when Amma came for the first time to Finland more than a thousand people came to see her. A crew from the main TV news channel also came to film the event.

One year, the Minister of Culture and Ecclesiastical Affairs in Finland, Tanja Karpela, who was my friend, came to welcome Amma at the beginning of the program. She became so attracted to Amma that she wanted to visit Amritapuri with her children. I was supposed to be her host. A big media affair started in Finland, since Tanja, being the Minister of Church Affairs, wanted to meet a Hindu guru in India. It had never happened in Finnish history. I told Amma almost daily about the comments made by the Prime Minister and the Board of the Church.

Then, two days before the Minister was expected to arrive in India, Amma told me to tell her not to come. I was shocked, but I wanted to do as the guru said. Soon, I realized the reason for this. The Minister would have arrived at the āśhram just when the 2004 Asian tsunami hit and poured into the āśhram — Amma did not want that to happen.

The darśhan program on the day of the tsunami was supposed to take place in the big hall of the aśhram. However, Amma said in the morning that she will give darśhan in the Kālī Temple. Everyone was surprised as the crowd that day was very large and not everyone could fit into the Kālī Temple. We understood later why Amma insisted on this. Later that day, the waves of the Tsunami overflowed into the big hall, which could have put many people at risk!

That morning, I had planned to go to the seashore to swim, run, and walk. Before that, I needed to go ask Amma what I should tell the Finnish media as to why the Minister was asked not to come to the āśhram. I saw Swami Shubhamritananda talking to Amma. Swami said he could not ask Amma, because they came to know through the internet that a tsunami had hit the east coast of India; many villages had been destroyed and people had drowned. Amma continued giving darśhan and I sat next to her, waiting for an answer. I waited at least an hour, thinking, "Why is Amma taking so long to answer me?" I was anxious to go enjoy the seashore.

Then, I heard a terrible sound of rushing waters and people shouting "Veḷḷam, veḷḷam! Water, water!" I realized that the tsunami was now hitting the āśhram! I got up from Amma's side and went to the doorway. All the āśhram yards had become like rivers, but the waters did not reach up to the level of the temple hall. I understood right away that this was the reason why Amma did not let me go to the seashore. I would have drowned. Amma had saved my life! Not only me — everybody was saved by Amma! Nobody died in the āśhram that day, even though 186 people died in the village areas on the peninsula surrounding the āśhram.

I informed the Finnish media that the Minister could not come to the āśhram because of the tsunami, but I did not tell them that Amma had asked me to inform them to cancel their trip two days earlier.

Eight months later, Amma came to Finland and I drove her from the airport to the house where she was staying. When I opened the car door for her, she asked me, "Rishi, where were you when the tsunami happened?" I said, "I was right next to you Amma!" Like a child, Amma innocently replied, "Ooooh!" and walked to the house, acting as if she did not know where I was at the time of the tsunami.

Some time later, when I was sitting near Amma, I asked inwardly for her to give me a sign if she had really saved my life during the tsunami. In that exact moment, Amma turned towards me and gave me a beautiful, all-knowing smile. Thank you Amma, for saving my life. Now I, and all of us devotees, need to be saved from the tsunami of māyā – ignorance.

***

Over these twenty-nine years of being with Amma, I have had many wonderful and also painful experiences. I have understood that the meaning of all of these experiences has been to weaken my vāsanās and to help me to get rid of them. At times I have climbed upwards and at times downwards on the ladder of spiritual development – yet with Amma's grace, I have been able to continue climbing.

One time, I heard Amma explain that the *mā-ōṁ* mantra is a mahāvākya – a great saying of truth. That had a powerful impact on me. 'Ōṁ' represents wisdom and pure awareness and 'mā' represents divine and selfless love. When we have both, then we have everything.

Many years ago, I was wondering, will I ever become fully free of the six enemies of the mind – desire, hatred, greediness, attachment, pride, and miserliness? That same day, Amma came to her yard and started to give prasad to the devotees. Her back was towards me, and I prayed, "Please Amma, throw me one sweet." Amma immediately turned around and threw me a sweet! I was able to easily catch it, as it landed right in the middle of my hand! It felt that this was one of Amma's miracles. I realized that Amma was telling me that the satguru will send the prasad of divine knowledge at the right time to the devotee, but he must pray for it and receive it.

Once in a group darśhan in her room, I asked Amma, "If Vālmīki[11], who started out as a robber and a murderer, could attain God-realization — is it also possible for us?" Amma replied, "Yes, but you need to have the same intensity as Vālmīki had." A Finnish lady asked, "How can we get that sort of intensity?" Amma answered, "Pray for it!"

Amma please bless us, your children, with intense longing — so that the tsunami of māyā does not swallow us, and we may attain the highest goal of liberation.

[11] Sage and author of the great epic *Rāmāyaṇa* who was transformed through an encounter with the Seven Sages who gave him the 'Rāma' mantra, which he chanted fervently over years until he attained self-realization.

6

Guiding Seekers of All Traditions

Nirupama Orona - USA

This story begins on June 14, 1988 in Santa Fe, New Mexico. I was in my studio apartment, getting ready for an art show. Back then, I was a professional fine artist. On that particular day, I was painting the Aztec god, *Quetzalcoatl* — the Winged Serpent. Suddenly, I heard a knock on my door and I went to answer it. It was two female friends of mine. They told me there was an Indian woman saint visiting Santa Fe, they were on their way to see her and they stopped by to see if I would like to go with them. I replied, "No, I'm not interested," and sent them on their way.

The afternoon rolled around, I had my lunch and went back to painting. Again, there was a knock on my door. I opened it and to my surprise, there stood another two female friends coming for the same exact reason. However, my answer was the same, "No, I'm not interested!" and I sent them on their way.

Next, the evening rolled around, I had my dinner and continued painting the Aztec god. Guess what happened? Yes, another knock on my door, and yes, it was another two female friends. "There is a holy woman from India and we came to take you to see her."

So, now I started listening. I thought to myself, "Gosh, I guess I'm supposed to go see this holy woman!" The reason I kept turning away my friends was because I already had two spiritual teachers in my Native American tradition, I knew nothing about Hinduism and was not looking elsewhere. However, it was strikingly obvious that I was supposed to see this woman saint.

So, I jumped in the car with my friends and we drove up into the mountains above Santa Fe. We parked the car and walked a distance through the Piñon, Juniper, and Ponderosa Pines till we reached a large tent. I walked into the tent with my friends and sat on a pillow on the floor. I had no idea what to expect. The first person I saw was a western woman in a white sari standing at a table. There was a stage at the back of the tent with saris draped as curtains. Three skinny, young Indian men about my age came to the right side of the stage. One was standing, dressed in yellow, and the other two in white sat on the floor and began to play Indian instruments. The brahmachārī in yellow began to sing accompanied by the other two in white. Then, I heard chanting from the other side of the sari curtain that was still closed. I heard a bell ringing, saw smoke coming up from the other side of the curtain, and then, the curtain opened. Taken aback, I gasped in awe! I thought to myself, "Oh my God, she is a high soul!"

This mysterious woman in a green sari radiated like the sun — her eyes, big and dark, looked as if they contained the endless depths of the universe. This wonderous Goddess peered straight into my eyes! As our eyes locked, she looked into the depths of my soul, seeing everything and the most inner parts of my being. Incredibly, I knew that everyone in the tent was experiencing the same exact thing I was! Amma never moved her head but looked straight into the souls of all who were there.

When Amma started darśhan, I got up on my knees to get a better look. She laughed, sang, and was talking to the people around her. Enjoying herself, and in no rush at all, Amma gave ten-minute darśhans to each person. To be honest, after seeing Amma, it was as if everyone else in the room disappeared.

My eyes fixated on her — this wondrous Goddess. Then, a subtle being, probably a *Kachina*, a Native American nature spirit, put his hand on the back of my head and began to push it to the ground, saying, "She is worthy of your adoration." I could not resist my head making its way to the floor, and when it touched the ground, I began to cry.

Why do we cry when we meet Amma? She didn't even have to touch me, but I was touched — my heart overflowed and cried a river of love. I prayed, "Oh darling holy lady! Thank you for coming to my motherland, to our people, the Pueblo people."

I did not get darśhan that night and just sat with my friends watching Amma for some time. My impression was that she lovingly accepts all, regardless of who they are. I had to leave when my friends were ready to go, as they were my ride. So we left, even as the saint was still enjoying and giving darśhan.

***

Meeting Amma for the first time in Santa Fe, New Mexico is actually a miraculous thing for me since this is my ancestral homeland. I am a Pueblo Indian woman and my ancestors are the ancient Puebloan people.

I would like to quote a passage from Swami Paramatmananda Puri's book, *On the Road to Freedom, Vol. 2.* Here, he is referring to the first U.S. tour in 1987 and the first time Amma stayed in Santa Fe, New Mexico.

"On the night of her arrival in Santa Fe, Mother could not even get a wink of sleep. She told us in the morning that the entire night was spent giving darśhan to some funny looking subtle beings who were living in the neighborhood. When asked what they looked like, Mother replied that they had the torso of an animal and the legs of a human being. She said she had never seen such beings before. By some strange coincidence, in one of the rooms of the house where we were staying, there were a number of figurines that answered exactly to Mother's description. When asked what they were, the owner of the house said they were the images of gods, called Kachinas, that are worshiped by the local tribes of Native American Indians. From this, we understood that such beings do exist and can be seen by those who have eyes to see. Apparently, they recognized who Mother was and flocked to her for her blessings."

The Kachinas are the gods, or dēvas, of the natural world in Pueblo country. They are known as Bear Kachina, Owl Kachina, Eagle Kachina, and Cactus Kachina, among others, and are very sacred to us, the Pueblo people. They are our guardians, spiritual teachers, disciplinarians, and guides. The Kachinas also represent the different clans and high priest societies to which the Pueblo people belong. I, for example, belong to the Spruce Clan, a very sacred pine tree, known for its gift of bringing the clouds and rain. It is said that these ancient Kachinas followed the Pueblo people from the previous three worlds to the present fourth world, guiding and protecting us along the way.

One evening in Santa Fe, I was awakened by the Owl Kachina Mother, who is believed to be very ancient and wise. She stood at the foot of my bed, enormous in size! She spoke to me, saying, "There are realities beyond God." I thought to myself, "What is this reality beyond God?" It was not until I declared Amma as my guru and spent time with her that I realized what the Owl Kachina Mother had been trying to tell me. Amma is, indeed, the reality beyond God. She is the Creatrix, Ādi Parāśhakti, the Supreme Being.

With a satguru, a perfect master like Amma, any sincere seeker can be guided in their own tradition. Being around Amma for so many years, I came to many "Aha!" moments, when I thought to myself, "So this is what our elders were speaking of. This is what the Kachina meant when she spoke to me." Amma has deepened my understanding of my own native Pueblo traditions, making them crystal clear and more potent within me. Under her care, love and watchful eye, the flower blossoms no matter what variety it is or from which place of origin.

***

Even though I met Amma in the summer of 1988, I did not see her again for another six years. Amma would visit Santa Fe in the summers and this was when I was usually on pilgrimage with one of my teachers and participating in seasonal ceremonies like the sundance or pow wows.

There was one gathering I was invited to at the Six Nations Indian Reservation that changed everything for me. I was asked to speak at the seven-day gathering. One day, 400 Native American women gathered together in a big hall, and one by one, the invited guests began to speak. The brave, tribal women were relating to all of us the conditions on their reservations and in their tribal communities. Stories of poverty; substance abuse; domestic violence; lack of food; loss of land, water and hunting rights; loss of language...it was utterly heartbreaking to hear what our people were going through. I was supposed to speak, but heartbroken, I thought to myself, "What can I possibly say to these women that will uplift their hearts? What words of hope and comfort can I give to them?" Then it dawned on me – I need to become perfect. I need to become a light in this world, for my people, for all my relations.

I decided that the next year when Amma would return, I would go to her. For some reason, I knew that Amma could take me to that place of perfection and teach me about love and service.

Even though I had two Native American traditional spiritual teachers, they were not perfect, and in my heart there was always a yearning to be with a perfect master. One of my spiritual teachers' names was Guadalupe de la Cruz Rios, a traditional Huichol Mara'akame, or shaman, from Mexico. Guadalupe received darśhan from Amma in 1995. I remember Guadalupe was speaking to Amma during her darśhan. Amma looked at her with such love and tenderness, listening to her attentively. I don't know if she spoke to Amma in her native tongue or in Spanish. I had never seen Guadalupe so happy, she was overjoyed like a child in Amma's arms. After giving darśhan to Guadalupe, Amma said, "There are still spiritual masters among the Native American Indian people and if you want to see them, they will show themselves."

My other teacher's name was Pat Kennedy. He was a Chippewa Cree ghost dance medicine man from Montana. Because he was a Plains Indian, I was able to participate in traditional rituals that were different from the Pueblo traditions. One such rite was the sundance. This involves a year of abstinence and fasting, culminating in the actual sundance, occurring during a full moon in the summer months. During the sundance, we dance as the sun rises in the East and sets in the West while fasting from food and water for four days. As Amma has said, "The sun is a representation of God in nature."

In preparation for this sacred ceremony, I was taught by an elder about the White Buffalo Calf Woman, the holy woman who brought 'the seven sacred rights' to the Lakota tribe. The tradition says that she was a very beautiful woman dressed in white buckskin and bearing a bundle on her back, appearing from a herd of buffalo, and then returning to the buffalo.

After teaching the people and giving them her gifts, White Buffalo Calf Woman left them, promising to return. She let them know that she wouldn't return for a long period of time and asked the Lakota to integrate the rites into their lives till then and work with them eagerly. According to her prophecy, her return would be in a time of great crisis and upheaval, shortly before the prophesied 'great cleansing of the earth.' She would return to support nature and all tribal peoples.

Learning of this and knowing that we have reached this critical juncture on earth, I began to fervently pray to this holy woman. My constant prayer was, "I am waiting for your return, Mother. Please save our people!"

***

In the summer of 1995, a friend and I decided to drive to Seattle, Washington from Santa Fe, New Mexico to be with Amma at the beginning of her U.S. tour. After the Seattle programs were over, we made our way to the San Ramon program via Montana. We drove through the famous Yellowstone National Park, considered to be a very sacred place to the local tribes. The park is full of buffalo, elk, deer, and other indigenous animals.

As I was driving through this very beautiful and holy land, I was trying to make up time and drove a little faster than was advisable. I was so focused on the two-lane highway that I did not notice a herd of buffalo grazing on the right side of the road. My companion in the car, Kathy, suddenly yelled, "Watch out for that buffalo on the side of the road!" I put my foot on the brake to slow the car down and looked to my right where the buffalo were grazing.

As we slowly drove past them, one little female calf that was closest to my car picked up her head and looked straight into my eyes! My heart jumped into my throat – for who did I see staring back at me? The big, beautiful black eyes of my beloved Amma! It wasn't that the buffalo's eyes just looked like

Amma's. That beautiful little calf with eyes full of tremendous love, compassion, and tenderness, *was* Amma! The experience was so intense and profound for me that I could not speak and remained quiet for hours. Kathy finally asked me if I was alright. I did not say a word, I could not. I just kept my eyes on the road in silence, deeply contemplating what I had seen.

For me, this vision was Amma's confirmation that she is indeed the sacred woman I had been praying to. She has kept her word that she would return to us during this time of great crisis and upheaval. How blessed we are! The White Buffalo Calf Woman has returned for the people, the land, and all my relations. I remember once Swami Purnamritananda Puri said to me, "God will appear to the people according to their traditions."

As Amma has said, the main Goddess for the Native American Indian people is Mother Earth. We do not need to build temples because Mother Earth is our temple. The mountains, ocean, rivers and birds, the four-legged, the trees and flowers are the chapters in our scriptures. We learn how to live in a dharmic way by being with nature, loving nature, and respecting nature. We learn how to live in joy through nature. We learn how to worship God by observing nature. We do not see ourselves as separate, but as related to all of Her creation, our brethren. All have equal value and are sacred children of the Mother. To love the Mother is to love all beings, the trees, flowers, and all of nature. May all beings live in this joy, love, and harmony.

7

"Find *You*! Find *That*!"

Devapriyan - France

The only scripture I have studied in this life is Amma's words, gazes and actions, so I will share how they have influenced me and transformed my life beyond what I could ever have expected.

My parents were always very kind to my sister and me, and they showed a sincere interest in spiritual matters. Despite all their love and efforts, in my younger years I was engulfed by deep resentment towards myself. I perceived myself as not being fit for this world and unable to interact in a normal way with others. I felt like a lion in a cage, unable to express myself, and all this energy that could not be expressed would turn back against me. I was completely lost on how to approach life, and communication with others seemed impossible.

Around this time, in 2001, my parents met Amma. On the way back from our holidays, we stopped at the new āśhram in Pontgouin, near Paris in France. There, I met people that inspired me and seemed driven by a different perspective on life. They seemed happier than I was. Swamini Amritajyoti Prana was living there, trying to share with others the unexplainable magnificence and depth that she had experienced with Amma. I am really grateful for all her years of service.

I was seventeen years old then. In my family, the focus was all about getting good grades and a good job. Amma says, "There are two kinds of education: education for life and education for living." While 'education for life' focuses on making life meaningful and beautiful, my family's priority was acquiring an 'education for living,' solely for the purpose of obtaining a good income to live a comfortable life. This led me to build everything around my intellect. Yet I was yearning to move from my head to my hands and heart.

That year I started coming regularly to the āśhram to learn to use my hands instead of my brain, to sing bhajans, and to dig holes in the cold, all of which I enjoyed very much. Finally, this was something real and straightforward, much less complicated than all the thoughts and emotions that were overwhelming me.

Still, in my head, I was sure that spirituality was all about being serious and dealing with very important concepts. This mindset made me judgmental towards others, and myself. I had such a narrow understanding of spirituality that there were very few people who fit the image I had in my mind of what a spiritual person should be like — certainly not myself!

To be honest, when I attended my first Amma program I was not really impressed. The innocent enthusiasm and devotion I witnessed were not corresponding with my preconceived notion of spirituality. The program was nice, but I expected spirituality to be a whole different kind of affair, appearing much more serious. However, with her infinite grace and softness, Amma started patiently unweaving the threads that made up the jail that confined my mind and heart. Just like a wildflower finding its way through a tiny crack in the heavy, dark pavement of a road, Amma was already searching for an opportunity to shine through the layer of darkness covering my heart.

***

Until then I had taken refuge in academic recognition and success where I found things came easily for me and where I felt

I could be acknowledged and recognized as a good person. Academics was the entry point that brought me closer to Amma. In 2003, I decided to come for a month of academic exchange at Amrita University. Originally I had planned to stay at the Ettimadai campus, seven hours from Amritapuri. However, Amma apparently had another plan. By her grace, I arrived on the very day Amma was starting her program near Ettimadai.

It was my first trip outside of Europe. When I arrived at Amma's public darśhan program, I hadn't slept for thirty hours, had only eaten a snack purchased from a train vendor, and was dealing with an upset stomach and a confused mind. Arun, an āśhram resident living at the Ettimadai campus, spotted me in the crowd and spent most of his time patiently guiding me through the program. He asked me whether I would like to go to Amritapuri rather than Ettimadai for my academic exchange. I agreed and he quickly worked out the details with Swami Abhayamritananda Puri.

Arriving at Amritpuri and living in the āśhram were quite a shock. While all the students and most of the āśhram residents I met were really nice, I was overwhelmed by the heat, the charged atmosphere, and especially, the schedule for spiritual practices that I was taking very seriously. I just could not figure out how to make it all work. I felt trapped and began to understand that the real cage was within myself. I felt like a circus lion, not knowing how to escape from the dungeon of my mind. Until that moment in my life, I had thought that my mind was a safe haven protecting me from the outside world. Slowly I was starting to realize that my mind itself was actually the problem.

At one point, during a question and answer session in the Kālī Temple, I spontaneously burst out in laughter at a joke Amma had made. She spotted the crack in the wall of my mind and looked at me immediately with intensely shining eyes. The memory of this gaze has stayed within me for years.

I came back to Europe in the cold of winter, only knowing that I absolutely needed to go back to India as soon as possible for a longer stay. I had touched the possibility of interacting differently with the world, transcending the limitations of my mind. I could not figure out exactly what this meant, but I knew that Amma could teach me.

One year later, I joined the Journalism Postgraduate Diploma at Amrita University's Ettimadai campus. One day, a professor innocently asked why I was always securing the first page article of our campus newspaper. I suddenly realized that by always fighting to capture the first spot, I was barring others from the chance and unnecessarily taking more opportunities for myself. Other students also needed to write first page articles to support their future job applications. I was doing what I thought was best for me, but was unaware of the needs of others. Since I was lacking confidence in myself, I had an overwhelming need to be rewarded as the best student. This left no space for considering others in my mind. I could not listen to anything other than my craving to be accepted, recognized, and acknowledged.

The example set by many of the professors at the college has been a guiding light in my life ever since. These professors had obtained the highest recognition they could hope for from the world, with access to the best jobs in their respective fields, yet they decided to forgo all of that and dedicate themselves to a life of service.

***

What I saw of Amma's work in India deeply touched my heart. I came back to France with a fully new perspective on life. I realized that real success for me would not be limited to an engineering degree and a good job; it would include learning to interact with others in a more relaxed and compassionate way, and finding peace within myself. I strongly felt the need to sustain and foster my connection with Amma if I wanted my life to evolve in this direction.

Being away from Amma's physical presence compels us to be creative in finding our own connection with her. Since I am quite an action-oriented person, the easiest way for me has been to associate with the many dimensions of Amma's global family.

Amma makes sure that her āśhrams bring together diverse groups of people, countering our tendency to gravitate towards those who are similar to us. The people I encountered at the French āśhram were often very different from me, perfectly pushing my inner buttons to highlight issues hidden under the surface.

I had been doing sēvā with some guys for a few weeks and I got really irritated by them. One day, during a program in Europe, I went to Amma and expressed my frustration. She looked at me deeply, her eyes expressing the exact same anger that was raging in my heart. But at the same time, there was a tiny smile at the corner of her lips, showing that all of this was just a play.

Suddenly, I realized that it was actually my own choice to either make the situation difficult or to witness the līlā, the divine play, and not take it so seriously. After speaking to Amma, I walked away and ended up standing next to one of the people who had been driving me mad a few minutes before. We simply stood there together, watching Amma give darśhan. Amma had not said a word, but she had shown me the way through the situation.

I often feel that the moment we step into one of Amma's āśhrams the inner work starts. It is as if these deep, underwater currents inside are set into motion. You know something is cooking up for you, but you don't know what it is. It's both scary and exciting.

Being involved in the French Pontgoin āśhram near Paris was the first way I found to stay connected to Amma's grace. Doing handy work on the weekends was an incredible relaxation from the tensions of studies and work during the week. I loved it! At some point, Swamini Amritajyoti Prana asked me to participate in the cleaning of the āśhram. I thought to myself, "If Swamini had visited my home and seen the mess, surely she wouldn't have such a crazy idea as asking me to clean!"

It was sēvā, so I tried my best. I learned a lot about brushes and how to use them in different ways. More importantly, I discovered that when I started seeing an action as a service to Amma, I could start appreciating something I had previously disliked.

In order to stay true to my desire to balance my life, I had made a commitment to myself to never engage in intellectual sēvā, but to focus only on hands-on tasks. Amma soon helped me reconcile these different aspects of myself through sēvā.

***

In 2008, during an academic project for my engineering school, we had the opportunity to secure European funding to build an eco-friendly bee-house with other young people in the French āśhram. This project brought together the different parts of my life, allowing me to make use of my studies while participating in āśhram sēvā. I understood that everything we do can be related to Amma, no matter where we are, as long as we have the right attitude.

Doing hands-on work that summer with other youngsters that shared similar values was an incredible experience. I began to understand that my serious attitude about life was not doing me any good, and that interacting with other people my age would help me be a happier person.

I decided to contribute to the exciting adventure of AYUDH, Amma's youth movement, which was rapidly developing in Europe under the guidance of Swami Amritaswarupananda Puri, Swami Shubhamritananda Puri and Swamini Amritajyoti Prana. They always remained so youthful and dynamic, and I was sure their association with AYUDH was one of the reasons for it. I had found the elixir of eternal youth described in the 358th name of the *Lalitā Sahasranāma*:

> *ōṁ taruṇyai namaḥ*
> I bow down to Devi, who is ever young.

Ten years of association with AYUDH didn't stop my hair from falling out or turning gray, nor did it prevent wrinkles from appearing around my eyes. The real impact it has made in my life goes beyond these physical changes. Young people are always open to new ideas and projects, as long as it makes sense to them, and they feel a sincere sense of urgency regarding the state of the world. Most of all, young people don't tend to take life too seriously. It's this attitude that has been my long lasting, inner friend.

During the famous *Mātā Rānī* closing bhajan session by Swami Amritaswarupananda, about three hundred of us would dance and sing during the final night of our youth summer summits. The scene would invoke the feeling of being with Amma during her Dēvi Bhāva[12] programs. We would feel this in Europe in the

[12] 'The divine mood of Dēvī' when Amma reveals her oneness with the Divine Mother.

midst of July, even though Amma would physically be 9,000 kilometers away, usually on tour in the U.S.

Several youngsters have told me that they never imagined there could be such joyful gatherings without any alcohol involved. It's incredible to see hundreds of youngsters, half of whom had never met Amma, discovering a new perspective on life, especially at a time when they are exposed to so many negative influences in the world. This is one of the rare things that has succeeded in cracking my inner walls and led me to shed tears of joy in the last few years. I've seen what a difference it made in my life to be exposed to this environment during my difficult teenage years, so seeing others go through that process is still very touching for me. The joy, simplicity, and enthusiasm that AYUDH has brought me has rubbed off on my personal and professional life, and has been instrumental in helping me understand others better.

***

Amma has also taken care of the more material aspects of my life. After my studies, I found a job working with an NGO (non-governmental organization) next to the French āśhram, helping farmers produce local and environmentally friendly food. At the end of a sabbatical year spent with Amma in 2014, I asked her advice regarding coming back to France. She said,

"The world is like a supermarket. We have to know why we go there and not get distracted from the things we really want."

Amma's grace helped me keep this focus. I was able to turn my full-time job to part-time, so that I could tour with her regularly and have time for sēvā in France.

Participating in Amma's world tours was an important part of my 'stay-in-touch with Amma' plan. Concrete and down-to-earth sēvā has been Amma's perfect antidote to taking myself too seriously! I will always remember how Swami Ramakrishnananda would very casually join us in the kitchen at any time for preparing Indian snacks, such as frying papadams or rolling pooris on busy Dēvi Bhāva program nights. The feeling of brotherhood that is created when cooking or packing up a program together, exhausted in the wee hours of the morning, is a unique experience in life. When you spend six weeks in a row just rolling and frying pūrīs with the same guy all day and night, you can't hide much of yourself from him. This feeling of togetherness brings immense satisfaction, since it reduces our sense of separation and isolation in life. From participating in the tours, I gained the understanding that community life and brotherhood were powerful ways to go beyond my own mind.

When I started thinking of where to settle down, it only made sense to be close to Amma's āśhram near Paris. I joined a small group initiated by the āśhram coordinator that was discussing the idea of building an eco-village nearby. With Amma's grace, this idea quickly became a reality. For Nirmukti, my partner, and me, living just by ourselves made little sense.

The night before the French government imposed the first lockdown, Nirmukti and I decided to seek refuge in the French āśhram. We stayed there for several months, with twenty other people who had made the same decision. This was an incredible experience, juggling to combine remote work and managing the daily functioning of a newly formed, diverse group that had never experienced a situation like this before. It was a bit crazy sometimes to answer important workcalls in the middle of a bhajan rehearsal that was due to be streamed live a few minutes later. There was no space to rest and sit idle, yet the intensity I felt was deep and nourishing. It also fostered and deepened my spiritual practices. I was actually happy when the second lockdown came, since it gave us a good reason to temporarily move back to the āśhram once again.

The community of Amma's children has given structure to my life and helped me grow, providing so much support and inspiration. I feel so much happier now, and I feel that the best is yet to come. These experiences have repeatedly shown me that when Amma is first in our agenda and we do our best, all the rest falls into place by itself at the right time.

***

The next step for me is to put Amma first, not only in my outward life, where she has gently settled, but in my daily thoughts and emotions as well. I've always had the strong vāsanā, or tendency, to analyze and pretend to understand the trajectories of society and the world. I've wasted a lot of time reading endless news articles and I'm still struggling not to do it too much. There is one thing for certain: we're now in Kali Yuga, the age where materialism and unrighteousness predominates, and it's a pretty dark business. Dwelling in that energy does not do good. What does good however, and actually guides us through any difficulty in life, is the remembrance of our beloved Mother.

History has shown us that in the darkest of ages, light can always find its way through. With all our vāsanās and our conditioning, we sometimes feel helpless to change. Yet we should always try our best to decide the influences that we expose ourselves to. Science and epigenetics are clear on the fact that our environment conditions the way our genes are interpreted, and therefore influences our body-mind continuum, the interconnectedness between the physical and mental and emotional states. Amma makes it extremely simple:

"Let us sow good thoughts and reap good actions. Let us sow good actions and reap good habits. From good habits and behavior, we can build a beautiful life. Through living a good life, we can rewrite our destiny."

Once, I went to Amma and enquired about the meaning of life. Amma replied by pointing her finger at my heart, and said, "Find *You*!" Then, she pointed her finger towards the Infinite, saying, "Find *That*!"

I've made some progress towards knowing myself, and about the infinite, only God knows. What is for sure, is that to go any further in both these directions, I need to let positive influences sink deeper and deeper into myself to change my thoughts, words, and actions. Only this can help me overcome the fears, tensions, and habits from the past.

Mother, please give us the grace to always seek refuge in the remembrance of you. Please give us the strength to live up to being sons and daughters of the all-pervading Mother of the Universe. May we rise to become your disciples, and in whatever small way we can, make ourselves fit and available for your work.

8

Amma's Grace

Anadi - Finland

I didn't look for a guru and I didn't believe in God. I was very happy with my atheistic life and truly believed that *me, myself,* and *I* were in charge of my destiny. I didn't have any sorrows — my life was filled with work and I was moving fast in my career. Without Amma's interference, I could see myself as a very tough businesswoman, climbing to the top of the company hierarchy with high heeled shoes and a tight skirt, pushing others out of my way without empathy or compassion. Amma saved me, my near and dear ones, and my co-workers from that horrifying future. I consider this as the first time that Amma saved my life.

In January 1997, Amma came to me in a dream. She hugged me, fed me some bread with a lot of butter on top of it and said, "I am your mother." When I woke up, I felt like I had been in India (where I had never visited) and I knew something profound had happened. I couldn't explain it. I felt that I had experienced something that was greater than *me, myself,* and *I.* There was God.

Two days after this Amma dream, I was in my birth mother's house. The doorbell rang and I ran downstairs to open the door. A family friend was standing there and he handed me a book with Amma's face on the cover. It was Amma's biography. I immediately grabbed the book and said, "This is for me." I couldn't put the book down. I found out that Amma was coming to Stockholm in August, so I started to organize a trip and eventually there was a bus load of people traveling to meet Amma from our city.

When we arrived at the venue in Stockholm, I can only remember the peace and love radiating from the building where Amma was giving darśhan. I remember sitting in a line for hours, but I don't remember my darśhan. I don't remember much after that either, except that I was wandering in the streets of Stockholm during the night and wondering about the miracles of life. I remember feeling so profoundly happy and content.

We soon received permission from Amma to start a spiritual center in our city in Finland. My life was full of sādhanā and sēvā during that time. We organized courses, gave free yōga lessons, and held satsangs. I stopped drinking alcohol and coffee, and tried to be a good devotee while praying to Amma for self-realization.

However, several coincidences led me back to worldly life and other things filled my time. My work with horses was fulfilling and I didn't feel any more need to do sādhanā. I was slipping further away from my spiritual path, but then, something happened. One spring night, when I was driving back home, I felt a strong desire to leave everything and go to Amritapuri. I still remember the spot on the road where this happened. I gave up my apartment, lived at the horse stable where I worked, and saved money for the trip. Before leaving, I even shaved my head. I still don't know why I did that, but in my mind, it was a part of the process of going to India.

Before leaving for Amritapuri, I went to see Amma at a program in London along with my son. He had turned eighteen and was living in his own apartment. When we went for darśhan together, I was inwardly praying to Amma to take care of him while I was in Amritapuri. After darśhan, Amma squeezed my cheek saying, "We will see." I was stunned that she knew that I was coming. When I came to my senses, I started to look for my son. Amma had asked him to sit beside her. She definitely had been taking care of him always, and would continue to do so during my stay.

In Amritapuri, a revelation hit me. Why had Amma picked me up from Finland when there were so many people coming to have her darśhan? I feel Amma brought me to Amritapuri because I could not find a way to do sādhanā while staying in the world as there were simply too many desires to follow.

***

Even to this day, I can never understand the amount of grace Amma poured on me when she saved my life, and not only that, guided me to serve others and understand the true goal of human birth. My path hasn't been straight. I have been circling, stuck and slipping, but Amma has always been at my side. My faith in her has never shaken.

Everything was so simple when being around Amma. My bosses asked me, "Why do you travel with Amma so much?" I had to think before I could reply. "Whenever I am in Amma's presence, everything is very clear."

From the beginning it was obvious that sēvā was my way to receive Amma's teachings. In fact, Amma has only spoken to me verbally three times during the twenty-five years I have known her. At one point, I was very jealous of all the people having conversations with Amma. But instead of speaking to me out loud, Amma has kept speaking to me through sēvā, and that has kept me doing sēvā with all my heart.

Veggie chopping sēvā has been a great teacher. Garlic taught me that even if something looks rotten and bad, I should never give up! Underneath the rotten surface, there is something good inside. Cilantro taught me that we have to remove our negative vāsanās or latent tendencies (the very bad cilantro leaves) in order to have only the good qualities. The café sēvā taught me that compassion and love will melt our anger. Each sēvā has taught me something, and I can always feel Amma's presence while taking part in it.

Amma gave me a nice lesson about how I should never question any sēvā I am given. I was attending the Paris program and doing dishwashing sēvā for three days. There were not so many people to help, so we washed all day long. When the program ended and I took off the washing gloves, I noticed that my hands were sore from being immersed in water for so long. I decided to continue to follow the tour to the Netherlands program. There, I showed my hands at the sēvā desk and said, "I will do anything else, but I don't think I am able to wash dishes." They said, "Okay, you do security." My reaction was, "Oh, what a boring sēvā!" How wrong I was! I got the chance to stand near Amma's room when she finished the darśhan and help with security during a pūjā ceremony. They told me, however, that I was not a very convincing security person, because I was simply crying the whole time!

Even though I was not performing any japa and living a worldly life, I felt that Amma was always near me. In 2007, I was traveling with my husband in Europe on a motorbike. He was an atheist, but accepted Amma. He had a brand new bike and he enjoyed driving very fast. I didn't enjoy it, as you can imagine. He explained to me that he carefully checks everything before speeding and that he could control the situation. I told him that you never know what could happen. His speeding was a topic almost every evening during our trip.

We arrived in Finland and were driving pretty slowly in a light rain. We changed lanes and as we crossed over a slippery road-repair area, he lost control of the bike. He hit his head on a concrete drain pipe and died almost instantly. I still remember the feeling of being carried very smoothly, just a little above the ground, and then dropped beside the bike. There is no doubt who was carrying me — Amma! This was her second time saving my life. I only had a few minor injuries and was released from the hospital the next day.

At the hospital, the doctors and nurses offered psychiatric help, but I replied, "I have my own help." And indeed, I had. This may sound very strange, but the next few weeks were the most peaceful and tranquil in my entire life. I felt Amma's presence so strongly all the time — tears would come in the middle of a shop or street, because Amma's grace was flowing, and I just knew that everything was as it should be. My husband received his greatest teaching in his death and it was exactly how it was supposed to happen. Friends and relatives called to comfort me, but it always turned out the other way around. I was comforting them and reminding them that we are not the ones deciding our lives. God knows best when and how it's time for each one of us to depart this world.

I realized that I had been prepared for this. The concept of death had been in my mind very often. I would ask myself if I could really accept God's will, or was it only theoretical understanding which would collapse when it would happen to me or someone close to me. I can't say that it was me who passed that test — it was only Amma's grace that gave me the understanding and acceptance. I am so grateful to Amma for having given me this experience and teaching.

***

The next year, in 2008, Amma came to Finland, and I was responsible for the café. My asthma had been very bad for many years, and during the previous year, I had not been able to sleep more than one hour at a time. During the night, I used to drink hot cocoa and sleep on a chair because the coughing was too bad to lie down. I was quite a zombie during those times and I came to the program in bad shape. After serving the four-hour café shift during the Dēvī Bhāva, I lost my voice and it became painful to breathe. I finished my sēvā and thought that I would go and finally have darśhan.

Two doctors from our satsang group saw me and said that I needed to go to the hospital. I strongly objected because I hadn't had my darśhan yet. They insisted and put me in a taxi with someone from the Helsinki satsang group to watch that I didn't escape back to the program before a doctor's examination. I was very innocently surprised when they told me at the hospital that I had an extremely high fever. Amma's energy was so strong when doing sēvā that I didn't even feel the fever.

Amma's program ended and I was very sad that I had not received darśhan. Later, the doctors found out that I had abscesses surrounding both my lungs, requiring immediate surgery. One week after the surgery, the abscesses came back and I had to be operated on again. I was in the ICU and the doctors told my mother that I was very close to dying. My mother remembered that two ladies from our satsang group had left to attend Amma's program in Ireland. She immediately sent a message to them saying that I was near dying and if they could please ask for Amma's help. One of the women turned on her mobile at 3 a.m. in the morning and saw the message. They managed to get in front of Amma, crying hysterically. Amma comforted them and said, "She is going to be fine." From that very moment, I started to recover. This was the third time that Amma saved my life.

I remember an incident from my time in the ICU. My mother and stepfather were visiting me and of course they were very worried. I gave a thumbs up signal, trying to express that everything was fine. No matter what happens, everything is fine. I found out many years later that they understood that as a sign that I am going to fight. I wasn't fighting, I was surrendering. I am ever grateful to Amma for this powerful lesson.

Despite all the grace Amma showered on me, I still didn't do any sādhanā. Drinking champagne and smoking organic cigarettes were still part of my life. I visited Amma's programs in Europe every year, but in between, I was caught by the nets of the world. I am grateful for this time also, because I would have never met my second husband without having gone through this period, and I would not have gained an understanding of people who are not on a spiritual path. It was very comforting to hear that Amma once said, "Everyone is at the right place in their path." By saying this, Amma has given the understanding that there is no need to judge. Everyone is walking their own path, just where they need to be.

My husband Jari, whom I met in 2011 by Amma's grace, has become a true Amma devotee. Today, he praises the Divine Mother of the Universe every evening on his knees, with his hands toward the sky. He gave up a lifetime of bad habits such as drinking and smoking and now chants the archana[13] every morning with me, does sēvā, and serves others. This transformation, which took seven years, is truly a miracle of Amma.

***

In 2014, I had severe problems with my stomach, and even if I drank a cup of water, I got very bad pain. No one knew what was wrong. I felt a strong need to go and see Amma, so I planned a trip to San Ramon. This new pain was exhausting and I thought, "I will now go and finally ask for help for myself." Although I

[13] Chanting of the 108 or 1,000 names of a particular deity (e.g. *'Lalitā Sahasranāma'*).

trusted that Amma knows what is going on even without me telling her, I remember thinking, "This time, I can't manage. I need Amma's help!" So, my plan was to go to San Ramon at the end of May. But, just before I was supposed to leave, the pain finally forced me to the hospital and after many tests they found out that my white blood cells were attacking the intestine.

The doctors said that it would be very dangerous to fly and that I should stay at the hospital. I wrote to Jani, the accommodations coordinator, telling her that I was not coming because I was hospitalized. When I pressed the send button, tears started to flow like a river. The only one who could help me was Amma and I needed to go to her! I sent another message, "Never mind, I am coming!" I booked a flight and called my husband to come and pick me up.

I arrived in San Ramon in the afternoon, got darśhan in the evening and explained the situation to Amma. I was able to eat from the very first night without any pain. During this time, I used to meditate and command my white cells not to attack, telling them to calm down. I am sure the universe had a laugh while listening to my command attempts. This was the first time I ever asked Amma for help for myself. I had in my mind that I could only ask for help for others. Even during the difficult period I struggled with asthma, I never asked for help from Amma for myself. I came back home not only fully recovered, which was a miracle in itself, but Amma had also opened me up to an indescribable joy and fulfillment that lasted for months.

Soon after this, I found a prasād ring blessed by Amma, and in Milan, my husband and I asked if Amma would marry us. She said yes, and in 2015 we were married by Amma. Marriage presents its challenges, but my husband plays the role of an exceptional teacher in my life. I will be ever grateful to him for walking this path with me, and I will always treasure our relationship as a gift from Amma.

The year 2017 was a transition year. Very effortlessly, by Amma's grace, I felt the need to start doing archana again. I started to wake up before five, take a cold shower, do archana and meditate before going to work. One evening, while in the shower, I thought I should stop smoking. One morning the thought came to my mind that I should also stop drinking coffee. I would have never been able to quit smoking and drinking coffee, but I was finally blessed by Amma. She took the attachments away and the desires just vanished. I don't feel I gave up any bad habits, I simply realized that they were useless.

Thank you Amma, for keeping an eye on me and giving me everything that is best for me. My only prayer is that I get what I need, not what I want, and that I get a bit of strength to cope with what it is that I need.

I began to organize satsangs every week in our home. I also started waking up with only one thought in my mind — enlightenment — as I used to have after meeting Amma when I was younger. Back then, I really didn't know what I was asking for, but very sincerely prayed, "Amma! Please give me anything, I can take anything, but please enlighten me." What a bold prayer it was!

***

Even though I traveled to meet Amma in many places, Amritapuri stayed distant from me. At the end of 2017, I got a call from a person in our local satsang group who wanted to go to Amritapuri. He asked if anyone would like to join him. I sent a message to our satsang group asking if someone would like to go. He called me a few more times to follow up. Then, in January, he called and said he had booked tickets. I was thinking, "Why is he calling me? Good for him, he's going!" But as soon as I hung up, tears started to flow. It was Amma who was calling me. I called my bosses, booked the flight, and within a month I was in Amritapuri again. It was only for nine days, but it felt like I was there for many months.

The way our Amma manages time is beyond our understanding, but it is an incredible grace to always get what we need. I came back after one month for another short trip, and in 2018 I came again with my husband during Amma's birthday. He used to say he can visit Amma in Europe, but he won't go to India. Then he said he can go to India, but he will not go at the time of the birthday. In the end, he could not resist you, Amma!

When the announcement came about Amma initiating new sannyāsins and brahmachārīs, my tears again started to flow. All of them are a constant reminder for me of how life should be lived. We can only try to develop that dedication and renunciation while living in the world. I shed tears for being so far away from such a life and felt left behind. I then went to meditate and I got very clear instructions from Amma on how I should change my sādhanā. It should be done at exactly the same time every day, and the mind should not be able to negotiate. If negotiation ensues, then the mind is winning.

From that morning, we have been performing archana at 6 a.m. and chanting *lōkāḥ samastāḥ sukhinō bhavantu*[14] 108 times in the evening. When Covid-19 hit, we started to hold the chanting online on Zoom so that our satsang group could join whenever possible. Even after the restrictions were lifted, we continued doing this. This showed us how important group support is. Without our satsang group and without my husband I would

[14] 'May all beings in all the worlds be happy' – a prayer for universal peace.

have probably failed a long time ago and my mind would have won.

***

All is Amma's grace. My own effort is so small, but with Amma, there are no limits. The greatest grace is to have a guru who can lead us to self-realization. There is a passage on the last page of the book, *The Timeless Path* by Swami Ramakrishnananda Puri, that touched me very deeply.

Swami explains the eternally unbound nature of consciousness, that the question of bondage or liberation exists only for a mind, and that "the jīvanmukta (a self-realized person) has come to understand that he is not the mind nor was he ever." "He considers himself to be nothing but eternal, blissful consciousness." Later on, Swami assures us:

"This understanding will come to all of us. For this, we have the promise of both the scriptures and Amma. 'It is only a question of time,' Amma says. 'For some this realization has already occurred; for others it will happen any moment and for others it will happen later. Just because it has not happened yet nor may not even happen in this lifetime, don't think that it is never going to happen. Within you, immense knowledge is waiting for your permission to unfold.'"

When I first read this, my tears started to flow. I had to open that page every day for a month, and each time I read it, I cried. This is the greatest grace of all — a promise from Amma — that one day she will come, take our hand, and lead us to freedom.

Please, Amma, accept my very small self-effort and lead me to the goal, so that I may contribute to the well-being of others as much as possible.

9

Nothing Greater than the Guru

Surya – USA

There is one phrase from the *Guru Gītā* that really sums it all up for me:

> *na gurōradhikam*
> There is no truth higher than the guru.

Amma, our guru, took birth out of her pure, selfless compassion for the world. I can unabashedly say that taking full advantage of being in her physical presence as much as possible, unless she directs you otherwise, is the smartest way to spend the short time of this fleeting life. Doing all we possibly can to serve her and her mission, striving to embody her immensely potent teachings, and doing our daily sādhanā is the intelligent way to spend our few breaths in this life.

Those of you who have nothing standing in your way are the luckiest people on earth. We are so absolutely blessed to have Amma in our lives. I don't know how people go through life without a guru. We should take full advantage of every moment because, as Amma often tells us, we should be like birds sitting on the dry branch of life, ready to take flight when the branch breaks.

I can speak straightforwardly about these things because I am an absolute expert in wasting those breaths. Even though Amma told me in 1991 that I could come to the āśhram in India whenever I liked, it has taken thirty-one years for that to finally happen in this lifetime. I allowed vāsanās (latent tendencies), samskāras (accumulated impressions), prārabdha karma (results of past actions from previous births), and the ridiculous ideas and excuses of the mind, to keep me from being with Amma in Amritapuri. Amma often refers to the distractions of the world as 'glittering seashells.' I foolishly allowed various types and levels of these 'seashells' to distract me. Meeting saints and sādhus (wandering monks), visiting holy places and going to numerous Kumbha Mēlas[15], are all just more glittering seashells. More spiritual or sāttvic seashells, but still just seashells nonetheless.

There is no reason to go anywhere else but to Amma. Her feet are the ultimate place of pilgrimage. What a waste of so many precious years that I could have spent with Amma! Time that I can never get back.

At least I drew the line in the sand, like the three-hundred Spartans at the Hot Gates[16], to go on all the North American Tours since 1990. Often, I didn't have enough money, but somehow, it always worked out. I have also been actively involved in the local satsang group for decades. It is not that one needs to come to Amritapuri to have a relationship with Amma. However, if one comes, one gains insight into the context of the tradition that surrounds Amma, and can more deeply understand who she really is.

I often go to the ocean near my home at sunset and think of Amma by the ocean in Amritapuri. Seeing the little town by the sea I live in and how my house has vintage photos of Amma hanging everywhere just like Amma's birth house has now, I can see that something from Amritapuri was inside of me all this time.

---

[15] Major Hindu spiritual festival occurring every three years in one of four sacred riverbank pilgrimage places in North India.

[16] Reference to a battle in 480 BCE where 300 Spartan warriors made a valiant stand against the invading Persian army, delaying their advance. It symbolizes defiance against overwhelming odds.

***

From a very young age, I had a strong devotional and spiritual inclination. My family did not. My mother passed away when I was nine years old, just one day before her thirty-third birthday. At the age of twenty, a latent kidney problem was discovered, and the doctors advised her not to have children. But she wanted kids so badly that she didn't let anything deter her. She gave birth first to me, and then my sister soon after. This was the intensity of the love my mother had for me. She often expressed that love by showering me with affection and 'Eskimo' kisses – affectionately rubbing her nose softly against mine. I have passed on the essence of my mom's love to my two daughters, Kanyakumari Devi and Vismaya Devi.

The intense grief I experienced from her death broke something inside me. I had been very interested in school prior to that, and was enrolled in an accelerated program for gifted students. I would say from that point on, I simply coasted on my intelligence and never really applied myself again. I developed a deep dispassion for the world and focused on reading all I could about the astral realms and the occult, in hopes of somehow communicating with my mom. I followed the teachings of Taoism, Zen, learned meditation, and then discovered the yōgic tradition at the age of sixteen. That later blossomed into studying numerous other great spiritual traditions of India. It is said that intense grief and trauma is something that can awaken the spiritual energy within you, and I feel that is what happened to me. So, I often say that my mom dying when I was young was both the greatest and worst thing that ever happened to me.

My father remarried very quickly, not allowing me time to fully grieve for my mom. This caused great resentment in me. He was not a very emotionally available man. I know he loved me, but too often he was verbally and physically abusive to me as a child. This became worse after my mom's death. I often felt that along with my mom, I had lost my dad as well. It happened often enough that I never felt safe in my home and had conflicting feelings of loving my dad dearly while being afraid of him. I graduated high school a year early to get out of my house and started college at sixteen. The anger and resentment caused by these traumas has haunted me my entire life. My dad passed in November 2019, and I am still in the process of forgiving and letting it all go. Amma's presence and teachings have helped me greatly in this process. I know he was simply running the software he was given from his childhood, going back generations, and simply was who he was. My mom's death was hard on him too, I'm sure.

At eighteen, an intense desire to find my guru awakened in me. I became quite distraught and desperate about it. I never dreamed that great mahātmās, or self-realized masters, would come to New York City where I was living. Suddenly, starting in 1988, I met several saints, one after another, in New York. They were all great beings, but none of them was my guru.

Some satsang friends told me that a great saint called Ammachi was coming, and that she was said to be an incarnation of the Divine Mother. I was so excited that I couldn't wait! On the evening of July 5, 1990, which was Guru Pūrṇimā[17], I was blessed to see Amma for the first time at the age of twenty-two. I remember my very first thought when I saw her from across the hall at the Universalist Church in New York. "Oh my God, I am looking at God!"

I remember getting so blissed out at the program, and I went into a kind of drunken stupor after my first darśhan. After that, all I could think about was Amma. I was drifting between worlds, hearing celestial sounds, and longing for when I could

[17] Full moon day in summer, dedicated to worshiping the guru.

see her again. I came back for the Dēvī Bhāva program two days later. I didn't know if Amma was my guru yet, but I knew she was my mother and that there was a deep connection. I took a mantra that night and when asked what form of God I wanted a mantra for, I didn't know what to say. I was then asked what form brought spontaneous love for God, and I said, "Amma's form!" So I was given a mantra for her. Absolutely perfect!

After the program ended, I stayed to help clean-up. The programs were small back then, only very few stayed to help, and no one was waiting for Amma to emerge from the temple on the stage. I became engrossed in cleaning up the flower petals on the floor that Amma had tossed on us all at the end. I was just so overjoyed to be able to do sēvā for a real saint. Suddenly, I felt someone affectionately touching my arm. Then, I looked up and saw it was Amma. There was no one else around anywhere close to us. Our eyes met, and I heard Amma's voice inside me say, "Son, you were one-pointedly serving the guru, so of course the guru had to come to you." I looked down and saw Amma's feet and quickly prostrated myself before them. I didn't realize it at the time, but this moment, which was arguably the greatest moment of my life, was the moment she hooked me forever.

I followed Amma up to the last programs of that tour – a retreat at an old barn in New Hampshire. It was a beautiful setting and such a potent time with Amma and so few people. I remember coming into the hall one day during darśhan and seeing immense light filling everywhere, only to realize it was emanating from Amma. She gave us all such powerful darśhans. I remember her putting her finger with sandalwood paste on my third eye and holding it there for a long time. She pushed my head back with so much śhakti, or spiritual energy, that people six-feet away on either side felt it and asked me afterwards what had happened. She let me stare deeply into her eyes for a long time. They became big black pools and I saw that there was no one inside — no individual personality. There was only pure love, pure consciousness, and endless bliss. These experiences had a profound effect on me and deepened my connection to Amma. At the end of one program, Amma danced and went deep into samādhi, her mind fully absorbed in the divine. We all rode that wave with her — such stillness and bliss, thick as a Kerala monsoon.

***

The next few years of tours, I dove even deeper into sēvā. Back then, we didn't have sēvā departments like we do now. There were just a few of us who would run from task to task, doing whatever was needed. It was such a magical time. I couldn't get enough. My way of approaching sēvā was, and is, just to say 'yes' to anything I was asked to do. I never asked to do anything close to Amma, but somehow, by doing all the other sēvā that few among the few there wanted to do, I was asked to do things close to Amma. So I said yes to those opportunities too. This really is my experience with Amma. When you are not focused on taking from Amma but instead on giving, when you are content with anything and don't fight to be the closest to Amma — that is when she really showers you with grace. So much more than you could even think to ask for.

There used to be a quote in the snack tent at Amma's San Ramon āśhram that said something like, "When a disciple matures, he doesn't want to take from the guru, but instead, only wants to give to the guru." That really influenced me and has been an aspiration that I try to live up to more and more.

Back then, there was only one small camper that had to be packed just right to fit everything that needed to go from program to program. Later, that became a small truck. Often, it was just a devotee named Haran, myself, and another young man named Shakti packing the entire truck by hand, unlike today where we have teams of people helping with pallet jacks and forklifts. It was really one of my favorite things to do.

This reminds me of a sweet, funny story with Amma. I had been working as a private exercise trainer and nutritionist for a number of years. With the focus on the body seeming to be the antithesis of what Vedānta and yogic philosophy stressed, I wondered if I should continue with this work. It was heavy on my mind. We were meeting Amma at the airport in New York and Amma was walking ahead of the rest. The path was steep, and I was afraid maybe Amma might fall, so I came forward and offered her my arm to hold on to. She took it and then squeezed my bicep saying, "Good muscle." Then she picked up her arm and flexed her bicep for me. I politely squeezed it and said something like, "That's cute, Amma." That one little action removed all my doubts about my work, and Amma has since commented numerous times on my strength in a positive way. It has been a great help in many different sēvās.

Amma always knows who is doing what and if anyone hasn't come for darśhan. Back then, we would all go for darśhan every day. Once, in 1992 or 93, Amma came out to the truck after the program. I was there with a couple of others, including a man named Ramana. He hadn't gone for darśhan as he had been busy organizing the truck, and Amma knew it. I didn't go to the truck early because I didn't want to miss my darśhan and time near Amma. She came to the truck and called him to come to her. He was reluctant to come into her embrace, as he said he was sweaty and dirty. Amma insisted, and as she embraced him she said, "The sweat of sēvā is Mother's tears." I really took that moment and what Amma said to heart. She doesn't miss a beat.

***

Most of us often wonder if Amma knows us. Does she know our name? Absolutely silly thoughts, as a mother knows each of her children and loves them equally. We don't even know ourselves, but she knows us. For the first program of the summer tour around 2015, I was sitting close to Amma assisting the darśhan line, which I often did. As usual, I was there from before Amma arrived until she finished. Though I was right in front of her, she didn't look at me or give me a kind of 'What's up?' head-bob greeting like she would often do when first seeing me on a tour. Darśhan finished and everyone lined up to see her leave. The thought spontaneously came to me, "Does Amma know me at all?" I had known Amma for over twenty years at that point, and she called me by name many times. However, this thought just arose out of the longing of my heart, not in an effort to test her or attract her attention. A minute later, when Amma got to where I was standing, she tapped me on the chest and said, "Oh Surya!" Yes, she knows us all.

***

Who knows what would have been different if I had come to the āśhram right away in 1990 or 1991? Most of us wonder why we didn't get to meet Amma earlier, but at least we did meet her at some point this lifetime and know her now. There is no use in speculating and looking back at one's life, except to reflect and try to strive harder, moving forward with whatever time one has left in this life. When I saw Amma recently give the sannyāsa and brahmachārya dīkṣha — initiation into formal monastic renunciation — I felt sad once again that I have simply wasted so much of my life so far. I wish my karma had been different, and that I could have been of much more service to Amma and the world. All I can do is make better use of whatever short time I have left in this life.

All the times I went to the Kumbha Mela gatherings, Amma didn't go, but when I didn't go, Amma finally went. I was kind of upset about it to be honest, jealous of all my Amma brothers and sisters that got to go with her and get dunked in the Trivēṇī Saṇgam — the meeting point of the three sacred rivers, by her. Amma heard my mind. The next night, she came to me in a dream, manifested the entire Kumbha Mela, and gave me darśhan. That was beyond amazing!

***

My life fell apart in early 2011 when I entered an astrological period called Śhani Mahādaśhā. Within a few months, I lost my six-figure job along with my sixteen-year relationship, breaking up our family, and the home I had lived in for thirteen years.

I came on tour, but with very little money. I noticed after the morning program in Seattle that there was no jacket for Amma and I knew it would be cold at night. So I took the last little bit of extra cash I had, and I bought her a nice, soft fleece jacket. I knew it wasn't Amma's usual style, but I thought, just in case it was needed, it could keep her warm even just that one night as she walked to the car. Amma seemed to really like it and started telling everyone how nice and soft it was, and how I gave it to her. Lakshmi Akka, now Swamini Shrilakshmi Prana, Amma's attendant, told me that Amma often wore it over the next two years. I know she did this just to somehow keep me close during this very difficult time. Amma's love knows no bounds or distance.

When I finally made it to Amritapuri for the first time, Amma gave me a welcome like the prodigal son returning home. I was touched beyond anything I can express.

Years ago I had the realization that I am Amma's son, both s-o-n and s-u-n (like my name, Sūrya). Actually, I am simply

Amma's. That is all the realization I could ever need. I don't want mōkṣha or liberation, but only to keep coming back to serve her every time she chooses to take on a body.

Amma is my mother, my guru, my Goddess, my everything, and all her children are my true family. There is nothing greater than the guru.

10

Happiness Is a Decision

Praseeda - France

The following story marks the beginning of a quest that led me to Amma. I am twelve years old, and find myself in a dark classroom. The tables are U-shaped, and I am sitting in the back row opposite the teacher. This is my second year of Spanish. In this language, there are two verbs meaning 'to be' — *ser* and *estar.* The verb *ser* refers to permanent states, whereas *estar* is used to express a temporary state.

The teacher, Mrs. Perez, gives us sentences, and we have to choose which verb to use. This is when the example appears: 'I am happy.'

"Which verb do you use?" she asks us.

I don't remember the answer to the exercise, but it raised a question beyond that Spanish class, a question I've thought about many times in my life. Can I really say, "Soy feliz," I'm permanently happy? Every time I thought about it, I was confronted with the fact that life is made up of ups and downs. To what extent is it possible to be permanently happy?

Without knowing it, Mrs. Perez had led me to the heart of the philosophy of Sanātana Dharma, which would later become my goal: sat-chit-ānanda — existence, consciousness and bliss.

Reflecting on my life, I realize how I have always searched for happiness. With every decision I have made, the purpose has always been to find happiness. Meeting Amma was a decisive turning point in this quest.

One of Amma's most powerful statements is, "Happiness is a decision." Honestly, I never fully understood it. When sad or angry, if I say to myself, "Now, be happy!" it doesn't really work and I don't feel immediate happiness. However, Amma certainly does not say this for nothing. What happiness is Amma talking about? Let's investigate!

When I was seventeen, I remember being shocked by the words of my philosophy teacher who said, "All the actions that man carries out, he does because he evaluates that they are good." Flabbergasted, I expressed my disagreement, "Sir, what about criminals? Are they not aware that their actions are wrong?"

This was a perfect gateway for him to expand on his point. Amused, he replied, "Criminals are not looking for the ethical good, but to do something that will do them good. Even if, in their madness, they actually commit an unjust and cruel act." I understood then the difference between 'acting for the higher good' and 'acting to feel good.' He added, "The purpose remains the pursuit of happiness."

Our life is a sequence of actions aimed at our well-being. Since our birth, our first impulse is the search for external happiness in the satisfaction of ephemeral needs, or the avoidance of unpleasant situations. Personally, I have spent my life looking for happiness in the eyes of others by trying to be the right friend, wife, colleague, sevite, spiritual aspirant, and so on.

My first conclusion of this quest: the key to happiness is not found in the outer world. Amma tells us,

"Understand this great truth — happiness from worldly pleasures is only a faint reflection of the infinite bliss that comes from your own self."

In martial arts, the strength of the opponent is used to make him fall. Similarly, the Indian tradition is infinitely rich in texts describing the inner battle that Dēvī leads against our negative tendencies. As a true master of the 'internal martial arts,' Amma uses the strength of our negative tendencies to bring down our ego. When the ego is down, we can then change our perspective and look at life with fresh eyes.

My husband Ojas and I met when we were both twenty-one. Today, we are thirty-seven. We only got married after nine years of being in a relationship. In France, being in a long relationship at such a young age can be seen as something to worry about. People would say, "You are too young," or, "You should have more romantic encounters before you make a serious commitment."

I've long agreed with these maxims. So, it took me years to accept the concept of commitment. For me, commitment was an impediment to freedom, including the freedom to break up if one day the relationship became too complicated. I would say, "If Amma marries us, we have to be sure of ourselves!"

I felt anxious about the commitment of marriage, and losing the freedom to change my mind was unbearable and made me feel very insecure. The infinite patience shown by Ojas, never asking for anything, his deep trust, as well as Amma's grace, got the better of my resistance. Something in me let go, and I accepted my dharma was to be married.

In 2014, during a Paris Dēvī Bhāva night, I very 'romantically' proposed to Ojas in the sevite's parking lot. Amma married us the following year to a somewhat unsettling melody for that occasion — the *Mahiṣhāsura Mardini Stōtram.* This is a rhythmic chant depicting Dēvī battling the buffalo demon that represents the ego. It was one of the most powerful moments of my life — both of us at Amma's feet, inwardly asking Amma to teach us to see her in the heart of the other.

Once married, I gradually felt the inner freedom that the commitment offered me. Many of the questions that had existed until then were no longer relevant and disappeared.

The mind was partly unburdened. Even in a modest way, I had gained inner freedom. I understood that the spiritual path awakens us from the illusion of outer freedom to the experience of true inner freedom.

The great promise of Sanātana Dharma is not to find joy in heaven, but to realize the eternal joy here and now, in this body. This state is accessible to one who has attained complete inner freedom. In the *Bhagavad Gītā*, Śhrī Kṛiṣhṇa says:

"Supreme joy verily comes to the yōgi whose mind is calm, whose passions have been appeased, who is freed from all impurity, and who has become brahman." (6.27)

Swami Ramakrishnananda Puri in his book *Living Vedanta* states,

"If we want to find ultimate happiness — true bliss — then we must understand that happiness does not come from external factors, but is our fundamental nature. As Amma says, 'We have to move from 'I love you' to 'I am love.''"

Once, I had a dream about this. I was alone with Amma, bathed in her loving gaze, with her hands in mine. Full of joy at being so close to Amma, I wanted to say, "Amma, I love you," but the memory of Amma's teaching stopped me dead in my tracks before the words came out of my mouth. Instead, I said, "Amma is love; I am love." Amma then looked at me very surprised.

In retrospect, instead of letting my heart speak, I had recited a lesson. But honestly, that's where I stand. There is some intellectual understanding, but not yet an understanding of the heart. Let's go back to the statement we are delving into, "Happiness is a decision." What keeps us from accessing this understanding of the heart?

***

A month into our marriage, around midnight, Ojas and I had an argument. This is not a common occurrence. I don't actually remember what it was about, but as I remember it, he was wrong and spoke in very bad faith! He even had the nerve to end the exchange by suddenly saying, "I'm going to sleep now."

Here is a sample of my inner speech, "Unbelievable! He doesn't understand anything, he leaves me like that, he's unfair! He doesn't understand my needs or my point of view." Disillusioned, I suddenly got up, left the room, went down the stairs of the building, and started running down the street without knowing where to go. I ran into the cold of the Parisian night. The streets went by, when all of a sudden, I bumped into her — Amma! She looked so beautiful in a gold-colored sari, the one from the Dēvī Bhāva she wore for our wedding.

I came out of my thoughts suddenly. I was still in my room. Ojas was sleeping peacefully. I was completely agitated and insomnia was setting in. I thought, "One thing is for sure. Amma married us, so there's no way I can run away!" I got up, went to my altar and prostrated myself at Amma's feet. I started to pray, cry, and then to meditate. I deeply felt Amma's presence — her love soothing me. I went back to bed and miraculously, I fell asleep.

The next morning, as soon as he woke up, Ojas looked at me. His first words of the day were, "I dreamed of Amma last night and... I apologize!" He was in a great mood! Let's be honest, this is not the classic scenario. This was, in my opinion, a gift from Amma at the beginning of our marriage to show us the way.

The lesson for me was twofold: Firstly, we cannot expect a limited mind, such as a spouse, co-worker, or friend, to make unlimited efforts to meet the needs arising from our own limited mind. Having expectations of others is one of the first obstacles to open-heartedness and to happiness. The idea is to learn to love rather than to expect to be loved.

Secondly, let's put ourselves in Amma's hands first. She is there with us at every moment. The only way to face mutual misunderstanding is to accept our mutual limitations, to rely on Amma, and to let our true nature express itself.

The 17th century French philosopher Descartes said, "I think therefore I am." I think I have practiced mostly, "I do therefore I am." However, it seems to me that Vēdānta teaches us simply, "I am."

For Vēdānta, existence is not a question. On the contrary, the scriptures affirm that existence is the ultimate truth, and this existence is pure awareness and bliss. It is neither thought nor action that gives us access to it; it is an inner experience. The action carried out in sēvā is a preparation for this inner experience — a purification process.

Even if the love I have for Amma and my brothers and sisters is a strong motivation for my actions, and even if I try to act selflessly, I cannot deny that the need to be approved and loved is mixed with my intentions.

Among the sēvās I have had the opportunity to do in recent years, the most effective in wearing down my tendency to seek approval and love in the eyes of others are those in which I have played a coordinating role. In these situations, I am very visible, and so are my mistakes; my choices are subject to criticism, and I can easily get into ego fights when I try to defend a point of view.

These adventures facilitate the observation of the monkey mind because it will oscillate a lot between hopes and worries about the future, and the regrets of the past. Let us not be mistaken, it is not the sēvā nor the sevites that induce agitation of the mind. The sēvā simply amplifies these oscillations so we can become more aware of them. In the same way that a microscope is needed to observe the movements of molecules, sēvā is a tool that helps us to see the fluctuations of the mind. Amma tells us that only when we serve others with the right understanding, with love and faith, will we be happy and at peace.

***

Ojas and I have been coordinating Amma's charitable activities in France under the guidance of Swamini Amritajyoti Prana for the past ten years. This sēvā consists of creating opportunities for devotees to serve those in need by practicing selfless service together.

Recently, a brahmachārī explained that the translation of the Sanskrit word 'dānam' as 'charity' is not complete. When we give, we receive. Amma says, "My children, this is what we should be about: the desire to give. Only those who give can receive. In giving, we find inner peace."

Early in 2022, a dozen sevites led an initiative to help Ukrainian refugees in France. Afterwards, it was striking to hear them all say, "I feel like I received so much more than I gave." This feedback, which is often heard following sēvā, resonated with the words of the brahmachārī who defined the term 'dānam' as 'sharing.'

The sevites all felt that the smooth running of the project was not of their own doing but clearly attributable to Amma's grace. They expressed, "When my attitude is right, it is not me who does, but Amma who acts through me." Sēvā is a tool that transforms our egotistic intentions into a humble attitude, and also allows us to grasp deep concepts through direct experience. This is the magic of sēvā!

Every year for the past seven years, we have welcomed homeless and undocumented people for a few days of vacation at the French āśhram. We welcome people who are in terribly painful and unjust situations — living in a world very different from ours. In order for the experience to go well and for the distance between them and us to diminish, there is only one solution — adopting a listening attitude with an open heart and staying in the present moment. To do this, we try to remember the incomparable example that Amma offers by unconditionally welcoming each of us during darśhan.

When we engage in sēvā to help people in unjust situations, we often feel helpless. These sēvās teach us to discern between the situations over which we have control, and those over which we do not. Remaining humble regarding our actual capacity while keeping the genuine will to serve is so important. We can offer our time, a smile, and a listening ear. What else can we do but lay the rest at Amma's feet? For me, remembering that we are only an instrument of God is a key to happiness.

In the *Bhagavad Gīta*, Chapter 6, verse 34, Arjuna says:

> "For restless is the mind, O Kṛiṣhṇa, turbulent, powerful and unyielding; I consider it as difficult to control as the wind."

Arjuna is a hero of the great Indian epic *Mahābhārata*. He, along with his brothers, the Pāṇḍavas, represents the path of dharma, right action. If Arjuna had such an intense experience of trying to control his mind, what about ours?

Śhrī Kṛiṣhṇa answers him in verse 35:

> "No doubt, O mighty-armed, the mind is difficult to control, it is wavering, but by practice and non-attachment it is held, O son of Kunti."

By the force of the latent tendencies of the mind, known as the vāsanās, we spend our time forgetting the path and the goal; we even forget the power of Amma's love. Only constant reminders can sustain us in this work of disidentification from the senses and the mind. That is why Kṛiṣhṇa invites us to constantly repeat our efforts.

What helps me in this endeavor is performing my spiritual practices every day and continuously recalling the moments I have spent with Amma. These experiences testify to the unique power of her unconditional love, the divine mystery that she is, and her presence by our side at every moment. I would like to share one of these experiences of Amma's grace.

In 2009, at the age of twenty-three, Ojas and I innocently arrived in Amritapuri when Amma was on tour in the U.S. We discovered the āśhram with curiosity and were impressed by its power.

I had been an insomniac since I was eighteen. One night at the āśhram, the insomnia set in and I could not fall asleep. Exhausted, desperate, and terribly sad, I prayed to Amma, "If you are the one they say you are, then why don't I sleep?" I then instantly fell asleep and dreamt that Amma was in front of me giving darśhan to a child. When it was my turn, I hesitated to approach and looked at her shyly. She then sternly signaled me to come to her. My first view of guru bhāva. I had no idea that love could take this form. The rest of the dream will remain secretly in my heart forever.

The next day, without understanding why, I cried throughout the bhajan session in the evening. These delightful tears were a blessing to my spiritual practice until today. Mysteriously, since that experience, I have not been subject to insomnia for years. Infinite gratitude to Amma.

***

Let's summarize some of the ways we have identified to overcome the obstacles to eternal happiness: abandoning our expectations; observing the oscillations of the mind through the practice of sēvā; discerning what is within our power and what is not; remembering that it is Amma who is the doer; and constantly reminding ourselves of our path and the goal.

I can make the decision to try to apply these methods that bring me closer to happiness. But how much can I decide to be happy? Śhrī Śhankarāchārya tells us in *Vivēkachūḍāmaṇi*:

> *Actions help to purify but they do not, by themselves, contribute to the attainment of Reality. The attainment of the Real is brought about only by self-inquiry, and not in the least by 10 million acts.* (Verse 11)

> *Neither sacred baths, nor any amount of charity, nor even hundreds of prāṇāyamas can give us the knowledge about our own self. The firm experience of the nature of the self is seen to proceed from inquiry along the line of the salutary advice of the wise.* (Verse 13)

Let there be no mistake, Śhankarāchārya does not criticize all the practices mentioned so far. He invites us to continue them with the awareness that they are not an end in themselves. He acknowledges that they play a role in purifying the mind in order to develop inner maturity. This preparation of the mind gradually induces the inner calm necessary for the complete integration of Amma's words and the teachings of the scriptures — "I am That; I am supreme happiness."

Amma tells us, "Happiness is a decision." Let's inquire into ourselves sincerely. Do I have the maturity to make this decision consciously? Honestly, have I fully decided that my goal is to realize the self? What happens when I cut my morning practice time short to make sure I have time for breakfast? Or when I spend my meditation time thinking about an argument I had with a friend?

Many ancient stories from the Indian scriptures describe how certain spiritual seekers were able to quickly achieve liberation. I used to think, "The ancient ṛiṣhis (sages) were so spiritually strong. It sounds so simple in these stories, but in my case, it's much more complex." Now, after studying the scriptures, I understand it in a deeper way. In fact, these stories are about seekers who had already reached a high level of maturity at the time of meeting the guru. With their hearts wide open and their minds calm, they could immediately become impregnated with the master's teaching.

To be able to be happy by making the decision, one needs to be completely unified within and focussed on the ultimate goal. Needless to say, I still have to patiently walk the path of making the necessary preparations. At the very least, I can make the decision to do everything I can to prepare myself for experiencing the state of true happiness. That, in itself, is already a source of joy!

Patience is the key to happiness. I would like to share a story Amma once told on the beach in Amritapuri.

On his way to Vaikuṇṭha, Lord Viṣhṇu's world, Sage Nārada met two monks meditating under a tree by the side of the road. They called out to him and said, "Sage, since you are going to Vaikuṇṭha, could you please ask the Lord when we are going to attain enlightenment?"

He agreed and went on his way. On returning, he told the first monk, "The Lord says you will attain enlightenment in as many lifetimes as there are leaves on this tree." Shocked and desperate, the monk left his meditation seat and returned to a worldly life.

"What did the Lord say about me?" asked the second monk. Sage Nārada replied, "The Lord says you will attain enlightenment in as many lifetimes as there are leaves on this tree." The monk was amazed. "Thank you so much, sage!" He jumped for joy. "The Lord has given the assurance that after this many lifetimes, I will finally attain the goal!" At that very moment the man attained enlightenment.

At the end of the story, Amma, with a mischievous air, added a conclusion that made a deep impression on me; "Infinite patience leads to immediate results."

I conclude from this that if the decision to be happy is made with full awareness, with a completely open heart, and with the firmness that only a purified mind can have, the result will also be immediate.

Amma, may your infinite grace open our hearts to experiencing our true nature. May we develop a sense of gratitude. May your light illuminate the hearts of human beings so that they will favor peace, mutual aid, and a life respectful of our Mother Nature. Amma, may each moment become a prayer in my heart to feel your presence in me.

11

Amma's Way to Wellness

Dr. Shankar Logaraja – India

By some credible estimates, about one in eight people worldwide, which is nearly one billion people, are living with mental health ailments.[18] Aside from those who are formally diagnosed, there are many suffering silently and countless others experiencing issues related to burnout, fatigue, fear, and sadness. These are challenges that all of us have experienced at one time or another. On top of this, society stigmatizes mental health issues, making it even harder to discuss them openly or seek help.

Amma has given us the gift of spirituality through her teachings and actions. She is truly the embodiment of wellness, and her teachings help us all find the way to lasting peace of mind. I would like to share strategies that I have found helpful for day-to-day mental well-being. These methods have helped me to feel closer to Amma when I am away from her physical presence, reminded me of her words, and strengthened my devotion. I'll start by sharing my journey with Amma, and the lessons that have helped me find a path to wellness.

I met Amma in 1996 when I was four years old. I was just out of the age range for the traditional 'first-writing' ceremony with Amma, which is probably why my handwriting is so terrible. My only contribution to meeting Amma at that time was likely

[18] The World Health Organization website states that 970 million people globally were living with a mental disorder in 2019. This number is also said to have significantly increased during the Covid-19 pandemic. Accessed in March 2024.

buckling my seatbelt in the car ride to the program, although I'm not sure if I even did this.

I credit the development of my current relationship with Amma today to the unwavering devotion of my parents. They gave me the stability to find my own understanding of the guru and spirituality over all these years — an understanding I am still developing. I have deep respect and admiration for many of you who did not have this support and overcame familial and other interpersonal conflicts to be with Amma. To those of you who did have such consistency and support, please remember to thank the people who provided it in your lives, as I certainly took this for granted for many years.

Amma has given me countless blessings in this life, and has been a part of every milestone and blunder. As I got older, around the age when I started using computers instead of pencils, I feel that my relationship to spirituality was marred by a transaction-oriented mindset.

Although my family is from India, I have spent my entire life in the West. In my experience, temple worship can sometimes be easily corrupted by the pursuit of materialism and gain. Without proper guidance, people often engage in 'prayer,' only to fulfill their materialistic aims. I have participated in, and contributed to this phenomenon on many occasions, despite having Amma in my life. I distinctly remember taking part in an abhiṣhēka, the ceremonial bath of a deity in a temple, while negotiating scores in my head on an upcoming test. I tried to think of what seemed like a reasonable 'ask' for the time I was spending there that day without putting any actual effort into studying the material. Needless to say, I did pretty poorly on that particular test and many others that I approached in this way.

This attitude stifles growth because it makes your happiness, or perception thereof, contingent on the outcome you desire. In my experience, this approach leads to anxiety and attachment to the result without even putting in the necessary effort to achieve it. The desired outcome itself is constantly changing and poorly defined.

Taking our prior example of scores — was it the score itself that mattered or the future success insinuated by a good score? In the case of the latter, does success refer to access to further educational pursuits, financial gain, approval from peers or family, fame, or something else entirely? The list goes on! Going about life in this way feels like swimming while holding your breath even when you are above water. It is a complete waste of effort and counterproductive.

I used to get so caught up in this process that I would use my precious time during darśhan to ask Amma for aid on tests and school work, without even properly studying for them. Amma, as she always does, met me at my level. She would give me the most loving smiles, never made me feel guilty for asking a satguru questions like these, and thankfully, didn't allow me to completely fail!

To my school-going and test-taking brothers and sisters, Amma has taught me, time and time again, that defining your self-worth by scores or achievements is not sustainable. None of them are actually the *be-all* or *end-all* we make them out to be. I am by no means above this mindset, nor have I completely rid myself of it. However, now that I have identified this way of thinking, I am consciously trying to change my attitude.

Most of the time, the results we seek may not actually be the best for us after all. Unfortunately, our expectations, stemming from this mindset, do not have the wisdom to know that. Only Amma does. As Amma regularly emphasizes, our sincere personal effort, surrender to the guru, and detachment from the outcome are the keys to our salvation from sorrow.

Amma has a beautiful quote from *Awaken Children* about this topic: "Live a detached life. Don't attach yourself to work or to its fruit. Perform it as a sacrifice. Then your actions will become beautiful and beneficial to others."

***

The sacrifice Amma mentions in this quote leads me to the next point I would like to make. It is important to remain cognizant of our intentions when performing actions, irrespective of the action itself or its perceived quality. Our intentions, though directed outward, still have a profound effect on us internally. Working on them can definitely bring us closer to Amma.

One of my favorite examples of this is my father. His favorite bhajan is *Vāgadhīśhvarī.* Now it's the favorite of everyone in my family. Whenever we were in the car together, it was almost always the first bhajan played. He liked *Vāgadhīśhvarī* so much that once, when Amma asked my father how far away we lived from the āśhram, he told her that the drive takes as long as the length of *Vāgadhīśhvarī.*

One summer about fifteen years ago, at a program held in Amma's San Ramon āśhram, he had the opportunity to sing *Vāgadhīśhvarī* for Amma. Although never trained or gifted in singing, he jumped at the chance. He would constantly listen to the bhajan on loop with a pair of headphones and practice singing the lyrics. When the time eventually came, he sang the song to the best of his ability. The whole hall went silent as people tried to figure out if someone had gotten injured. He got through the bhajan only with Amma's grace. In his darśhan afterwards, my biological mother, as any well-intentioned family member might do, commented on his seemingly lackluster performance. Amma corrected her and said that it was not the singing, but the bhakti in his heart that she enjoyed, showing that Amma sees the devotion and intention of our actions, and not necessarily the perceived result of them.

***

Regarding the importance of the intentions behind our actions, I remember an incident from when I was working in a medical research laboratory. We were using genetically modified mice to study cancer in the pancreas, which is the organ responsible for producing insulin and digestive enzymes in our bodies. I felt uncomfortable with the prospect of sacrificing mice, considering they happen to be Lord Gaṇēśha's vehicle in the Hindu tradition. I expressed these concerns to a very knowledgeable devotee who gave me some valuable advice. He explained that these types of studies were essential for the advancement of medicine, and even the pain medications we commonly use today were tested on animals at some point. The intention behind using mice was to benefit people in the future. Regarding the symbolism of the mouse, he said that it represents the ego, which Lord Gaṇēśha had conquered and therefore rode upon. It should not be taken literally. Again, it is the intention behind an action that is most important.

Bad intentions can result in both physical and mental pain. I recall an experience that clearly taught me this. Some time after I had received the guidance about mice, I met another commonly used animal in medical research: fruit flies. They appeared on a bunch of old bananas I had left out. I don't have anyone else to blame for this situation but myself.

One day, I had enough of the flies and spotted a particularly unlucky one on the countertop. I thought I would send a message to all the other flies, using this one to set an example. I put all of my frustration and emotion into a booming downward slap! I completely missed the fly — who actually did not even register my attempt and continued to sit there. I had miscalculated my trajectory so much that I bent my finger back on the edge of the countertop and managed to cause a complete fracture of one of the metacarpal bones in my hand!

I could not bring myself to believe this had happened, and for a few weeks I refused to get an X-ray and suffered as a result. When I finally suppressed my ego enough to do so, it showed the fracture. My negative intentions caused me both mental anguish and physical harm. Not only that, my ego was badly bruised by the fact that I had, quite literally, lost an altercation with a fruit fly! Not only that, I was the aggressor. Luckily, I have had no problems with my hand thus far — thank you Amma! The fly in this instance made me its vehicle by conquering my ego. It serves as a reminder that bad intentions can harm our physical and mental wellbeing.

***

What should be our intentions when performing an action? I believe a passage from a dialogue with Amma in 2004 answers this perfectly:

"Action performed with a spirit of selflessness is far superior to action performed with selfish motives. A person who is inspired by the ideal of selflessness is less attached to the action and more dedicated to the ideal of selflessness. This attitude of selflessness has a beauty of its own."

In discussing the practicalities of implementing this strategy, Amma went on to say,

"So in the beginning, just feel inspired by that very ideal (selflessness). Love the ideal; be inspired by it. In the beginning, it is a conscious and deliberate attempt. As you feel more and more inspired by the ideal of selflessness, you start working from your heart. By the very performance of the work, a joy will spring forth from deep within you. Eventually, it will become spontaneous."

Here, Amma refers to the internal wellbeing that results from an intention of selflessness!

Along with keeping pure intentions, I personally have found great benefit in visualizing Amma alongside me. As part of training in the field of surgery in the U.S., we spend dedicated periods of time working in the Trauma Service. This program oversees the evaluation and treatment of all injured people that come to a hospital as a result of motor vehicle accidents, violence, falls, and workplace injuries. After an individual is picked up by an ambulance, we are informed of their arrival and wait for them in a room with resuscitative medical equipment. People can be injured in very grotesque and unsettling ways, and at times, despite everyone's best efforts, they may pass away.

Sometimes, I, the guy who lost the fight to the fruit fly, am the most senior individual present during these resuscitation efforts. These situations often fill me with anxiety and fear. During some of the most difficult times, I imagine Amma at the bedside with me. We both wait for the patient to arrive, look onto the stretcher together when they do, and assess them from top to bottom. She stays close to me if I have to do any procedures and guides my hands while I do. She comes with me to the operating room, especially when there is an intimidating senior surgeon or a difficult surgery, and even walks beside me in the hallway at the hospital! I hope I remember to always feel Amma with me, giving me the strength to conquer my fears and continuously do my best.

In *Awaken Children*, Amma shares some beautiful advice on this sentiment. A devotee asked,

"With what attitude should I visualize God?"

Amma answered,

"It can be imagined that 'I am God's child.' God's existence will also become more convincing when one's resolve becomes stronger and stronger."

Remembering, "*I am Amma's child*," will undoubtedly put a smile on our face!

***

Another insight I would like to share is the importance of gratitude to the guru. A large portion of my thoughts are spent amplifying and reliving negative experiences, even though they have passed. In fact, if I were to calculate the proportion of time spent occupied by these events compared to the time I actually experienced them, the number would be astronomical. This could be chalked up to human nature, but because of Amma's teachings, we know that this cannot be an excuse. The burden of negativity is a weight we drag around with us wherever we go.

We never question when good things happen to us, expecting these occurrences and thinking that we deserve them. However, when bad things happen, we immediately question them without fail! We complain, "Amma, why did this have to happen to *me* of all people?" To add to our woes, our mind also creates unnecessary reactions to the circumstances of others.

As Amma explains, "There are two kinds of happiness and sorrow. When we don't get what we want, we feel sad; but when others get what they wish, our sadness is even greater. Similarly, we are happy when we succeed in something, but we are happier when others fail. This is a serious disease of the mind. Pray for a heart that rejoices in the happiness of others and empathizes with their sorrows."

The first time I read this, my eyes welled up from the sting of the accuracy of her words. I feel that gratitude to Amma is a powerful way of combating this tendency and reducing the burden of negativity and sadness. We all have more than we can comprehend to be grateful to Amma for, even at the most superficial levels.

I was recently sent a video of a darśhan that Amma gave to our family many years ago. In the video, my biological mother was tearfully explaining an issue while Amma listened sincerely and consoled her. When we discussed it, neither my mother nor I could remember what she was distressed about at the time of that darśhan; but I know Amma remembers. I cannot even recall all of the times Amma has guided me through the now forgotten issues that, at the time, seemed like life or death.

I apologize to Amma that I cannot fully appreciate how much she has done for me, even through our visible interactions. Not to mention all the other subtle ways the guru assists us in our lives. Despite this shortcoming, I have a lifetime of gratitude, multiple times over, for what I can remember.

One example is how Amma supported us when my father passed away nearly thirteen years ago. When compared to the circumstances others face in the world, I feel privileged for all the time in this life I did have with him. I know he is now with Amma. By Amma's grace, she was visiting San Ramon for the November program that year and met with us immediately. Amma sat on the floor with us and we mourned his physical loss together. Amma did not dwell there though. She addressed the practicalities of life moving forward, quickly arranging for my biological mother to live in the āśhram in San Ramon, and providing us with resources, support, and connections. Amma even recommended that I go to counseling, which helped me immensely.

I have no idea what life would be like without this support. To this day, I have peace of mind due to the interventions and support of Amma, and any accomplishment I have experienced or will ever experience in life is a direct result of it. These sentiments and remembrance of Amma's love have helped me to feel her presence and have reversed negativity and sorrow in my life.

***

Amma provides us with so many tools to improve our mental wellness and imparts teachings that she herself exemplifies. These include the importance of detachment from the outcome of our actions, purifying our intentions, visualizing Amma alongside us, and cultivating gratitude to our guru. I hope we can all keep these ideas more salient in our minds as we go about our day, improving our overall wellness and keeping Amma closer to us.

To me, it is this mental proximity to Amma, or devotion, that aids our mental wellness, especially when we are living far away from Amma's physical form. I used to believe devotion was a binary quality, either present or absent in our lives. Now, I perceive it as a spectrum, wherein the beauty and benefits increase exponentially the more we cultivate it. Devotion requires practice. Looking back at the times I have felt the burden of my mind the most, they undoubtedly coincide with the times I made the least effort in this regard. Let us all pray that Amma strengthens our devotion day-by-day, until there is never any distance between her love and us.

Amma, I don't know what boon was granted to all of us to gain you as our mother in this life, but I dare not question it. I pray to you that I do not squander it. Thank you for hand-carving a path to salvation in the unforgiving terrain of this world and being our navigator step-by-step, regardless of our pace or whether we falter. Thank you for giving this life the only meaning that matters.

Amma, I pray that you remove the cataracts of worldliness from our eyes, which cloud both our vision of your full glory and our true nature. I pray each one of us hears your affectionate words in our ears, sees your divine gaze with our eyes, and feels the warmth of your caress on our skin, every second we are away from you. I pray we go out in the world as an embodiment of your love – giving strength to others, taking less than we receive, and striving to improve the environment for all those around us in some way.

12

Indescribable Longing

Kavyakala – USA

We all know how Amma has deeply touched our lives and have heard countless stories expressing the complete awe that we are all in — transfixed by this radiant form of the Mother as our guru. Amma holds the very light that illumines existence, and this light reaches far beyond our perception. With this light she helps us awaken within and also shows the exterior path to follow. In fact, she helps us go beyond all these concepts of exterior and interior, and gives us love that has no boundaries or limitations. Our eyes constantly crave to see Amma because she is the embodiment of this love, ever familiar and yet so vast that it is hard to comprehend.

The topic I will try to share about is the indescribable place of deep longing. These stories are arising from my personal experiences and are just one way that I have personally felt this longing. In fact, each one of us seems to have our own unique expression, yet in truth, this longing is universal and undivided. Longing is the very core of existence and propels us all forward towards the ever-present source.

The question naturally arises: What are we longing for? Anything we name — happiness, relationships, family, friends, objects — everything falls short. If these were all that were required to make us happy, then the moment we attained them, we would be content and no longer seek for more. The longing continues, thus proving there is something unnamable at the source. This is where Amma has come to guide us past the seen to the unseen, the outer to the inner, the separate to the inseparable.

So here begins my story. Perhaps if we all look within, we feel that Amma has always been there, and in truth, she has. As stated in the bhajan *Abhīṣhṭa Varadāyikē*, "Right from the earliest days, as far back as my memory takes me, I felt that I was the flower that was offered for your worship."

The year was 1987, Amma's first world tour, and I was a struggling teenager living in a remote town near Mount Shasta, California. I remember standing at the window in our living room, looking out at the majestic, volcanic mountain and hearing that a woman 'hugging saint' from India was coming to the area. I only had a vague idea of what a saint was, let alone a hugging saint from India. Although it was not quite time to meet Amma, just hearing about her opened up a new world of spiritual exploration.

I grew up without any specific organized religion. My parents loved nature and from the age of five years old, we would go backpacking to the alpine lakes and mountainous areas of northern California. The silence of the still lakes in the morning and the spacious pine forests became my first spiritual connection. As I grew, I developed a fascination with religions and went to almost every church in our small village. I was interested to see what they were saying and why they were apparently separate. I loved the stories, started to read the bible, and felt the fundamental principles of Christianity were kindness and love. My eight-year-old mind could not see any separation, and even as a child, I could feel that these principles were not exclusive to the Christian faith. When I asked my parents about other religions, they told me to explore all of them and that I could be part of any religion I wanted. The doors were wide open. So when I heard that a 'hugging saint from India' was in our local area, a sudden revelation dawned on me. There must be a wealth of spiritual teachings from the East that I needed to investigate.

Living in the Bay Area of California was like a huge supermarket of spiritual practices. I was hungry to figure out what was the purpose of this life, and which spiritual path resonated most. I explored so many paths, and there were a variety of valid teachings. Yet something was missing, and I noticed that my insecurities, anger, anxiety and judgments only seemed to be increasing. At one point, I heard the saying that digging a lot of shallow wells will never bring you to water, and I realized nothing was really bringing me closer to true understanding.

***

The twists and turns of the world brought me to New Mexico, and I became a midwife, assisting women as they gave birth. Here I was, at the precipice of birth and the fragile experience of new life. The mother figure became my focus, and unknowingly, I started to worship the Divine Mother. At that point, I did not have a set form for the Divine Mother but felt like I could hear and feel her presence all around. I felt the Divine Mother unified all these so-called different belief systems into the one all-inclusive aspect of motherly love. From then on, I could hear the word "God" and equate it with the Divine Mother.

My internal relationship with the Divine Mother grew through working as a midwife. As I assisted the mothers, unbroken prayers for each emerging baby would fill my mind. Each birth taught me how powerless I was, and showed me how limited my thoughts and actions are compared to this vast ocean of creation. Prayer became very natural in this setting. What else do you do when you have seemingly endless hours of waiting, and you know you are not the one in control? On one such occasion, looking up into the star-filled night, I put out a prayer that would change my life forever. The delivery of the child had stalled and I felt helpless and uncertain of how to proceed. It was all a reflection of my inner journey. I stepped outside to get some air and cried, "Oh Divine Mother! I really need you! I don't know how to move forward in life. I am so confused and need your guidance. I need to see you and for you to show me the way."

The baby was born safely, but this longing and inner cry for help remained. Here is where the longing became known to me, but I was still unclear of what I was truly longing for.

Soon after, I was at a bookstore and randomly pulled out Amma's *Awaken Children* book. I purchased it and could not stop reading. Here, Amma expressed the deepest spiritual truths in such a straightforward, simple way. I heard for the first time that God alone is our eternal support, that there really is no one to call our own, and that this ever-changing world is not our true self. Amma's words were straightforward, and a deep longing to meet Amma took root.

In 2008, an opportunity finally opened where I could take leave of the midwifery practice and make the pilgrimage to meet Amma at a program in Albuquerque, New Mexico. I brought my six-year-old daughter Kenya, and my eight-year-old son Quinn. It was on the occasion of Dēvī Bhāva and we were ushered into a huge room full of people sitting on the floor. We waited...

When Amma walked into the room, I instantly burst into tears. I knew my prayer had been answered. Here was the Divine Mother in a physical form! The children looked at me with concerned eyes saying, "Mama, what is wrong?" I could not even respond — tears were streaming down my cheeks and I was speechless. It was like the sun entering the dark cave of the mind. Here was the Divine Mother that I had prayed to countless times.

The following year, the children's father, Amarnath, joined us. All four of us went to see Amma, and this is when we asked if we could come to Amritapuri. After this, our yearly three to five month pilgrimages to India began.

Amritapuri felt like our second home, and the children grew up knowing the bliss of āśhram life. They experienced chocolates in Amma's room, running after Amma, greeting the swāmīs and swāminīs, and sitting at Amma's holy lotus feet on the special days when Amma would serve food to everyone in the temple.

Amma had other plans for me. Along with the bliss she would turn up the heat, and my unending tears would flow. As Amma says, "My children, you are unaware of the way a mahātmā works on you. Mother operates from the inside, very deeply, without any external incisions. Mother operates and makes deep transformations. She removes your vāsanās (latent tendencies) in subtle ways. It may be necessary to remove many things. Mother is removing the pus from the wounds within you, and this will occasionally be painful."

This is one aspect of what I had been longing for — inner transformation. I felt very willing to lay down on the operating table, knowing that it was more painful to keep living with my negativities. Whenever the time came to leave Amritapuri, it felt like I was falling into a deep, dark well. All I could think about was how to get back to my Mother!

Back in New Mexico, singing bhajans alone, reading spiritual books, and walking in nature, became my way of surviving the time away from Amma. Morning archana, mānasa pūjā and mantra chanting were my anchors. "Where is my mother?" I would cry, "You can't abandon me now!" Just in the nick of time,

Amma would glide into the U.S. or carry us back to Amritapuri. The longing felt intense, but Amma made it clear that it needed to get more intense.

***

In 2010, I was sitting in the Kaḷari[19] after a pūjā for world peace. It was then that I heard someone speaking about the earthquake that hit Haiti, devastating the country. We all prayed sincerely for the peace of all those that lived there.

A month later when we returned to New Mexico, I got an urgent message from an organization called Bhumi Sehat, calling all midwives to come to Haiti to help with the relief effort. I didn't really have to think twice and knew it was another journey set forth by our beloved Amma. It was time to set aside my own comforts and serve.

What a contrast going from the heaven of Amritapuri to the hell of demolished Haiti. The stench of death and the force of birth met head-on, and here, my whole world-view shattered. I was on the front line of the two extremes, thrown into the deep waters of disaster relief service. It was here that I first witnessed the depths of suffering, and what it is to truly have no one to call your own.

One young mother's story awakened a new level of understanding within, and became a pivotal point on my spiritual journey. She had lost her home, parents, and her husband when the multitude of buildings crumbled down. The shattering waves of the earthquake had left her with only her unborn child in her womb. She was so young, pregnant and alone. I had just arrived and was assisting the primary midwife. It was a long, challenging labor with many complications. Finally, the new

[19] Original small temple where Amma used to hold Kṛiṣhṇa Bhāva and Dēvī Bhāva darśhans.

life emerged, and a spark seemed to light up the eyes of this mother for the first time. Waves of maternal love saturated her very being.

A few days later, however, the newborn started to decline. Nonstop efforts were put in to try to save this new life, yet tragically, the baby died. This fragile, little light flickered and went out. It was the first and only time in my twenty years of being a midwife that I witnessed a life passing; a new, fresh life that passed so quickly. The angelic face of this little one was painful to see, but what shook me the most was when I looked into this young mother's eyes. They were vacant, revealing a deep absence. She walked away from the tent hospital with absolutely nothing.

A few months prior, she had a family, a home, a new baby on the way, and in an instant, it was all gone. The extremes of birth and death collided, and the impermanent nature of this human existence became crystal clear. Right then and there, everything shifted. I witnessed firsthand how there is truly nothing to call our own. All the relationships that we have are like trying to hold water in our hands. This was when I truly understood what it meant to be an orphan.

For me, I knew the only cure to this level of suffering was to wake up, and Amma was the guide to help me do this. The love of the mother is what every orphan longs for, and the guidance of the guru is what every seeker lives for. This manifested a new level of inner longing within me, to awaken to Amma's love, the true self.

After many intense and heart-wrenching experiences in Haiti, I returned to our small farm, friends, and family in New Mexico. But I was not the same. I knew, without a doubt, that I needed to focus my attention on 'that' which is permanent. The longing to go beyond this world of life, death, sorrows, joys, and continual fluctuations became urgent. I knew then that I needed to be with Amma, she was the only one that could show me the way.

***

Of course, time and my dharma, or sacred duty, as a mother were not yet aligned, and it took twelve more years until I could live at Amma's abode. Every year, I would ask, plead, and beg Amma to allow us to come live in Amritapuri. But it was always shown that this request was not in the best interest of the whole. I could not abandon my duties as a mother, but at the same time, I knew there was no time to waste. So throughout the days, I would be a mother, midwife, teacher, friend... and the minute I could, I would dive deep within myself and cry endlessly. In fact, I'm not sure how this body was able to produce so many tears. I cried and cried, and then I sobbed and sobbed.

I would pray from the depths of my heart, "Oh, Amma! Take me in your arms! I am lost. Please show me the way! Please do not forsake me Amma, this child is all alone. Who but my Divine Mother can show me the way? Please don't let go of this child's hand. Hold tight so I do not fall."

Some of us are really hard nuts to crack, and so need extra force to break the exterior. Finally, the children were grown and Amma had given permission for me to come live at Amritapuri. My possessions were reduced to a few suitcases, and all arrangements were in line. The family was supportive, and I was ready to embark on the journey home. Then, the entire world shut down due to the pandemic. Now the fire of longing became an inferno. I would walk through the pinyon forests of New Mexico with tears streaming down while praying and calling out to Amma.

In June 2020, I got a call from the GreenFriends Montessori School at Amma's Chicago āśhram. They needed some consulting for their emerging elementary program, and since I was an elementary trained Montessori teacher, I felt like it would be a good way to serve. Amma sent a little lifeline so that I could at least be at one of her main U.S. centers during the pandemic.

I thought I would be there for a few months, and then go right off to Amritapuri. Since patience and acceptance are some of my challenges, I got to really practice these essential qualities. Two months turned into one and a half years. Amazingly, the tears never stopped, and I have so much gratitude to Swami Shantamritananda Puri for his kind guidance, and all the dear friends that kept encouraging me.

When India opened its doors to foreign travelers, I quickly made arrangements to come. Arriving back at Amritapuri I felt such a loving welcome, and with Amma's infinite grace, I am now able to call Amritapuri my only home and refuge. I cannot even begin to express my gratitude to Amma and the Amritapuri family.

***

Honestly, everything has been so divine, and Amma has been holding all of us throughout this. Amma showed me that she heard every one of those prayers and each tear was a flower petal at her divine feet. Once I fully placed everything in Amma's hands and became empty, I could see Amma was holding me the whole time.

As Amma sings in the bhajan *Ḍar Ḍar Maiṅ*:

When You uttered, 'You are mine,'
I realized that I am no longer an orphan.
You have given me so much,

but I have nothing to give You in return.
I surrender this life at Your sacred feet,
O Immortal Goddess!

As I reflect, I can see that I am only at the very beginning stages of longing, and have a huge mountain to climb to attain the level of longing that the gōpīs had for Kṛiṣhṇa. This highest level of longing culminates in unity. The merging of the jīvātmā, the individual soul, with the paramātmā, the supreme being.

I have just started to understand that spiritual longing is not a weakness but a spiritual practice. As we focus our minds on uniting with our Mother, the source, a cleaning out of the unwanted thoughts, emotions and actions will occur. It is like the tsunami wave that removes everything in its path, the giant wave of emotion that swallows up all the small waves.

For all of Amma's children, whether physically away from her or living in her physical presence, I pray that we can all allow the longing to continually expand. Although it is often excruciating, it also binds us to the ultimate goal, transforming into the one burning desire for self-realization.

I would like to conclude with a short poem. These words came to me after looking in Amma's eyes, and are just a little expression of love.

Translucent eyes
Looking into the depths
Allowing only light to emerge
Unveiling the source to sip the nectar
The mind flits around seeking a landing place,
Plummeting down to the thick density of the world.

Oh the desire to soar high,
Longing to feel the expanse of the eternal sky.
How to release this tether that binds?

Your feet show the pathway
I try to follow but the thorns draw blood and fear grips
Trembling, I cry out for you to hold me.

A child like this cannot make it alone
Through this quickly growing jungle.
Come close, Oh Mother, Come close!
Guide this child to the source.

13
Gratitude and Grace

Devanath - Spain

Amma once told me that cultivating gratitude was essential for my spiritual progress. Gratitude brings many benefits in disguise. It increases awareness of one's own selfish tendencies, develops humility, and opens the heart to allow the ever-present divine grace to flow in. I'll start with a story of how Amma's grace blessed me, allowing me to be here today.

One night when I was a child, I awoke from my sleep and saw something shocking. A black figure less than a meter tall, with a red tongue, was smiling at me mischievously. It had either four arms or perhaps only two, but it moved them so rapidly, up and down, that they appeared as four. A thought arose in my mind, saying, 'You should not be seeing this.' So, I fell asleep again.

This incident happened on the night of January 5th, a very special night for Christians in Spain. It is the night when the Three Wise Men from the East, who came to witness the birth of Jesus Christ, are believed to bring gifts to all children. I thought I had seen a strange version of one of the Wise Men — the one usually depicted with dark skin.

The next morning, I told my cousin what had happened, but he was not so convinced. It wasn't until a few years ago that I realized that the image I saw that night resembled the divine Kālī idol in the Kālī Temple in Amritapuri.

Fast forward to when I met Amma. One day, one of my co-workers started to talk to me about Amma. I was not so interested in gurus, especially one in a woman's body. Soon after, I started to attend English classes, and interestingly enough, my classmate was the sēvā coordinator for Amma's program in Spain. There was no way I could escape meeting Amma. The next year, I went with my classmate to see who Amma was.

I committed to attend Amma's program and do sēvā for five days. We finished setting-up around midnight on the night before the program. I wanted to sleep, but someone said Amma was supposed to arrive in *only* one and a half hours, and that we should wait. I thought they were crazy.

Nevertheless, since my companions intended to wait, I decided to do the same. As people started to chant ōṁ namaḥ śhivāya[20] while dancing, I got my confirmation that indeed, these people were crazy — and I was supposed to spend another four days with them! I tried to think of an excuse to leave the program the next morning, but something inside told me to wait. Finally, Amma arrived...

Amma was greeting the devotees, stopping and touching people's hands, talking with them and smiling at everyone. When she reached the spot where I was, she did not look at me and kept walking. Yet, as soon as she passed me — oh, my God! — from the very second she walked by, I felt an indescribable joy, something completely unknown to me. I felt such divine grace that I knew without a doubt that Amma was the answer to everything I was looking for in my life. I knew I must be with her, so I wanted to ask her permission to come to Amritapuri. I had been looking for a perfect master, but from my egocentric viewpoint, I never thought I was qualified enough to become the disciple of such a great master.

Maybe this is one of the reasons why Amma has come as a divine mother who welcomes all of her children, no matter

[20] A prominent mantra meaning 'Salutations to Śhiva, the auspicious one, the inner self' that is used as a greeting in Amma's āśhrams.

how unworthy they may seem. If she were only taking on the role of a guru, how many of us would be qualified to be with her right now? Surely not me. However, in my ignorance, since the beginning, I have thought of myself as Amma's disciple. The reality is, I'm only a newborn baby in spirituality and incredibly lucky to be one among Amma's children.

The next day, the program started and I joined the line to give prasād to Amma.[21] While giving prasād, I was unaware that Amma was waiting with her hand open. I thought, "I should be paying more attention." But my very next thought was, "Well, my delay is not a big deal since it's only a couple of seconds." As soon as this thought appeared in my mind, Amma turned and looked at me with a face that I'm still unable to describe. It happened only for a millisecond, but I was shaken to the core.

Despite that incident, I continued in a state of bliss for a week. I felt, for the first time in my life, that the people around me were my brothers and sisters — I felt love for everyone and everything.

Someone told me that each morning, ten people would get a chance to ask a question to Amma while she was giving darśhan. Since many people wanted to ask questions, a type of lottery was held to choose the ten for that day. I felt this was my chance to ask Amma's permission to come to the āśhram. I had been staying up very late at night during the programs, so to attend the early morning lottery I had to reluctantly give up my most beloved attachment — sleep. Every morning I would attend the lottery, hoping to be one of the names drawn. However, my number was not amongst the lucky ten.

---

[21] Each person who comes to receive Amma's darśhan, also receives prasād from Amma, a blessed offering in the form of a vibhūti (sacred ash) packet and a candy. 'Prasād giving' is where devotees receive the opportunity to place this offering in Amma's hand while she is giving darśhan.

After three days with little sleep, on the last day the first winning number was mine! I felt Amma saying, "My son, you are definitely on my list, but you should first put in some effort to receive divine grace." Amma finally answered my question by giving me permission to come to Amritapuri. I got leave from my job for as long as I wanted, and I left my home, girlfriend, and family to come to India.

***

Upon my arrival in Amritapuri, I saw that one of the daily activities was archana at 4:50 a.m., so I thought I would attend it once to see what it was all about. During my first archana, I got a headache from reading the thousand names (of the Divine Mother) at that early hour. However, after a few days, I felt that if there is anything I could offer to Amma, it should be what I cherished the most — sleep. So, I started to get up early to come to the hall daily at 4:15 a.m. after a shower. It became the most beneficial habit I have ever developed and I can feel its benefits every day.

Amma's tours were fast approaching and I started to dream of traveling with her around the world — but I had no money. Before the tours started, my biological mother told me that she had won a lottery prize and unexpectedly gave me the money. It was the exact amount it would cost to travel with Amma for an entire year! I felt that Amma manifested her grace through my mum's selfless donation.

I went on the South India tour and after returning to the āśhram, I started to have tooth pain. On my birthday, the pain became so intense that I had to urgently go to the āśhram hospital. It is said in astrology that whatever happens on one's birth date has a special karmic reason behind it.

The next day, I noticed that I could not open my jaw more than half an inch. I was barely able to put a spoon between my teeth and suck the food. When I went to the dentist, she told me it was a normal side effect from the anesthesia she had given me the day before, and gave me a muscle relaxant. However, when I went back to her three days later with the same problem, she started to fret that something was wrong. One of the doctors said I would need to undergo surgery and have part of the muscles of my mouth cut, and another dentist said that it was too late for the muscles to come back to their normal position. Everyone agreed I must go to AIMS Hospital.

The doctors at AIMS also said that it was too late for the muscles to come back to their normal position. They gave me a splinter for my teeth and mouth exercises to be done daily, and said my jaw would open normally again after...*one whole year*! I left AIMS and joined the North India tour starting the very next day.

To add to the līlā, or divine play, it just so happens that one of the best dentists in the world for jaw-related problems is from my country. Many people told me to go back to Spain and see this doctor, and many other people told me to talk with Amma about my issue — but I did neither. I felt that this was a test coming from the guru to see what I wanted first in my life. I trusted that if I stayed in Amma's physical presence, everything would be fine.

As the tour was going along without any improvement in my jaw, I started to feel anxious. One day, feeling truly miserable, I shed many tears and finally inwardly surrendered to the situation. That night, I fell asleep mentally exhausted. The next day, I felt divine grace filling my whole being and tears started rolling down my cheeks. At that moment, I noticed I could open my jaw half an inch more than before, but still not enough to get food inside.

I contacted the famous Spanish dentist and he told me to do an orthopantomography, a specific x-ray of the jaw, and send it to him. I could not find any clinic or hospital with the proper equipment to take the X-ray while touring. Once we reached Bangalore, I walked for miles, stopping to inquire in about ten hospitals, until I finally found one with the right equipment. Once the orthopantomography was done and sent to the doctor, he said I needed to come to Spain to undergo an operation, as there was no other way for the jaw to be opened.

I did not say anything to Amma. I felt connected with her and trusted that everything would work out through her grace. Also, I did not feel worthy enough to bother her with my problems, and still I do not. Yet, it's one thing to not bother Amma, but it's another to lack the discernment to know when to talk to her openly.

Because of my feeling of unworthiness, and also because of my cowardice to speak to Amma openly, in the past I have not talked to her when I should have. Only with her grace, from now on, I'll be able to have the discernment and courage to talk with her when it may be required.

***

After the North India tour, I continued on to the Singapore, Malaysia, Australia, and North Kerala tours. In Malaysia, when Dēvī Bhāva was finishing, someone asked me to come near Amma to move the pīṭham, Amma's seat, as soon as she stood up after darśhan. I approached and sat near Amma's feet. However, Amma did not get up, but instead, started to talk while seated on the pīṭham for about forty-five minutes. I felt so blessed to be sitting at the Divine Mother's feet. When Amma got up and left, one brahmachāriṇī told me that I had not looked at Amma's face even once, and she asked me why. I told her the truth. I didn't feel worthy of being with Amma, and I was scared even to look into her eyes. However, I was immensely grateful for the opportunity to be at the Divine Mother's feet. That day, I could open my jaw another inch. I again felt divine grace pouring into me.

Soon after this, I joined the Japan, U.S. and Canada tours. Those two months, I felt so much joy and gratitude for being able to travel with Amma. One day, during the Atlanta program, I cried out of pure happiness without knowing why. At that very moment — I could finally completely open my jaw again after almost six months!

I went to the stage and sat close to Amma. Remember, I had not told Amma anything about my jaw issue all this time. She turned to me, took a big ball of peanut candy and threw it to me. I caught it and looked inquisitively at Amma. She pointed to her jaw and said twice, "You can eat." Even writing this now, seven years later, tears come to my eyes. It's beyond my ability to express my gratitude to you, Amma. Thank you, Mother.

***

That year and the next, I was able to travel with Amma everywhere she went. I remember an incident that happened at the airport in Réunion. Amma had been sitting and speaking to the devotees for a long time, when finally, she stood up and passed beside me as she headed to the boarding gate. I had a feeling of not wanting to bother her by trying to get close to touch her hand. Instead, I went and sat near the chair where she had been seated to feel her presence and grace. As I was about to sit, I saw a flash of a white sari and smelt a heavenly fragrance. Yes, it was Amma! She had come back.

Just as I started to sit in the adjacent seat, I felt four arms grab me and pull me away from Amma. Two of Amma's Western children with fierce expressions were pulling me out of their way while saying, "These are *our* seats!" Surprisingly, although I looked closely, I could not find their names written anywhere on the seats.

While I was pulled away from Amma, by her grace, I did not feel disturbed. However, when I tried to sit on the floor in front of Amma, there was not even a single spot left, as it was all taken in one second by the rest of Amma's children flocking around her. I was standing only on one leg, trying to maintain balance and not fall. Seconds passed, I started to hear everyone laughing, but nobody moved an inch to make room for me. Suddenly, a gracious arm and hand rose to offer me something to hold on to. It was Amma! I knew that it had a deeper meaning for everyone. Whenever we may be stumbling or close to falling, the guru, the Universal Mother, will be there to hold and support us. As the others saw that I was also a child of Amma, someone moved a little bit and I could finally sit.

After the Mauritius program, I was feeling sad as Amma was continuing to Singapore and I had to return to India. I also felt disheartened that I never had the courage to talk to Amma. I was in the airport, and I went alone to my boarding gate, while the group traveling with Amma went their way.

Suddenly, I saw Amma approaching. She looked at me and asked, "Singapore?" I replied, "No Amma, Amritapuri." In a tone that reflected my sadness, Amma said, "Oooh!" as she came towards me, took my hands, and kissed them. Without letting go of my hand, she then started walking towards the boarding gate for Singapore, gently pulling me along. I couldn't believe what was happening, so I did not start to walk. Again, Amma gently pulled me by the hand to walk by her side. I felt the deeper meaning — whenever you may be stuck on the path, the guru or Divine Mother will pull you by the hand and walk beside you. My mind was blank and I felt the desire to embrace her. As soon as this thought appeared, Amma stopped walking and gave me darśhan. I felt so divinely overwhelmed that I could only say, "Ōṁ namaḥ śhivāya." Then, she gave me a second darśhan and continued on her way to the boarding gate. I might have considered it all a dream, had it not been for the fact that Amrita TV was filming the entire scene.

It is beyond my comprehension how much compassion Amma has to come down to my level — embracing me with the same love that she has for all of her children. When I had my jaw issue, Amma's body was undergoing some painful teeth problems as well, and I felt she was taking a huge karmic burden from myself and many more of her children.

A biological mother cannot take away the physical, mental, and emotional suffering from her children — but the Universal Mother can. She takes it upon herself, and does so with an infinite number of her children, and her entire creation — a sacrifice far beyond understanding. I used to pray to Amma, "Give me dispassion, discrimination, devotion, selflessness, strength, and faith." It was only very recently that I began to ask her in my prayers, "What I can offer?" rather than what can I receive — even if all I have to offer are my mind's impurities and negative tendencies.

***

After the Africa tour that year, I asked Amma's permission to become a renunciate. I must say, soon after my first arrival in India, I felt more identified with my Indian brothers and sisters than with my Western ones. I ate only Indian meals and I avoided going to the Western Café or mingling with my Western brothers and sisters. I also liked to do sēvā with brahmachārīs, and even though there was a language barrier, I still felt like one of them. I feel a deeper connection to this sacred land of India, the great Bhārat, than to my own country.

So, when I became a renunciate, I wanted to be assigned to some department where I could do sēvā with brahmachārīs, be in silence as much as possible, and be far away from the Western canteen area. But guess what department I was assigned to?

Yes, I was assigned to work in the Western Café and canteen! Not only that, I began my sēvā during the busy season, with more than three hundred Westerners coming to each meal shift. So, in the end, I needed to talk with many Westerners while attending to them. As my Western brothers and sisters were talking to me, forgiving my shortcomings and mistakes with kindness and tenderness, I also felt Amma's grace and love flowing through them. Whether from India or any other country, all of you, Amma's children, have blessed my life. You are all an inspiration and example for me.

Eight years ago, I came to Amritapuri trying to get self-realization. However, what I have learnt is that the most important thing in life is not what we finally get, but how we live it. I have realized that true fulfillment lies in making our lives an offering to others. That feeling of fulfillment is truly the goal of life, and liberation in itself.

14

Amma's Inner Presence

Hansa Bhaskar – USA

Many of us who are unable to be with Amma for an extended period of time, find ourselves struggling without her physical presence. Amma often tells us to be strong, and assures us that she is always with us. We know this intellectually, but most of the time we don't have the experience and awareness of this truth.

I want to share a few of my experiences of being able to feel Amma's presence, even when I was physically far away from her. In 2007, my brother and I went to India to be with our father. He had broken his hip and suffered a heart attack, and he needed to stay in bed for one month before receiving surgery. I was very sad to be in India and yet not be with Amma. I felt so far away.

My brother was part of a group that met regularly to send reiki, healing energy, to my father. One day, one of the group members offered to do energy work on me. He asked me to close my eyes as he began his work. When he was finished, he asked me to open my eyes and began to tell me in amazement, "I just had darśhan of your guru!" I asked him what had happened. He said, "I could not even see you. A beautiful lady in a white sari was sitting in your chair the entire time. I am so thankful to have seen her!" This experience gave me the confidence that when we are alone and missing her, Amma is so close to us that her form can actually be seen in place of ours! We don't have the eyes to see her, but she is certainly with us.

Amma also clearly hears us when we are not with her. Once, I was driving home from Amma's āśhram in San Ramon,

California after the evening program. I was driving along on a dark, lonely road and did not notice that the gas tank of the car was empty. Suddenly, I realized that I was pressing the gas pedal, but the car was not accelerating. Horrified, I quickly pulled off the road. By Amma's grace, there was just enough gas for that. I had no cell phone with me. I realized that if my lights were off, a car could easily hit me. However, if I turned them on, my battery would run down. I started asking Amma for help. My voice slowly became louder and louder. I kept repeating, "Amma, I surrender to you. Please help me!" Soon, I was shouting, but nothing happened.

After some time, I gave up shouting and I just sat silently. I thought, "Whatever happens is in Amma's hands. I cannot stay in the car all night." So, I got out of the car, looking like a ghost in my white sari on the dark, lonely road. A man in a pickup truck stopped when he saw me. I prayed to Amma and got into the truck. I told him I had run out of gas and needed a ride to the next town. He simply nodded and drove in silence. I was so relieved when he drove me to a gas station. As I stepped out of the truck, to my amazement, I saw one of my former students working at the gas station. She had a huge smile on her face and ran to me and gave me a hug. Not only did she send someone to put gas in the car and drive it to the gas station, but she also fed me food and gave me a nice, hot cup of coffee as I waited for my car to be delivered. Amma had definitely heard me and saved me! She waited for me to be ready to accept whatever might happen, and despite feeling scared, to make the effort to get out of the car. At that moment, Amma did everything necessary to save me.

***

The seven years before I met Amma were the most difficult and traumatic years of my life. It felt as though every time I held onto something or someone for support, it disappeared like a mirage. I was left alone to deal with so many problems, and felt helpless and extremely disillusioned with the world. I wanted to hold on to something that would not be a mirage — something that was divine and changeless. At the same time, I was wandering aimlessly in the world, and had completely lost faith in spiritual teachers.

In June 1989, I reluctantly agreed to see Amma for the first time in Palo Alto, California, at my sister-in-law's request. As I joined the darśhan line, I noticed people crying as they received Amma's embrace. I thought this was expected and became worried that I would not be able to cry. Amma was beautiful and familiar and loving, but I was only worried about how to ask the many questions I had prepared in the few precious moments of my darśhan. However, as I moved up in the line, my mind became quiet only from being in Amma's divine presence. When I finally came in front of her, only one question came to my mind. I told Amma that I wanted to see God. I hadn't yet understood that I was already seeing her right in front of me.

Amma answered lovingly, "Daughter, if you can hold on to that intense feeling of longing for four years, that is enough." I felt very happy that it was possible to have the vision of God, but of course, my mind immediately went back to its old ways. Amma's divine presence alone had made me ask a question that hadn't even been on my list.

The following year, I called the āśhram to find out about Amma's San Ramon retreat. I was told that the retreat was limited to only a hundred people, and it was already closed. I was very disappointed. A few days later, they called back and said the retreat had opened up to 150 more people and I could now attend. It was wonderful to spend two and a half days immersed in Amma's presence and to stay onsite. I received a precious mantra from Amma during this retreat, and I treasure it as my unchanging connection to her.

Five days after the San Ramon retreat, I went to my parents' house in India. They had arranged for me to give a small house concert on the veena. Ever since I was a child, I was used to waking up in the morning to the lovely sound of my father playing the veena. I naturally loved the instrument and was happy to play.

One of the people attending was an ardent worshiper of Dēvī. Towards the end of the concert, I played a song to the Divine Mother called, Śharaṇu Śharaṇu Śhāradā. As soon as I started playing and singing that song, all the lights in the house went out. I was surprised, but I did not stop. I finished the song in the dark and the lights came back on. The Dēvī devotee asked me to play the song again. As soon as I started, the lights again went off, and once again, I played the whole song in the dark. Immediately after, the lights mysteriously came back on. After the other guests had left, I asked the devotee what had happened. He explained that the first time the lights went off, he saw a brilliant light — like a thousand suns — surrounding me. He wanted to test this, and so he asked me to play the song again. Again, it became dark and in the darkness he saw the brilliant light. Witnessing this blessing, he advised me to sing that song every day.

In my heart, I realized that this brilliant light was Amma, whom I had just spent three days with. I felt the Dēvī devotee had witnessed Amma's viśhvarūpa, her universal form, as described in the *Bhagavad Gītā*, Chapter 11, verse 12:

divi sūrya-sahasrasya bhavēd yugapad utthitā
yadi bhāḥ sadṛiśhī sā syād bhāsas tasya mahātmanaḥ

> If the effulgence of a thousand suns were to blaze forth all at once in the sky, such would be the splendor of that mighty being.

This experience had a profound effect on me. I knew that Amma was not only my guru, but that her greatness was beyond comprehension and incomparable. I felt a deep gratitude that God had heard my prayers. My faith in God and the guru came back stronger. I still felt numb from my seven difficult years, but suddenly there was hope. By grace, I finally had a divine guru who was not a mirage, whose feet I could hold on to forever, and who would listen to even my smallest prayers.

***

Everything to do with Amma was just like magic during those first two years. Normally, my mind would run from one problem to another like a rat in a maze. By her grace, whenever I was in her presence, my mind would quiet down and become more focused. I was able to experience peace of mind – something I had not known before. There was nothing I could have done to deserve it. It was all Amma's compassion.

I soon started going to the San Ramon āśhram for satsang and began getting more involved. The following year, I attended Amma's San Ramon program. One Dēvī Bhāva was truly unforgettable. Before Amma arrived at the hall, some people started moving towards the place where pāda pūjā, a traditional ceremony to welcome the guru, was being set up. I was standing a little further away.

All of a sudden, I heard Amma's voice inside me saying, "I will never leave you. I will always be with you." She said it once, but I heard the echo again and again and again. There was an indescribable, absorbing feeling within and when I looked around, everything happening outside of me was like a movie that I could choose to be part of or not. I just sat quietly by myself all night, trying to stay with that feeling. It lasted till the end of Dēvī Bhāva.

I knew then that the formless God I was praying to all this time was Amma herself — the mother of compassion. I felt many wounds of the past being healed. All I wanted to do now was to center my life around Amma. There is nothing Amma needs from us, but I felt so much gratitude that I wanted to try to sincerely follow her teachings.

From this point on, I would spend my time either touring with Amma and doing sēvā, or at my job teaching. In school, I tried to see every student as someone sent by Amma, so that I could help them in the best way possible. On the weekends, I gave the students free extra tuition, and also brought them peanut butter and jelly sandwiches and milk for lunch. They still remember that help and the sandwiches.

I also was able to see the sixteen years that I spent taking care of my father as a sēvā given to me by Amma. I was the only one taking care of him except when I was at school and a caregiver would come. My father was in so much pain that he needed to sit up and change his position almost every hour at night. Since to me it was a sēvā given by Amma, she gave me all the strength and energy I needed to stay up at night, as well as to get up early to cook lunch and get him ready before I went to school. Without Amma's energy, there was no way I could have done that for several years.

The last year of his life was during the Covid lockdown. Towards the end of the year, he got Covid and passed away. No one could come into the house for those ten days. It was heartbreaking and overwhelming to be alone. Without Amma's great support system, I would have had a complete mental breakdown. The daily webcast gave me an ongoing connection to Amma, and the daily meditation with her helped calm my mind. Swami Dayamritananda Puri offered me solace by speaking with me on the phone, and many days that was my only support. I was so grateful for Amma's support system and it was only because of her that I had the strength to handle my father's illness and death all on my own.

***

Because of Amma, my life has completely changed from the inside, even though the external circumstances may have remained the same. Amma always reminds us that what we have to change is our attitude towards the external situation, not the situation itself.

It was Amma's grace that I always got time off for each tour as I held a full-time teaching job. One year, I just could not find a way to get leave for the Australia tour. I bought the plane ticket, but I needed a doctor's note to satisfy the teaching contract and be given time off. As the time to leave for Australia came closer, I felt more and more sad thinking I might not be able to go. The day before I was supposed to leave, the sadness and the stress of trying to find a way to go was all too much, and I passed out in class. I was put into a small electric cart and taken to the school nurse. She made me lie down, but every time I sat up I felt dizzy. This incident convinced the school that I needed time off to recover, and through this, Amma opened the doors for me to go see her in Australia. Amma had heard me! The very next day, by Amma's grace, I was perfectly okay. All signs of the sudden illness disappeared, and I left for Australia for ten wonderful days with Amma.

This reminds me of another beautiful incident that happened during an Australia tour. I had just arrived at the door of the program venue as Amma was entering the hall. To my surprise, she turned to me and said, "I wasn't given my sandals." One of my sisters, who actually had the sēvā of offering Amma her sandals, was quite upset that Amma had asked me instead of her. I was very puzzled, and had to stop and think about why Amma had said that to me. Then, I remembered rearranging my altar at home before leaving for Australia. Amma's pādukās, or sandals, were still in a drawer. Because I left in a hurry, I had not set them up on the altar. I had not given Amma her shoes! Another beautiful example of Amma's omniscience and how she is always with us!

***

Reflecting on the tough period I passed through before meeting Amma, I finally realized that all the difficulties I had undergone were actually a blessing to make me ready to meet Amma. Instead of blaming my bad karma, or blaming God, I saw it was a gift. No matter what challenging situations are thrown at us in life, no matter what changes we face, we have to constantly remember that the only unchanging thing we have in this universe is Amma's love. All we need to do is to hold on to her divine feet — and everything will be alright!

I want to conclude by sharing a very beautiful answer Amma gave me when I got the golden opportunity to ask her a question on the last U.S. Tour. As we all know so well, when Amma sings, she transports us to a divine world — a world of blissful, poignant yearning for God. A place where we long to merge into her and our hearts are dancing in bliss. I asked her how we could go to that world ourselves when Amma was not physically with us.

When I thought of asking Amma this question, I imagined that she would say that you have to be a very good musician or that you have to sing with deep feeling or that you have to imagine your beloved deity in front of you. I was ready to do anything she said to enter that world.

The answer Amma gave me was totally unexpected. She said, "You have to see everyone as yourself." Then, she went on to describe, very beautifully, how she used to talk to nature. She told beautiful stories of how she used to talk to the waves and to the leaves. Her description was so inspiring — as she spoke of the divine world that she always beholds. Finally, she said, "Just let go."

Simple, but as with all of Amma's answers — so profound — encompassing the essence of the Vēdāntic truth of oneness! I pray that Amma blesses us all to achieve this blissful state, and takes us to her divine world.

15

Amma's Love — Lessons on Pain & Surrender

Uday Allendes - Chile

I am a Chilean devotee, and I met Amma for the first time in Milano, Italy, in 2018. After three wonderful days with Amma, I was left with so many questions. I could not understand how someone could sit in lotus posture, embracing people nonstop without any rest and without having food, simultaneously beaming with a radiant smile, skillfully correcting the musicians, making jokes, offering advice, and giving instructions — all the while hugging thousands of people each day!

It was the living image of the Goddess Durgā with eight arms doing eight different things simultaneously. I thought, "How does she do it? How does she have so much energy? Why has she been doing this for so many years without stopping?"

In the modern world, where there is a lack of values and spiritual tradition, many of us grow up seeing successful leaders who only amass wealth and power. On the other hand, here was a woman from India giving her entire life to serving others, without preferring or excluding anyone. To my mind, it was not logical at all.

After three days, I returned to Stockholm, Sweden, where I was living. I had received my mantra, and I was constantly repeating it. One day, I received a call from immigration saying that my work visa had been denied, and I was staying illegally in the country. I had two weeks to leave, otherwise I would be deported. I felt frozen and perplexed. Without any money for traveling or a plan, in the middle of the confusion, the image of Dēvī Bhāva appeared in my mind. It was like a light illuminating the darkness, but I found it even more confusing. Why is Amma appearing in my head? I kept trying to see what kind of options I had, and her image appeared in my mind again. At that moment, I asked myself if I should go to India? I immediately felt a deep internal peace. It was like the light had cleared all doubt. I felt like a child waiting to start a new adventure. I bought a one-way ticket, sold everything that I had, and came to India.

After arriving in Amritapuri, I joined the North India tour. In that month, love and devotion for Amma flooded me. Right at the end of the tour, I turned thirty years old, and I received the most precious darśhan — the experience of God. It was like when your mother is preparing a cake and gives you just a little taste — you haven't eaten the cake yet, but you know it's delicious. That day, Amma gave me a taste of how to realize the self. All my searching ended. I'm not thirsty anymore because I know where to find the water that quenches my thirst.

I had planned to spend only four months in the āśhram, but I stayed until the last day of my visa. Everyone in the āśhram told me, "Don't worry, Mother will arrange everything for you. Just do your sādhanā." So, with the last couple of bucks that I had left, I bought the cheapest ticket I could find to Australia to look for work. Not knowing where I would go, no contacts, no plan — I just trusted in the process. A devotee who just came back from the Australian tour told me that she had met a Chilean woman who had been in the āśhram and gave me her contact. I wrote to her asking if she could host me for a couple of days while I looked for a job. She replied the day of my flight, "Yes, I can host you for a few days." When I stepped into her home, I saw a large picture of Amma smiling as if to say, "Mother takes care of everything."

***

Rewind to the week before I left the āśhram for Australia. I visited an astrologer and he mentioned that at the end of 2020, I would suffer a severe accident and a strong blow to my leg that would not allow me to walk for an extended period of time.

On November 3, 2020, I was heading home on my motorcycle when a car in the opposite direction didn't respect the stop sign and hit me on my right side. All my bones rattled — I let go of the handlebar, and called out, "Amma!"

I don't remember how many meters I flew through the air or how far I was dragged along the asphalt. I couldn't move my leg, which was practically separated from my body. The shock was uncontrollable. I screamed and cried at the same time — my body trembling intensely.

I remember the voice of the first person who assisted me, it was a lady. She held my hand the whole time and the only thing she said was, "Everything will be alright." I was screaming so loud and I felt so scared thinking, "What am I going to do? No savings, no proper insurance and no relatives in a new country." This lady kept saying, "Don't worry, everything will be well." I didn't know her name or even see her face, but she just kept holding my hand, and kept me conscious until the end. Finally, the ambulance arrived and they had to get me onto the stretcher. When they moved my leg, I screamed so loud that I passed out.

Suddenly, I remember seeing my body writhing in pain on the ground. I was above everyone, about seven meters high, looking down at the whole picture. I saw the woman who hit me screaming and crying on the other side of the street and all the people around me. When I saw my body, my first thought was, "Why does that body suffer?" There was no emotion in me, and no sense of being identified with the body. I saw everything from the level of consciousness — the ātman.

Suddenly, I felt a warm and pleasant sensation, like on a cold morning when a beam of sunlight touches your skin. So I turned my attention to where this sensation was coming from. Several meters above me was a huge sphere of white light — a portal that was magnetically attracting me. When I was about to enter, I looked back at my body for the last time and understood that this was the end of my life. Without any complaint or emotion, I passed through the portal and was flowing through a tunnel with flashes of white light almost like electricity.

I saw the light at the end of the tunnel. When I came out of it, I was completely immersed in the middle of the universe — contemplating the vast darkness, infinite silence and the starry sky in all directions. What a gift! I cannot express the beauty of this experience. To see the universe and feel, at the same time, that I am the universe. To experience that I am at each point where I direct my attention. Like an ocean that vibrates and expands, the waves of sensations moved in all directions, in absolute bliss and pure consciousness. Slowly, I began to move without my will, faster and faster as if I had become a beam of sunlight that crosses the universe, galaxies, and planets.

I passed through another sphere of white light, and witnessed how I entered a human body as a baby. I saw the development of a human being from birth to death at the speed of light — witnessing all the activities and relationships through that person's eyes. I saw all of it as the impressions of a thousand previous lives. It was a profoundly beautiful experience. On the other hand, I understood the experiences of previous lives as only desires and suffering. After six hours of so-called 'unconsciousness,' I woke up in the emergency room completely drugged and with no idea what had happened.

***

One of the greatest fears of humanity is death, and one of the greatest mysteries is what happens after death. Sanātana Dharma teaches us about the cycle of saṁsāra. Saṁsāra is viewed as mere ignorance of the true nature of being. There is no difference between the soul and the divine. Due to avidyā, ignorance, the soul believes in the reality of the temporal and phenomenal world, which leads to the confusion and belief that the body is the self. That state of illusion is known as māyā.

Even though many spiritual seekers have studied this, the fear of death is still present in their minds. I believe that the greatest gift I have received has been to verify that there is life after life, and when we reach the end of this cycle, there will only be the pure consciousness of bliss.

I spent six months at the hospital and underwent ten surgeries. The day after my accident, a friend took one of Amma's photos from my altar and brought it to the hospital. I remember a social worker came and when she saw Amma's photo, she said, "I received a darśhan from the Divine Mother more than twenty years ago. Don't worry, I will do all the paperwork for you, everything is gonna be alright." Every time someone from the hospital saw Amma's picture, they took care of me with more attention. Countless times, hospital staff asked me, "Are you a follower of the Divine Mother? Are you Amma's devotee? The hugging saint is with you!" If they asked, "Who is that beautiful lady?" I replied, "That is my mother!"

So often, people without faith or a solid spiritual foundation believe that they are alone in this world. In my case, I was in a new country without family or old friends and in the hospital.

Yet, so many nurses and Amma's devotees became like compassionate mothers to me. They brought me my favorite fruits, and on one occasion, a nurse even attempted to prepare Chilean food. Another lady gave me clothes, and constantly asked me how I was doing or if I needed something. I received so much love from people who didn't know me. I saw how, in each one of them, it was Amma who was taking care of me. It was as if Amma was telling me, "Don't worry, Amma will take care of you."

In my second week in the hospital, the doctors stopped giving me intravenous morphine and started with pain pills. That's where my ordeal began. On the pain scale from one to ten, where one represents the lowest pain you have ever experienced and ten is when the pain is killing you — my pain was a nine.

We have all experienced pain in our lives. Amma always talks to us about the pain and suffering in the world, as she feels compassion for those who suffer. Pain, in broad strokes, is a subjective and completely valid experience, and very difficult to understand, even for modern science. When physical pain increases, there is a point where you begin to complain more and more. The moaning becomes louder, you begin to gasp, you start moving as if trying to escape the pain. When it continues to increase you inhale and hold back the pain like someone preparing to receive a blow. Little by little, the pain exhausts you.

As terrible as it is, our ego, with its different personalities, always tries to maintain control and possess our body. Still, constant pain possesses everything so that even the ego becomes exhausted. It is a fact that nobody wants to suffer or feel pain. We are afraid of it, and we do not know what to do with it. We want it to disappear as soon as possible. We want to escape our problems, and we don't want to look inside because it is too painful. Pain can lead to anxiety, insomnia, fatigue, or depression. All of this can be triggered by our minds. These are all common symptoms in today's society where people live with so much stress.

Once, the pain was so intense that I started to shout Amma's name. Then, I heard her voice inside me, "Yogic breathing." My first reaction was, "What? Yogic breathing!" Inhale deeply, hold the air, exhale everything, hold, inhale and repeat the cycle. Little by little, I entered an altered state. The pain was there, but it was less painful. My body was slowly calming down and feeling more relaxed. I didn't understand what was happening, but I felt as if I could witness the pain.

Another day, after so much pain, I was utterly exhausted and almost without strength. Suddenly, I felt a small hand on my shoulder, and I felt a gentle weight and pressure. For a moment, I thought it was one of the nurses, but then I felt a divine joy flooding every cell of my body and taking away my pain, making me feel as light as a feather. My divine guru was next to me, holding me in my pain. It was a mesmerizing experience that left me in tears.

Days later, I again didn't know what to do with the pain, and again I heard Amma's voice inside saying, "Mantra japa." I began to repeat my mantra. Little by little, the pain was less and less painful.

***

Amma's group in Byron Bay helped me in different ways. They also had some pūjās done for me in Amritapuri. After a few weeks, I got a letter from Amritapuri with vibhūti (sacred ash), kumkum, and Amma's picture. I was so happy that I applied the vibhūti on my forehead, on my wounds, and drank some with water.

A couple of days before that, I had started watching a TV show to distract myself from the pain. It was an old American TV show called the *X-files*, filmed in the early '90s, about an FBI couple solving paranormal cases. That day, I was watching the series, drinking water with vibhūti, when the FBI couple found a powder. One of the detectives visited an expert in paranormal affairs. They focused on him in the foreground, and speaking to the camera, he said, "This powder is called vibhūti. It is sacred ash from India with medicinal and mystical powers." At that moment, my skin got goosebumps. I began to laugh so loud. Outside of India, vibhūti is something completely unknown. I couldn't believe it! How Amma plays with the world's illusion — a TV program filmed in the year 1992 in the U.S. and broadcast in Australia on the very same day I received the vibhūti. In my mind, Amma was smiling and laughing, and so was I. That day, I felt like a simple puppet in her hands.

A few months later, I was traveling three times a week to the hospital for rehabilitation. One day, I was in the taxi trying to focus on my mantra, but still, my overwhelmed mind diverted my attention to thinking about my pain. All of a sudden, my attention was drawn to the radio program. Someone was talking about how chronic pain can affect one's general state of health. Just then, the person said, "Well, there are people in the world like the Divine Mother, Amma, the hugging saint from India who travels the world hugging people. With each hug, she shares her state of being with people undergoing afflictions of all kinds. People find healing and relief after their experience with her. It's incredible! She can take the world's pain and transform it." Amma! What are the chances that the driver will tune into the radio at that moment? It was Amma telling me again, "I am with you, can't you see?"

I was fortunate to have a highly skilled orthopedic surgeon that was able to save my leg from amputation. I took antibiotics for a year due to an infection in my bones. I went through painkillers that affected my memory and mental awareness. I suffered the side effects of post-traumatic stress. After I stopped taking strong painkillers, I experienced withdrawal effects like suicidal thoughts and horrible depression for a couple of weeks. Those weeks helped me understand the deep suffering that people with depression and suicidal thoughts experience. The understanding of others' suffering can open the doors of compassion at different levels.

The hospital staff constantly told me that they were surprised by my strong mental integrity. They told me that anyone in my position would be depressed. I was in a new country without family or relatives or a network of support. I remember that sometimes the nurses would carefully open the door of my room and observe me. They saw me looking at the ceiling and were worried about my mental health. They didn't know that I had my mālā in my hand and I was chanting my mantra. No one saw that Amma was taking care of everything — my pain and my problems. My refuge then and now, is the place where my mind dwells ever in God.

***

I cannot attribute a single gram of progress and rehabilitation to myself. I realized how fragile, weak, and vulnerable I am, and there is nothing bad about it. The idea of pretending to be strong and capable is exhausting. I surrendered to the ocean that is Amma and accepted to sail in the direction that she decided. Accepting the situations we are experiencing, however painful they may be, accepting that we do not have control, and surrendering, allows us to kneel and touch the feet of the guru. Everything becomes lighter and lighter. Little by little, with acceptance, the complaints cease.

How wonderful it is to complain less and less. The number of complaints that are spinning around in our minds is incredible and we suffer as a result. Complaining makes everything worse. By the grace of Amma, I could understand that even though I cannot control situations, I can decide not to complain. Every day, I choose to try not to complain, to embrace whatever happens and do what I have to do.

My rehabilitation process has been slow — at a snail's speed — but constant. I no longer have the same energy that I used to have. I no longer move at the pace I was used to. It's a constant reminder that nothing is permanent and that eventually, my other leg and the rest of my body will be less able to do things as well. I accept it and embrace it as a gift, and concentrate on living in the present moment. I don't know if my pain or energy will allow me to do something tomorrow, so I focus on what I have to do today. Embracing the pain also gives me more perspective on life.

We do not know how heavy and complex the pain is that people carry daily. We do not know how many people struggle every day to find a reason to live and not commit suicide. We do not know how many people live with chronic pain. Understanding the pain has been a blessing for me. It was like learning a new language. I don't need explanations if someone doesn't want to talk or isn't in a good mood. I know how it feels and I wish the best for them. This is what amazes me the most about Amma. The infinite love and compassion that lives in her and how she has embraced the pain of millions of people without distinction and without the slightest complaint.

The pain I have experienced has made me a more sensitive and silent person. This is something positive for a spiritual seeker on the path. I pray, "Oh, Beloved Amma, allow me to dwell in your silence." Every time I do my sādhanā, the joy and inner ecstasy are indescribable. This is not my merit, these are the gifts and teachings of the Mother. I have often asked Amma, "Why did you share these states of divine joy with me?" and the answer always is, "If you close your eyes, surrender, and leave your mind aside, everything is within the reach of your hand."

***

I remember a surgery I had on my spine. Just before going into surgery, my biological mother, who is not a spiritual person, or so I thought, sent me a bhajan about the Divine Mother. I started to cry with happiness. It reminded me — everything is gonna be alright by the guru's grace.

This whole experience with my accident has been a constant reminder to surrender to the silence of God. To trust in that silence despite all the things in the world and all the illusions of māyā. This whole idea that "I'm the one who does things and fights and pursues desires in the world," afflicts us. What an exhausting and tiring feeling. The pain we experience is a constant reminder to be present and give everything to God.

One time, I was practicing bhajans, and my pain was very high. I tried to surrender and let it flow. At one point, I began to experience a divine ecstasy that dissolved the idea of my body and the sense of 'I.' Only a fullness dwelled in me, simply from inhaling and singing the names of God. I could observe how, even while being in pain, a river of divine joy could flow in me. I felt how devotion can indeed alleviate pain and suffering. After that practice, I got into my car, and suddenly I felt someone in the back seat put their hand on my shoulder. A small, gentle and soft hand, but with the weight of the universe. I started to cry with happiness.

***

I have reflected on whether suffering is optional or not. Some people are really helpless and I cannot tell them they suffer because they want to — that would be a lack of compassion. However, from my own experience of sādhanā and my connection with Amma, I realize that it is an option to try not to complain and to do what I must do. I am sure that the study and practice of Amma's spiritual teachings can help us face any difficulty.

The day I arrived back at the āśhram, I saw Amma walking to her room after the program. I was so happy to see her physical presence! That same day, I was talking to my dear Chilean friends, and they asked me if I felt any difference seeing Amma after three years. Obviously, seeing the physical presence of my guru is indescribable. Her beauty is on another level. However, internally, I felt no difference. I feel that wherever I go and whatever I do, Amma's inner presence is always with me.

Amma has repeatedly said to not become too attached or dependent only on her physical form, but to also develop a strong inner connection. Our connection with the guru, our sādhanā, and her teachings, will keep us united with Amma wherever we go.

Thank you, Divine Mother, for everything!

16

Guru Vākyam

Meera Venkatesh – India

I grew up in a very religious family in Kerala. I lost my father at the age of seven, whereupon we moved to Kottayam to stay with our maternal grandparents. Although I did not know what devotion really meant, I was always surrounded by bhajans, cultural dances, and a prayerful atmosphere. We would visit Kṛiṣhṇa, Ŝhiva and Bhagavatī temples regularly. I used to spend all my free time drawing kōlams (floor designs, also known as raṅgōlī) and decorating the various deities in the pūjā room. These activities helped to develop a deep love and adoration for God. Growing up, my iṣhṭa dēvatā, personal deity, was Kṛiṣhṇa, but it gradually changed to Bhagavatī, the Goddess, after my marriage.

My husband, Venkatesh, whom Amma very lovingly calls Narayanan, and I moved to Seattle in 1988 with our sons Kartik and Nitish. In 1994, we had a chance meeting with Dr. Bipin and Dr. Geetha, and through them we came to know about Amma. However, having grown up in families focused on temple worship, the concepts of spirituality and having a guru were alien to us. It wasn't until two years later that we finally attended our first satsang gathering at their house. Subsequently, we attended a local retreat with Swami Dayamritananda Puri. During his satsang, he shared how Amma compassionately healed Dattan the leper. Just listening to that story, I was overwhelmed with emotion and I broke down. I did not hear anything else. I was simply consumed by the feeling that Amma was none other than the Bhagavatī whom I had been worshiping all these years.

Finally, the blessed moment came for us to meet Amma for the very first time. We reached the Fort Flagler retreat site just as Amma was arriving. The instant Amma stepped out of the car, she turned towards us and lovingly extended both her arms. We quickly joined the devotees gathered in front of the house prepared for Amma. Amma went around the circle, gently touching everyone's head. When Amma touched me, all thoughts ceased to exist, and my mind became still.

A funny incident ensued. In his ignorance, Narayanan thought that Swami Amritaswarupananda Puri was Amma's guru and gazed at him with adoration. However, when Amma came near Narayanan and tapped his head a few times, he quickly realized that it was indeed Amma who was the guru.

As Amma went inside the house, I just broke down and sobbed deeply for the next couple of hours. Soon after this, we were blessed with the opportunity to perform pāda pūjā and garland Amma, and later were both simply mesmerized by her soulful bhajans.

During our very first darśhan, Narayanan asked Amma about having an āśhram and Brahmasthānam temple in Seattle. Amma laughed heartily at his innocent request. Later, one of the senior swāmīs explained to us that Amma does not need an āśhram or Brahmasthānam temple, they exist solely for the benefit of the devotees and the world.

Although I was physically meeting Amma for the first time, I felt in my heart that she was my long-lost friend. With remarkable ease, I even asked Amma when she would visit *her* house. In my mind, I already considered my home to be Amma's home. Amma agreed to our request.

After returning home, I started preparing for Amma's arrival by cleaning the house, preparing the altar and making prasād and other delicacies. Expecting Amma around 3:30 a.m., and thinking we had some time left, I decided to take a shower when I suddenly heard a scream from Narayanan announcing Amma's arrival! In a dazed state, I somehow managed to wrap my sari and rushed down to the sound of Amma knocking on the door. I froze and did not even have the presence of mind to open the door. My entire being was in another world and I found myself unable to function. Swami Dayamritananda Puri had to dash in through the garage and opened the door for Amma. As Amma walked in she remarked that I should not keep the guru waiting.

Amma asked me to take her to the pūjā room and performed the pūjā. In-between, Amma asked for the children. Totally forgetting about my two sons, I mentioned, "Narayanan and I are here." Fortunately, a devotee friend had the presence of mind to wake up our children and bring them to Amma.

During the pūjā, I began to feel very dizzy and nauseous, so I slowly inched my way to the back of the room and leaned against the wall to avoid a fall. After the pūjā, Amma proceeded downstairs and started to narrate to everyone the story of Vidura and his wife.

Vidura had been longing for Bhagavān Kṛiṣhṇa to visit his house. Bhagavān agreed but decided to arrive unexpectedly. Vidura was absent and his wife had just gone to bathe so that she could welcome Bhagavān in fresh attire. When she heard Bhagavān arriving, forgetting everything, she lost all awareness of her body and came rushing to welcome the Lord. Overwhelmed with love, she peeled a banana, but fed Bhagavān the peel, discarding the fruit. When Vidura walked in, he was horrified to see this and reprimanded his wife, bringing her back to her senses. She rushed back to put on her attire and returned to properly welcome Bhagavān. However, this time, when she tried to offer the fruit, Bhagavān refused, as he was already full from the peels she had fed him in her state of total love and absorption.

Amma looked at me with a smile and told everyone that I was like Vidura's wife. She then lovingly called me to come close to her. As I sat beside her, Amma kept her hands firmly on my shoulders, mentioning to Swāmījī that something had overcome me during the pūjā, and that I was not feeling well. As Amma spoke, I felt something leaving my body and a surge of energy passed through me. Within moments, I felt renewed and well again. Amma looked at me and said I was free now and I could perform the pāda pūjā.

Though I had prepared only a small quantity of prasād, Amma miraculously fed all her children who had shown up unexpectedly. She even remarked that the container of prasād was an akṣhayapātram — an inexhaustible ever-giving pot.

***

In the year 1999, I was going through a difficult period, and it was during this trying time that I was immensely blessed with the opportunity to stay in Amritapuri for an entire year. Amma showered her grace on me and kept me by her side throughout this challenging time. She granted me the unique opportunity to spend time with her parents Damayanti Amma and Sugunacchan, as well as her brothers and sisters, and several longtime devotees, including Dattan. These were precious moments of my life that remain very dear to my soul. In addition to all this, I was able to accompany Amma on all her tours that year, despite struggling with severe back pain.

I was bathing in Amma's love and did not realize that the life lessons that I needed to learn were coming soon. Amma says, "In life, it is very important to learn to control our anger.

Anger is like a double-edged sword: along with the victim, it also injures the perpetrator."

Towards the end of the Europe Tour that year, Amma spoke sternly with me for a reason I did not understand. I was shocked and felt very sad. I could not use proper discernment and I let my emotions turn into anger towards Amma. My feelings continued to oscillate between grief, confusion and self-pity.

The following year, Amma came to Seattle and continued to bless us by visiting our house, yet I continued to hold on to my anger and resentment. On Amma's direction, Narayanan booked tickets for me to follow all the tours. However, I followed Amma half-heartedly for the next couple of years, as I continued to struggle with my feelings.

During one of the programs, Amma mentioned to me that there is no point in being angry towards her. I contemplated her words deeply and at last turned to the one thing I knew could help me overcome difficulties. It was prayer — the lifeline I had forgotten during this challenging ordeal. I started fervently and desperately praying to Amma to help me get rid of my negativities. By Amma's grace alone, I could feel all the anger melt away, and in about two months, it was completely gone.

I felt heartbroken to realize that, instead of counting all the special blessings Amma had showered on me, I had allowed anger to consume and overpower me. When I shared this with one of the senior swāmīs, he suggested that Amma might have created the situation to redirect all my negativities towards her. He went on to explain that Amma would not be affected by my anger, she could easily take it, and thus prevent my latent anger from being directed towards the world. In this way, Amma was compassionately saving me from creating more prārabdha karma for myself.

Ever since then, I have noticed that in confrontational situations with people, Amma somehow redirects my anger towards her, thus avoiding fallouts and ill feelings towards others. By Amma's grace, that anger quickly melts away. This shows me the depth of Amma's compassion, a mother and guru who exists only for the good of her children.

Over the years, Amma became the single most important thing in our lives. Hosting and attending satsangs and being part of the Amma devotee community was how we spent most of our time. Setting up Amma's altar rekindled my childhood love of decorating deities. I developed a habit of writing down the list of bhajans Amma sang in each of her world tour programs that I attended. This became a very precious collection of mine and I continue to add to it. Music has always been a special part of my life and Amma's bhajans have brought untold solace to me. Amma has told me that music is my life and has always encouraged me to sing.

Amma says, "Bhajan is a spiritual discipline aimed at concentrating the mind on one's beloved deity. Bhajan, concentration, meditation... This is the progression. Constant remembrance of God is meditation. Through that one-pointedness, one can merge in the divine and experience the bliss of one's true self."

In my experience, when we tune our minds to the lyrics during bhajans, it becomes a dialogue between Amma and us. In that instant, the bhajan session becomes a true prayer — a meditation.

Both of my sons started playing the tabla with no formal training. While I have always had an ear for music and could sing bhajans, I had no experience with musical instruments. However, there came a time when we had no harmonium players in our satsang. That year when Amma came, I mentally prayed to her that I should be able to play at least a few notes on the harmonium while I was singing. In only a month I was able to do so, and soon I was playing for the whole satsang group. While far from perfect, with Amma's grace I could play the harmonium to accompany any bhajan, as long as I remained focused on her alone.

***

Many of us, at some point in our lives, wish to win a lottery. Little do we realize that in Amma, we have already won the jackpot of all jackpots. Each member of my family has established their own special connection with Amma. Both of my sons were married in Amma's divine presence and live their lives built on a foundation of Amma's love and compassion. I am so grateful to Amma for giving me a family that has supported me in my spiritual journey with her.

I have been diagnosed with fibromyalgia for many years now, a medical condition characterized by chronic widespread pain, fatigue, sleep problems, depression, and anxiety. However, our beloved Amma and the opportunity to be with her during her world tours have given me a lifeline that I will be forever grateful for. It is only Amma's grace that has made it possible for me to travel all around the world with her. This, in itself, is a miracle. Health scares keep coming and going, but with Amma by my side, I feel safe and protected.

Amma says, "Through devotion, we are not searching for some God who is a limited individual sitting up in the clouds on a golden throne. God is the pure consciousness that dwells within everything. Through prayers, the perception that everything is God is developed. Through this, the limited self, 'I,' is lost, and the devotee becomes one with God. The life of the devotee itself becomes a prayer."

When I turned sixty, Amma asked me to come to Amritapuri to study pūjās and hōmas[22]. I had several doubts about my ability to do this. So, I re-confirmed with Amma twice. Amma said, "It's time for you to turn towards God. To call on God, keep ringing the puja bell, and God will come." At that moment, I decided to act upon it. Clearly, our guru knows more about us than we do about ourselves.

Amma asked the brahmachāriṇī who serves as the main pūjāriṇī in the Kālī Temple to train me. The going was tough and multiple times I told Amma that it was impossible for me to continue. Yet, Amma kept reassuring me, and asked me to practice for half an hour every day. She even had all the pūjā items sent to me from the Kālī Temple.

Three weeks into it, I was asked to perform a Gaṇapati hōma in the Kālī Temple – the holy grounds graciously blessed by Amma. My instinct was to fly back to Seattle immediately, but I knew that was not right. Though extremely nervous, on Ōṇam day, by Amma's grace alone, I was able to perform my first Gaṇapati hōma, followed by Bhagavatī Sēvā pūjā on Navarātri.

Both times, I could go for darśhan right after and Amma partook in the prasād. For me, this is simply another Amma miracle. I, who cannot comfortably sit on the floor for more than a few minutes at a time, was able to sit through the entire duration of the pūjās and hōmas. How does this happen? Where does this energy come from? Through these rituals, I was able to experience Amma's greatness. I can feel Amma's presence each time I prepare for them. I know and feel that it's not me, but Amma who is performing all the rituals. Amma gave me the best sixtieth-birthday gift I could ever imagine, and she keeps giving, giving, and giving.

---

[22] Pūjās are ritualistic worship ceremonies and hōmas are a type of pūjā involving a sacrificial fire into which sacred items are offered.

In 2018, a property was purchased in Seattle to be established as Amma's āśhram. Amma asked Narayanan and me to move there. Amma's words were, "All these years, your home was my āśhram. Now, my āśhram is your home."

People sometimes ask me what lessons I have learned from having Amma in my life, and I have often reflected on this. Every moment with Amma is an experience — a profound lesson. Over the years, I have learned to have more discrimination and to practice at least some detachment from relationships and physical and material comforts. I have learned that faith and surrender are the keys to overcoming difficult situations. It is not that easy, but as I mature, I see that many a time, it is the only way forward.

However, the most important lesson for me is guru vākyam — the guru's words. It is about cultivating the ability to listen to what my guru says to me, to show full obedience in following her words, and to accept that come what may, my guru will never forsake me.

We may have failed in this lesson several times before; we might fail again in times to come; but with Amma's grace, may we never cease to keep trying to fulfill guru vākyam.

17

The Two Moon Eclipses

Devanath - France

A long time ago, I told Amma, "Whichever path you want me to follow, whether as a renunciate or as a householder, tell me, and I will do it." Years later, Amma asked me, "What about brahmacharya? Will you become one?" I replied, "Amma, I am still waiting for your answer!" Amma said, "Amma will never choose for you. You have to decide for yourself." A part of me was waiting for Amma to decide for me and save the day. I answered, "Well Amma, then I don't feel mature enough to become a monk."

So, I decided to find a girlfriend, and I did. I came to Amma in New York, and when she saw me she said, "Do you know why Amma didn't look at you during darśhan? It is for you to feel 'Oooooow.'" Amma was referring to the fact that I was focused on her before, but now that I had a girlfriend, my thoughts were scattered.

The first relationship did not work. Later on, Amma asked,"You found another one?" "Yes Amma!" I replied. "Where?" Amma asked. "In your āśhram," I told her. Amma joked, "In the āśhram? Is it like a supermarket now?" I said, "Amma! Where do you want me to find a devotee? In the āśhram!" and we laughed together. This second relationship didn't work out either.

Amma kept joking about how depressed I was because of my relationship failures. I once said, "Amma, I am like Edison who invented the light bulb after 2,000 attempts. I tried two times and still have 1,998 attempts left!" Amma quickly answered with a mischievous look, "No, my son, Edison made his efforts for the benefit of humanity. That is not what you are doing!" Later on, she said to me, "The next one you find, you will marry her." As Amma's words are full of infinity, what seemed impossible became possible.

Once, in Amritapuri, Amma was giving satsang and I was taking notes. Suddenly, she started talking about a devotee and his girlfriends and how depressed he was. "Oh no, I think I know him," I thought to myself. I was embarrassed and wanted to become invisible! Later, when I came on stage, Amma turned and pointed her finger at me saying, "It was him! I was talking about him!" Amma continued to occasionally use these stories about me in her satsangs for some time.

Through these experiences, I was shaped to meet my wife Ahalya. Amma once said, "Without her, you have no muscles. You only grow with Kālī." Well, my wife is a mini-Kālī. I can't tell you how much I have matured by being with her. Amma knew that my level of maturity had room for improvement.

Once I was married, Amma asked me this question mischievously, "What is the thing you should never, ever forget in life?" I replied, "Uh, my mantra?" Amma replied, "Your wife's birthday!" We all laughed thoroughly.

One night, during a Europe Tour, Ahalya and I went to rest in the family sleeping area together. I began to moan and complain, "Look! These lights are so bright and people are snoring. Plus, it smells so bad here. It smells like feet!" Ahalya said, "I don't smell anything here." But after some time, she came closer to me and choked at the smell. "What is this?" She found the source of the smell was a stinking sock that fell down from my scarf to the floor. I have no idea how this sock ended up in my scarf. Later on, we told the story to Amma, and she told us it would be good material for a satsang — so here it is!

Amma says, "Only when we become aware of the burden of our own ego, will we be able to remove our faults. At present, we cannot bear someone else's ego or mistakes, but ours is alright. 'My ego is beautiful, but his is ugly.' This is our present attitude, and this attitude should go."

***

I was born in Paris. Since I was a child, there have been many tragedies in my family. My aunt died of cancer, and then my uncle drowned in the Arabian sea trying to save his own children. They were adopted from India and Columbia and became orphans for the second time. My parents are amazing souls. They took care of everything in a very righteous way, and do so even now, which is no easy task.

My sister and I grew up in an environment where the needs of others were always considered. The first words my mother said when she heard about her brother's death were, "What will become of the children?" With compassion, she put her grief aside, as did my father.

Amma says, "The spiritual path begins and ends with compassion."

As a child, I felt people didn't get proper answers to what happens after death. However, I knew that somewhere, someone understood the mysteries of life and death, and could take care of souls after their departure. I thought, "I will meet such a being and he will take care of me and all of my family, during life and after death too!"

Until I met Amma at twenty-six years old, I spent my life feeling as if I were in exile. I had spiritual aspirations without being able to name them and didn't feel understood. I felt really lonely. Fortunately, I could express my spirituality and my quest through music.

I clearly remember the inspiration that flowed through me when I composed my first poem at the age of seven.

> *When the Two Moon Eclipses rise, the God of Art will come.*
> *The Pollen of the Nine Rare Flowers will bring the Harp of Joy back to life.*

My mother put the poem on the kitchen wall at the exact same place where Amma's picture would hang many years later. This poem has followed me throughout my life, and its inner meaning has manifested in so many ways, especially since I met Amma.

When I was young, I used to pray to the moon. At the age of twenty, I first went through an experience of intense bliss and then one of severe pain. Two exceptional moments that eclipsed everything else in my life. In ancient times, when an eclipse would occur, people were afraid that the moon would never come back, and that the world would never be the same.

For me, these experiences were the *Two Moon Eclipses*. From this darkness, rose *the God of Art*. This God is Amma, whom I would meet later on. She is the one who has taught me the art of living the symphony of life.

The *Nine Rare Flowers* are the nine different forms of bhakti, devotion to God,[23] and *the Pollen* is the fragrance of that bhakti. We are each God's instruments. She tunes and plays *the Harp of Joy* for us to return to our forgotten nature. God wants us to play the wonderful music of eternal joy.

Once, I gave this poem to Amma, translated into Malayalam by kind devotees. They said, "Look, isn't it beautiful Amma?" Amma's answer was, "It is much better in French." I was deeply touched. This is the power of Amma's words. They can heal decades of exile in an instant.

---

[23] Expounded by Sage Nārada in the *Nārada Bhakti Sūtras*.

***

As a musician, I used to practice piano intensively. Sometimes, the sun would shine on a certain chord, or birds would come to me singing. I was playing music, and creation was playing with me! At other times, it felt as if I could touch eternity for a moment. Two seconds of this feeling were worth years of practice. I would play on and on in search of this feeling, through practice, concerts, and compositions. There was a mystery of life for me to decipher.

Amma says, “There is harmony behind every object and every place, no matter how insignificant it may look.”

When I was twenty someone said to me, “You know there are two moon eclipses tonight, right?” Obviously, this is impossible. However, as of this specific day, I started having life-changing experiences. I felt like a glass cup and an ocean wanted to enter into me. I could feel people as myself and I could sometimes see everything saturated with divine energy. I experienced that the logic we see in the world is not the real logic.

I was so happy, as I had been longing to see this reality for many years. I was amazed, and yet also scared at the same time. When I shared what I felt and saw, everyone thought I was crazy. I felt lonely in this experience. However, Amma’s hands were at work. It was Amma’s answer to a deep yearning, and she gave what was needed each step of the way.

Once, I felt a bridge in front of me as thin as a string. I had no other option but to cross it. On either side, there was an unfathomable abyss filled with pain. To cross it, I had to be devoid of everything, even of the sense of “*I*.” Only faith and humility could help me stand on the bridge. Later on, I understood, only a pure, humble instrument can withstand God’s powerful, divine music without breaking. Amma reminds us that in a great tornado, a mighty tree may fall, but the humble grass remains unshaken. In fact, I was not fit to receive this experience. What happens when you fly blissfully in the skies, but don't know how to land? You crash.

After a while, I experienced a mental breakdown, and it was the most painful experience of my life. For many months, I went through a dark night of the soul. I was experiencing an anxiety crisis that seemed to have no end. I felt like I was crushed into dust, and every part of my body and soul was being put together again, piece by piece, without anesthesia. Thanks to Amma's invisible hands, and the love and care of my family and friends, I could finally get through it. I would constantly chant a sentence from Pascal, a French philosopher, "More than the terrifying silence of infinite spaces, hear the silence of God." For me, this was a reminder that God is always with us, especially in the hardest moments.

Amma says, "We are like a musical instrument that is off-key. The guru wants to repair the keys that are off... In order to make the keys sound more pleasant, a little scratching, scrubbing, scraping, and removing is needed. You should be able to bear the pain caused by this, understanding its purpose is to make your life harmonious, as in a musical concert."

Amma once told me, "Now that you've reached Amma, you don't have to worry anymore." Even now, I feel it is Amma's profound blessing to have experienced such an extremely dark period and still be here. It is a never-ending source of lessons.

***

At twenty-six, I traveled to India. Unknowingly, it became a pilgrimage. I stopped at the tombs of great saints of all religions. The highlight was Ramana Maharshi's cave, Virupaksha. I stayed there for hours, feeling an amazing love filling each part of my being. Before coming to India, my mother told me about Amma, so I decided to go to Amritapuri.

When I arrived at the āśhram, I could hear Amma's bhajans. I was delighted to hear people singing with the same intention as me! That night, I had a dream. I was five years old with the old familiar sensation of exile which never left me. Suddenly I heard, "Happy birthday to you!" I opened the door. Amma was standing there holding a big illuminated cake and was surrounded by my family. Actually, in my life, every time I received birthday gifts, I was waiting for something very special that no one could give me. Subconsciously, I wanted to meet Amma. This dream was a gift in itself.

When I woke up, I could hear the sounds of the birds along with the chanting of the morning archana and the prayers emanating from the nearby temples. I felt at home and a deep joy rose inside of me. Later, I went to the Kālī Temple and listened to Amma's satsang. She was talking about music.

As Amma was leaving after the program, I thought, "If you really are omnipresent, then if I look at the wall, you will be in the wall too." As Amma passed by, I looked the other way. Someone said, "Hey look! Amma is looking at you!" I turned my head. Amma had stopped on her path and was staring at me! She then cast a glance at the wall with a beaming smile.

Later, Murali, a great musician and Amma's pianist, asked me, "Do you want to play music for Amma?" I didn't even know how he knew I was a musician. Sitting in the Kālī Temple, I closed my eyes and played with the thought, "If you are who you are, then you have heard my prayers all these years." Amma stopped the darśhan and looked at me, showing me a big thumbs up. Again, I got my answer.

The next day, I had four questions, including one asking for a mantra and one asking for a name! In the darśhan line, the assistant said, "No, four questions are impossible!" I thought, "Well, isn't she my mother?"

The first of my questions was, "Will you be my Master of music?" Amma answered, "Yes!" So, I finally found *the God of Art*! *The Harp of Joy*, the instrument she plays, which is me, eventually came back to life. My feeling of exile ended at that moment. I also received my spiritual name and my mantra that day.

On the train back, absorbed in writing poetry for Amma, I could smell her fragrance everywhere! Even after returning to France, my mother asked me, "What is this special smell around you?" Life changed radically and I tried to follow Amma everywhere I could.

***

Once, during a Dēvī Bhāva, Amma said, "You and I are the same! Crazy mother, crazy son." What an honor to have God utter these words, so full of meaning and mystery! Yes, we are the same, but only Amma knows it. The day I will get mōkṣha, in billions of years, Amma will still be far beyond my reach!

Each one of Amma's glances or words should be enough to hear the music of eternity, but I am one of those instruments that needs a lot of repair. My wood is soaked with the ignorance of her divine māyā.

During Amma's Europe Tour, one of my sēvās was to collect darśhan tokens during Dēvī Bhāva. Once, I was trying to help other sevites[24] close to me. They had two-hour shifts, standing very close to Amma and preparing the people to receive their darśhan. Sometimes they didn't know what to do so I would help them. They had to ask people questions like, "What is your language?" or "Did you come alone?" They also have to give instructions such as, "Place your hands on the pīṭham on

---

[24] A person who performs sēvā is referred to as a sevite.

each side," "You should come in front of your wife," "Let your children go first," etc. Often I would be first to interact with the devotees and then pass on their response to the sevites. This went on for eleven hours, and in the morning I prayed, "Amma I enjoyed this sēvā so much! Please put in a little more spice next time to see how I handle it!"

Well, we all know what happens when you ask the Divine Goddess these kinds of requests! The next day, it was Dēvī Bhāva in Paris and darśhan started very fast. I collected the tokens as fast as possible, but now the darśhan assistants were used to receiving my help as on the previous day. At this speed, I was overwhelmed with the amount of questions that came to me from all sides. I tried to answer, but I lost count of the tokens. At that moment Amma's assistant looked at me severely with a token in her hand. Someone had handed it directly to Amma! Well, my job was to not put extra difficulty on Amma. One token can be considered as a key to the divine abode. It is precious and meant to be used one time only. To prevent people from coming twice, we have to collect them. I had failed miserably, and that too, in my own hometown!

Someone suddenly took me by the shoulders and said, "Just collect the tokens, nothing else!" I said, "Can't you see I am struggling right now?" I spent the whole night on stage, ashamed and judging myself. Well, I was not as proud and quite far from the confidence I had in the last city! Amma emphasizes the importance of having awareness in every action. Through many similar experiences, Amma kept shaping me as a musical instrument, and believe me, there is still a lot of work to do!

Amma says, "There is an order to everything in the cosmos. There is a rhythm to everything — the wind, the rain, the waves, the flow of our breath and heartbeat. Similarly, there is a rhythm in life. Our thoughts and actions create the rhythm and melody of our lives."

***

As a child, I would wake up at night inspired to write poetry to the Divine Goddess. Twenty years later, one night in Amritapuri, I wrote a song. During one Europe Tour, Amma asked to sing it. We rehearsed together and I was mesmerized by her. So much so that I forgot the words of my own song. Everyone stared at me concerned. Then I laughed at myself out loud and even interrupted her divine singing. Amma stopped and her big laugh vibrated in the room. We laughed together. So much divine joy! Afterwards we went on stage with Amma to sing in front of thousands of people. Amma sang in French beautifully. We sang the same words I would write for the Goddess and keep for myself in my lonely childhood nights.

My most precious memories in life have been the nine occasions I have had the opportunity to sing with Amma — even twice under the stars and moon. On one of these occasions, Amma playfully drew on the song sheets. She made two faces in the shape of the moon — one sad and one happy. She even drew flowers too! *The Pollen of the Nine Rare Flowers* spread through these songs in my life, and has filled me with divine memories. *The Harp of Joy* was brought back to life.

Once, on the Europe Tour, I played music for Amma with my biological sister. Afterwards, Amma commented, "When your sister sings, bubbles come out of the self and become music." Then, Amma took my hand in prayer, saying, "Your sister has bhakti!" I felt unfathomable reverence to Amma, the goddess of art, for acknowledging the divine love in a member of my family.

On my 40th birthday, Amma blessed me by singing another song I composed, exactly twenty years after I had my *Two Moon Eclipses.* Amma chose the perfect time to sing it, as I was in France with my family. What a birthday gift! It resonated with the birthday dream I had of Amma singing with my family.

Amma says, "Love is not something that can be taught by someone or learned from somewhere. But in the presence of a perfect master, we can feel it, and in due course, develop it, because a satguru creates the necessary circumstances for love to grow within us. These circumstances created by the guru will be so beautiful and unforgettable that we will truly cherish these moments as something precious and invaluable. They will remain as a sweet memory forever and ever. One incident of this kind will create a big wave of love in us. More incidents like this, created by the guru, will make a chain of exhilarating memories which will produce waves and waves of love within us, until at last there will be only love. Through these circumstances, the guru will steal our heart and soul, filling us with pure and innocent love."

***

I have often felt a deep sadness inside, and at times it has been hard for me to come out of it. So, I once went to Amma and shared with her about this feeling. Amma pinched my cheek and clicked her fingers. From that simple gesture, a fire in my heart was ignited. Soon, I went to my room and began to meditate. Suddenly, I could hear very beautiful music coming from somewhere. It sounded like a choir. It was 2 a.m. in the morning, so I thought, "Who could be playing music so loud at this time?" I began to understand that it was coming from somewhere beyond — as if it was dēvas playing celestial music. I had an ecstatic feeling and tried to write it down. But it was impossible.

It was an unknown language filled with extraordinary bhakti. I listened to it for an hour and a half and felt a nectar spreading from my heart to my whole body. I had a feeling of serenity and divine happiness. I took it as a gift from Amma.

Later on, I discovered that through regular meditation and japa, I could overcome my feelings of sadness and pain. They were coming from me and me alone. Meditation connects us to the whole universe, to the great mystery surrounding us. Silence flows into us and allows us to hear the music of God.

The most beautiful feeling inside us is coming from Amma — inviting us to dive deep within and listen to her divine chant. The strings of our lives vibrate with her infinity. Spiritual practices can reveal this nectar in us and this devotion is my goal.

May my life sing the glory of God all the time. May I develop a receptivity to grasp this devotion even in the difficulties and trials of life. Amma, I apologize for being so slow to put your wisdom into practice. There are no words to express my gratitude, my joy to you.

18

Amma's Family

Ahalya - France

Ten years ago, I met my husband, Devanath, in Amritapuri. At first, I was surprised by the familiar way he addressed everyone in the āśhram. He would warmly wave to people as if they were family, "Hello brother, hello sister, hello auntie, hello mother!" I was a little skeptical and I told him, "It is impossible for you to genuinely mean that. Your feelings can't be the same for everyone as they are for your real family!" Back then, for me, there was only one family, and you could only use those words if you were sincere. In fact, he truly meant them, and now, so do I.

Every civilization in this world is built upon families, groups, and communities. Studies have shown that our family or caretakers initially help us grow physically and emotionally. Children deprived of emotional care don't experience the same physical, intellectual, and social development as other children. Sanātana Dharma states that the family we are born into is the direct result of our karma, showing that we have influenced the choice of our biological family.

I was blessed with a loving and open-minded family. I am very grateful to Amma that four generations of my family could meet her — from my grandmother and parents to my parents-in-law, and even my nephew. My mother possesses strong spiritual tendencies and my grandmother, who always lived with us, constantly spoke about her love for Jesus.

When my grandmother turned eighty, she and her sister suddenly became Sai Baba devotees. So I decided to take her to his āśhram in Puttaparthi, India. The first person I met there was an Amma devotee who immediately handed me Amma's biography. I read the biography in one go, and felt deep down that Amma was the one for me! It felt obvious and normal; it did not even feel like my life had changed. Instead, it felt as if Amma had always been with me.

Initially, we have a biological family, and gradually, we have the freedom to choose the families that best fit our ideals in life. Choosing which company to keep is said to influence us greatly.

When I was missing Amma during the pandemic, I had the opportunity to ask an online question to Swami Purnamritananda Puri: "How to soothe the pain of separation?" His answer was simple, "Be with your saṅgha, your spiritual family."

I believe one of the greatest gifts that Amma has given us is her saṅgha. Amma gives us sisters and brothers from around the world, of all ages, and from all backgrounds. From Los Angeles to Tokyo — monks, friends, children, fellow sevites, grandmothers, security guards, and the list goes on. We may only know some of these people from a distance, yet they inspire us so much, while others help us work out our issues by putting us through the fast cycle of 'the spiritual washing machine.'

***

A simple definition of a community is: A group of people who gather around common principles, values, and goals, and who have interest in living together. This definition applies well to Amma's family.

We all have the same supreme goal, even if as individuals we chase after various temporary goals. Some debate, "I want liberation" or "I am not interested in it." I believe we all want to be free from pain and desire spiritual growth. Mōkṣha or liberation is ultimately our common aspiration.

As a community, we share the same values. We all strive to develop compassion and train ourselves to discern the permanent from the temporary. We know we are here to purify our karma and we understand there is something higher behind our interactions than what the eyes can see. Therefore, we put in extra efforts to check our attitude when conflicts arise. Analyzing a situation through the lens of karma and growth is not so common nowadays outside of Amma's family.

During Amma's Europe tours, I participated in the assisted darśhan sēvā, where local devotees and volunteer tour staff collaborated to assist people with disabilities in receiving Amma's divine embrace. Once, five of us assisted a woman who could only survive for three minutes without her oxygen and medication. It required cooperation and concentration to make her darśhan a smooth experience. Implicitly, our shared values of compassion and service were the fuel for us to try to do our best.

Another time, we accompanied my grandmother in assisted darśhan. Not knowing she was family, a local devotee came to my mum and me and pointed at my husband, "See that tall guy with the beard? He is really rough with this poor old lady. He should not be allowed to do this sēvā anymore." In actuality, as my grandmother was starting to lose her mental clarity in her final years, we would affectionately tease and joke with her to boost her mood. Sometimes, there can be gaps between our reality and the reality of the other person. It's hard to judge a situation. My husband Devanath then brought my grandmother to Amma and said, "Wife," while pointing at my grandma. Amma joked, "New wife?" Everyone started laughing.

In Amma's spiritual family we may have many different objectives, but Amma and our spiritual growth are always our number one priority. The memories we share in our saṅgha are the most precious ones: Amma showering us with flowers during Dēvī Bhāva, or Amma dancing and laughing as we all gaze at her in awe. We share the joy of meeting her, the small and big signs Amma shows us that are so relevant for us, the synchronicities, and the million ways in which Amma knows and guides each one of us. Especially watching Amma bless all of us during Dēvī Bhāva before the curtain closes has been the most profound experience of my life.

I believe we are truer in front of Amma – we are stripped clean of the unnecessary, and what is essential in us is revealed. In that sense, we are all equal in front of her.

***

Amma almost never talked to me about my various sēvās. In contrast, Amma often said that I was "nice." Every time she said this, I experienced a feeling of love mixed with discomfort and unease. I spent years pondering about it. We went for darśhan once and she said to Devanath, "Your wife is *soooo* nice!" putting her hands on her heart as if I was the eighth wonder of the world. I thought, "He must have another wife somewhere."

Suddenly, it dawned on me. I always identified myself as a doer, a strong, result-oriented person, not as a sweet person. That's why it felt so unknown to me. By not talking about my sēvā, Amma was subtly stripping me of one of my identifications. By seeing myself through Amma's eyes, she helped me go beyond my personality. She helped me to recognize this *nice* place within myself – a place of love that we all have inside and that we forget. Despite our superficial differences, we share our most sacred and intimate treasure – the love that Amma gives us and the love we feel for her.

In our Amma family, one of the unique ways we spend time together, even before interacting, is being together in prayer.

The āśhrams and Amma Centers are saturated with the energy of spiritual practices. The benefit of just being in a Center or being surrounded by spiritual people is a blessing on its own.

During the second lockdown, I stayed in Amma's āśhram in France. Doing spiritual practices together and sharing simple moments of joy, even in silence, was very nurturing and the right answer to the Covid situation. As Amma has said, being able to participate in these Centers is like winning the lottery.

Isolation is rare within the Amma family. Once, I observed my eighty-year-old neighbor in Amritapuri walking outside, stopping people passing by to help her start a video call. It amazed me that it took her only thirty seconds to be assisted. In today's world, isolation and selfishness can sometimes become the norm, but within the saṅgha, whenever you face a problem, you will find people to help you. Obviously, it goes both ways. There are also many precious opportunities to help and contribute to others as well.

Amma's sēvā and the people we interact with teach us the best spiritual lessons. In 2019, a young man came to Denmark. He was completely paralyzed. Only his tongue and eyes could move. He had a small device attached to his wheelchair at his tongue level. Through this, he could talk a little. When he went for darśhan, Amma asked him how he was doing. He replied, "I have a happy life." His response was a profound lesson, reminding us to put our lives into perspective.

Two years ago, my husband was diagnosed with cancer and had to undergo aggressive chemotherapy treatment. Amma's invisible hand orchestrated everything through her children. Exactly when we received the news, I received an email from Swamini Amritajyoti Prana enquiring about Devanath's health. Instantly, she directed me to a woman who gave us valuable advice to improve his quality of life during chemo. Within days, a whole system was in place without us doing anything. We received tremendous help and prayers from so many people, from swāmīs and close friends to devotees we barely knew. For months, we had love and support without fail. We are immensely grateful to Amma and everyone for this.

There is nothing more meaningful than our relationship with Amma. Her family is a great source of meaningful relationships, and everyone works hand-in-hand with Amma for the benefit of humanity and our individual spiritual growth.

The *Bhagavad Gītā* points out that interaction with others and the world at large is inevitable, not optional. Without it, we could not fulfill our basic needs. How could we progress without learning to adapt to different people and viewpoints? How could we learn compassion if we had no one to share it with? Around Amma, we are taught adaptability, diversity, and humility. Even the conflicts help us learn to either define our limits and be more assertive, or less, depending on the situation. Amma says, "God has no separate hands, legs, eyes or body other than our own. The cosmic power inside us is God."

Once, I was asked to speak as an announcer during the French program functions. I started an inner negotiation with Amma. "Amma, 8,000 people is a big crowd! There is so much to do for my other sēvā, the main guest is an Ambassador and I don't know about the protocols! But okay, let's do it! Amma, give me strength and please don't add anything. I will not be able to take it." That's when I realized I had no formal stage clothes to wear, and then, as the function unfolded, I was given extra instructions and English revisions to be presented in the next few seconds in French. I just had to adapt. Amma shows us we can always do more with her by our side! Our potential is not as limited as we think.

Being such a large family, one of the most important lessons is to 'share Amma.' The small fights to be in the front row near Amma show how we compete subconsciously, comparing her love to a limited resource in time and space. However, regardless of the outcomes of our little competitions, Amma always blesses each of us in exactly the ways we need. I remember one experience that showed me this.

In 2014, Amma visited the Vatican, and Devanath and I flew to be there. We were not part of the delegation, but it held such great significance for us that Amma was coming to this holy place that we were happy just being there. Still, we hoped to have a glimpse of her. We did not know any details, except that Amma would be meeting Pope Francis. The day before, I had the intuition to go to Saint Peter's square. It was dark and rainy. In the distance, we heard a strong American voice. It was one of Amma's devotees alone in the middle of the square! Like spies, we observed where he was going. The next day, we went to the same place and found a dozen Italian devotees there. We did not know how they would react since, officially, we were not supposed to be there. However, the devotees were inclusive and welcoming. We stayed outside for two days together, waiting and praying to see Amma... and taking turns to order pizzas. In the end, we were able to see Amma many times and even received darśhan. Amma showered us with her love and made sure our needs were fulfilled.

A long time back, I was feeling discouraged and stuck. I declared that I was not fit for spirituality. I told myself, "Since my spiritual efforts don't help and I can't feel Amma is with me, I will now live a material life. I'll start by eating chocolate and watching TV." I sat on my bed with a jar of Nutella chocolate spread to watch a famous American show. The first scene takes place in the aftermath of a funeral. The widow proceeds to give her husband's friend one of his belongings. The dialogue starts with her saying, "Take this mālā. He got it in India. A few years ago, he met a spiritual leader who hugs people. Apparently, she has hugged over 30 million people!" Only one minute after my crazy declarations, Amma was compassionate enough to show me her presence, and rescued me through the TV show! Amma really uses every possible thing in our lives to teach us.

***

My husband is an incredible support in my spiritual life. Because of our love for each other, we learn to give more. We try to motivate each other in our sādhanā and because we are close, he can push my buttons like no one else can. I will share some examples.

When Devanath had cancer, he was very weak. I went the extra mile to make sure he was always comfortable. It was a full-time job teaching me to forget about 'me.' It was a revealing experience because I understood I could not have done that for someone else, but I also realized Amma teaches us to extend our compassion beyond our close circle.

Another lesson Amma taught me was particularly hard. I prefer keeping my life private, but my husband is a very open person. Before meeting me, he used to openly talk to Amma about his previous girlfriends and Amma would make jokes about it in return. Amma even told his story in her satsangs in the West.

The first time we went on tour together, at the end of a darśhan, the music stopped and a deep silence floated around. Everybody started gathering around Amma. Amma and Devanath started joking about Devanath's past. Everybody was laughing, but I was extremely embarrassed. I felt a burning pain inside and wished I had a magic wand to make it disappear.

Amma gave me the experience to face my fears, but at the same time, showed me the sweetness of her love. Amma was always supportive, joking with me how Devanath was like a big baby with a good heart.

That day, I was given invaluable advice by a good friend, Prof. Bhavani Rao: "Amma will work on you to help you overcome shame." I was not brave enough to tell Amma what I felt, but Amma knew. Once, during our darśhan she asked us mischievously, "Is it okay that Amma talks about you? Do you want Amma to stop?" Devanath replied, "Who am I to tell God what to do?" While a big part of me appreciated my husband's wisdom, I admit a less noble part of me thought, "Why doesn't he tell Amma how I feel? I'm so mad at him!" Obviously, he succeeded in the test and I failed. But gradually, I had to introspect and face the fear of shame in order to get past it. It took me three years to gather the courage to express my feelings to Amma. Thus, I began to slowly get rid of the unnecessary burden of shame in my life.

These experiences are not always pleasant but are the only way to really see where we are at. The true tests come when we interact with others and see how we respond. Through Amma or Amma disguised as one of us, we get opportunities to learn all of life's skills. Amma has already created all the conditions. It's just up to us to see clearly and grow.

***

Amma often asks us how we would talk about the principles of Sanātana Dharma to ordinary people. I believe the best way to touch people's hearts is by embodying Amma's teachings.

When Amma married us on tour, some of our relatives found it difficult to relate to the setting, as it can be quite a foreign cultural experience for Europeans. Nevertheless, they were impressed by the affection that the devotees showed us. Seven years later, my father-in-law still mentions our wedding as a strong memory of solidarity and love.

When my dad came to Amritapuri with no prior knowledge of āśhrams, many people took the time to sit and talk with him, even if he mostly wanted to talk about football and go to the beach. As my father used to be a professional soccer player, my friend Priyan went to play with him. Amma went so far as to ask him about his football team and its weekly results. Since then, he's been bragging about this great place, saying he had rarely seen a concentration of such intelligent people! Amma obviously takes care of us directly and indirectly through others. Knowing we are Amma's ambassador is a great exercise to check our attitude and to be more open to others.

In their satsangs, numerous devotees have shared stories of how one person was instrumental for meeting Amma for the first time, another to understand her better, another to be more disciplined, and so on. It shows how everyone can be a role model for someone else. Seeing people acting according to dharma, we are inspired to do the same. It's a ripple effect that has an impact on society at large.

Amma says,"We are all human beings, members of the world family. Belonging to a country or a religion comes only after."

Distributing clothes to the underprivileged in France, helping with the assisted darśhan on tours, or my job as a life coach — these sēvās have helped me to get glimpses of this truth declared by Amma. Deep inside, we are all the same. We have the same fears, insecurities, and doubts; and we all search for security, peace, and happiness. Our life circumstances may be different, and we might use different paths to get there, but we all strive for happiness and for realizing the true meaning in life.

From Amma's teachings, I understand we have two goals. One is to love and serve while being aware that human relations are temporary, to always remember that God is the substratum of everything, and that God alone will always be here. The other is to experience love through God's creation.

It is a lifelong journey to train our minds not to see others as a source of joy or pain. Since God's play can only unfold through us, we can practice seeing everything as a manifestation of God, or as sent directly by Amma. Let us start by acting in a spirit of brotherhood. This is the golden rule of every single religion. I am so grateful for this unique spiritual family that Amma has formed for us to grow, to practice giving, and to expand our capacity to love.

19

The Path of Love

Raghu Mannam – India

I am a Telugu native from Hyderabad currently living in Atlanta in the U.S. When I was young, I was introduced to spirituality by Swami Vireshwarananda, a direct disciple of Mother Sharada Devi. Later, in 1996, my family and I were told about Amma by Swami Paramatmananda Puri. We talked a lot about the spiritual experiences he had in Hyderabad, and discussed various Indian saints. That's when he suggested we have darśhan from Amma.

My first darśhan with Amma was in 1997 in her āśhram in San Ramon, California. When we arrived in the hall, the darśhan queue was very long. Seeing this, I decided to skip darśhan and made my way to the back of the hall, while my wife Arpitha joined the back of the darśhan line. Immediately, someone came and took Arpitha to the front of the darśhan line. To my astonishment, upon seeing Arpitha, Amma looked straight at me, gestured with her hand for me to come to her, and gave us both a beautiful darśhan together. We were amazed that she knew we were husband and wife!

For many years, Arpitha and our children, Viveka and Kaivalya, joined Amma on her North America Tour. I would get Amma's darśhan in Washington, D.C. or Atlanta every year. Spending time with Amma during the U.S. tours helped the children to imbibe values, build a strong spiritual foundation and prepare them for life ahead. Whenever my family would go for darśhan, Amma would always enquire about my well-being. Amma has been a guiding light to the whole family — bringing us closer together and transforming us spiritually. Being in her presence brings us the greatest joy.

Once, Arpitha, Viveka, and Kaivalya were attending Amma's program in Detroit, Michigan. I was traveling from Atlanta to India at that time. My family was a bit sad that I was not with them in Detroit, as I would not be able to get Amma's darśhan for another six months. When I went to the Atlanta airport to board my flight to India, after a few hours of flight delay, it was announced that the direct flight from Atlanta to Paris was canceled. Surprisingly, I was automatically rebooked on a new flight from Atlanta to Amsterdam — with a nine-hour layover in Detroit! I was dumbfounded. After landing in Detroit, I took a taxi to the Amma program venue. Within two hours, I got a token and received darśhan from Amma. I truly felt that this was Amma's saṅkalpa (divine resolve) to arrange for my darśhan. A devotee dropped me back at the airport, and I was on my way to India.

During my free time, I enjoy reading the Telugu Śhrīmad Bhāgavatam. I will share some stories that have deeply inspired me.

The Origin of the Śhrīmad Bhāgavatam

One day, Sage Vyāsa, the author of *Mahābhārata* and the *Bhagavad Gītā*, was meditating on the banks of the river Sarasvatī. He felt a lack of peace, but wasn't able to figure out why. Sage Nārada stopped by Vyāsa's āśhram and immediately recognized the disturbance within Vyāsa. Nārada pointed out to Vyāsa that even though he had clearly laid out all aspects of dharma in his works, he had not elaborately described the Lord's playful nature and the love between the Lord and the devotees.

Sincerely loving the Lord rapidly brings a devotee closer to God and ultimately culminates in oneness. This is because we fully identify ourselves with the one that we love. As love deepens, the lover and the beloved become one — the devotee merges with God.

Vyāsa understood his mistake and decided to write the *Śhrīmad Bhāgavatam* — highlighting the love between the devotee and the Lord. The *Bhāgavatam* describes the various stories of devotees who realized Lord Nārāyaṇa through love.

In the 1400s, there lived an innocent Telugu devotee of Lord Rāma named Pothana. One full moon night while meditating on the banks of the river Kṛiṣhṇa, Lord Rāma and Sītā Dēvī appeared before Pothana. Lord Rāma's complexion was like a dark rain cloud and Sītā Dēvī's was like a flash of lightning. Lord Rāma asked him to translate the *Bhāgavatam* from Sanskrit into Telugu. Acting as an instrument of the Lord, Pothana translated the *Bhāgavatam* with great devotion.

Pothana's exceptionally mesmerizing poetry depicts the soul-stirring love between the devotee and the Lord. I would like to share some passages from this Telugu *Bhāgavatam*, and share my perspective and understanding in the light of Amma's teachings.

The Realization of King Khaṭvāṅga

Khaṭvāṅga was a strong and powerful king, unmatched on the battlefield. The dēvas, or demigods, asked him for help in their fight against the demonic asuras. Khaṭvāṅga agreed and fought alongside the dēvas for many years until they finally defeated the asuras. The dēvas promised to give him a boon at the end of the war. Khaṭvāṅga claimed his boon by asking the question, "How much of my life is left?" The dēvas told him that since he had spent most of his life fighting the war, he had only forty-eight minutes left to live.

> *The King immediately gives up his elephant battalion and his large cavalry regiment of horses.*

He also gives up attachment to his beautiful wives
who loved him dearly.
He gives up attachment to all his friends,
family, relatives and teachers,
and takes to deep vairāgya (detachment).

Singing the names of Lord Kṛiṣhṇa
and deeply reflecting on the Lord,
giving up all fear,
the great King Khaṭvāṅga
merged his heart
in the infinite Lord
and attained kaivalya (liberation)
in less than forty-eight minutes.

Verses from Pothana's *Śhrīmad Bhāgavatamu*

When King Khaṭvāṅga was confronted with approaching death, the transient nature of the world instantly dawned on him. He immediately gave up his bondages and wholeheartedly immersed himself in the Lord. God is like the sky, and the body and our attachments to the world are like clouds. As soon as we give up these attachments — God alone remains and liberation is attained.

My understanding is that liberation cannot happen even if we have the slightest identification with the body and the world. In the context of modern times, we have to live in the world while performing our duties. But internally, we can remain free from the trappings of attachment. For this to happen, we need the presence of mahātmās like Amma in our lives.

Throughout the nineties, I had innumerable opportunities to buy a house in San Francisco, California. For many years, I regretted that I missed these multi-million dollar opportunities and I carried the baggage of these thoughts in my mind.

Recently, being in Amma's presence and the spiritual atmosphere of Amritapuri, these thoughts of missed opportunities have slowly withered away from my mind. Dropping these attachments has removed this obstruction to my spiritual progress. As

Amma says,"Everything is within us, but our attachments in the name of worldly love always pulls us down. Attachment binds, detachment uplifts."

The Story of Prahlāda

When we look at Amma's life, it reminds us of the incredible story of Prahlāda.

Prahlāda was a young prince — son of the great King Hiraṇyakaśhipu. From his childhood, his only focus was loving Lord Nārāyaṇa. This deep love for God enabled him to fully merge in the Lord, even as a child.

Seeing the Lord in his own heart,
he forgot to perceive the universe.
Completely merging his heart
in the thought of the Lord,
sitting all alone and shedding tears of joy,
he would lose himself in love for the Lord.

All alone, singing ecstatically,
knowing that this whole universe
is nothing but Lord Viṣhnu,
he would loudly laugh all by himself.
He would jump up and down with joy, saying,
'I have known the changeless,
lotus-eyed Hari!'

Prahlāda thus spent his childhood,
happily, all by himself,

immersed in the love of Lord Hari.
One day, his father, the King,
called him to his court and said,
'My sweet son,
talk to me about something
that is very dear to your heart.'

The young boy Prahlāda says,
'O mighty King and my dear father,
the feeling that I am an individual
and different from other beings
is like falling into a deep, dark pit.

Knowing that this whole universe is nothing
but the play of Lord Hari,
one can live anywhere,
even in the middle of a dense forest,
in total happiness —
merging the heart completely
in Lord Hari.

That alone is a day,
when it is fully spent in the love of the Lord.
That alone is education,
which teaches the nature of the Lord.
He alone is a guru,
who conveys and instills love for the Lord.

O dear Father,
he alone is a father,
who tells his son
to become one with the Lord.'

Śhrīmad Bhāgavatamu

Love is the thread that tied Prahlāda to Lord Nārāyaṇa. As Prahlāda's love for the Lord deepened, the omnipresent nature of the Lord was spontaneously revealed to him. Amma says, "One who has sincere love for God will see God's form everywhere, in everyone and in everything."

Śhuka

Sage Vyāsa had a son named Śhuka. Even from childhood, Śhuka completely gave up all attachments, immersed himself in Lord Viṣhnu, and was always aware of his oneness with the universe. One day, the child Śhuka, started walking away from his hut. His father Vyāsa, ran after him, loudly calling, "Dear son, dear son!" In response, all the trees in the forest responded in unison, "Yes, yes!" and the whole place was filled with the echoes of these sounds.

Śhuka was so filled with the sense of oneness with all beings that the trees responded in his place when his name was called. When we recognize that the feeling of multiplicity is caused by ignorance, we become one with the supreme Reality.

We read in the Lalitā Sahasranāma:

> *ōṁ nirbhēdāyai namaḥ*
> I bow down to Dēvī who is beyond all sense of difference. (178)
>
> *ōṁ bhēda nāśhinyai namaḥ*
> I bow down to Dēvī who destroys the sense of difference. (179)

As Amma says, "Bhēda-buddhi[25] will not be seen in one whose mind has merged in God."

---

[25] A perspective focused on differences and separation.

Reading this story, I am reminded of Amma's call to care for nature, as nature is not separate from us. Likewise, gratitude for nature helps us develop this sense of oneness.

Jeanne Guyon — A French Saint

Some years back, I was working on a project in Europe. After work, sometimes I would engage in spiritual discussions with my colleagues. Upon the recommendation of one of my colleagues, I read the autobiography of a French saint, Jeanne Guyon, who lived in the 1600s. I was greatly inspired by her life story and teachings.

At the age of twenty-eight, her husband died, and within a year, her son, daughter, and father all passed away as well. Despite such tragedy, she had a firm conviction in God. She prayed to God, "Father, since this is your will, this is exactly what I want as well." She urged that in order to see God, we should look for God within ourselves, and advocated that we directly approach God through love and prayer. She was later imprisoned for this teaching.

The saint's total surrender to God shifted her identification from herself to the divine. She was so fully identified with the 'Father within her heart' that she remained wholly unaffected by the tragedies happening in her worldly life. From this we learn that total surrender to God is a powerful way to attain oneness with him.

As Amma says, "Spirituality is the ability to turn within. Having surrendered everything to his beloved Lord, a true devotee is always in a pleasant, blissful mood."

May we all develop this attitude of surrender.

20

To Be Grateful Is to Flourish

Vikasita - Spain

I can't say I know myself. Only Amma truly knows us. I cannot comprehend the presence of God, but only marvel at such a mystery of love and mercy, and be grateful for it. Amma asks nothing from us, and wherever she is, her presence is always the most humble. Everything we can offer in return in life is a tiny bit of the love and joy that she has sown in our hearts.

I would like to share about the fragility of life and the proximity of death. You can't start living for God unless you die every moment. Every step that we take, when it is guided by Amma, is a step towards the death of the ego.

The subject of mystical death is known in all spiritual traditions. In my humble opinion, it is beautifully summed up in three words that I heard from Swamini Krishnamrita Prana. In reply to the question, "How do we stop fleeing from silence — from the death of the ego?" Swamini said, "You know, forget about yourself."

Forgetting about oneself — the more one dies to the ego, the more one begins to live for God. So, I will share with you how I began forgetting about myself a little. How this made it possible for God to enter into this poor heart of mine in the most beautiful form of all — Amma! How, since that moment, life has showered me with infinite blessings and lessons — all gifts of her divine love.

This daughter of Amma was born in Spain. The day I was born a nun came to the hospital room where my biological mother was, took all the flowers that people had brought, and put them on an altar of the Virgin Mary. When my mother told me about it, I felt that my birth was a flower offering to God.

My astrological birth chart ended in February 2008. An astrologer told me that somehow, my death had been averted, and that my life was going to be like a spring season from then on. So it has been every day, only by Amma's grace.

In February 2008, at the age of twenty-one, I woke up one night with two emergency doctors at the foot of my bed. An ambulance was waiting for me downstairs. I was taken to the emergency hospital and a series of visits to various hospitals over the course of the next six years began.

With each surgical intervention, a brain arterial malformation which had manifested as epilepsy was gradually being removed. However, it was not only the malformation that was eliminated, but also many memories, much of my personality, physical sensations, and the ability to express myself clearly due to a temporal aphasia[26].

My family says that from that moment on, I started telling more jokes and talking much faster than before. I felt as if time was slipping through my fingers. I knew that before time ran out, I needed to find God. In 2011, I began to search the world for God, and I started with India. Back then, I didn't know that knocking on God's door is an inward process.

***

After almost three months of blessed experiences in the holy land of India, I arrived in Kollam where a stranger told me that I had to visit a holy woman in a monastery. I couldn't imagine then that the holy woman he talked about was God in human form.

---

[26] A neurological condition that affects language comprehension and production.

Ever since my brave sisters and brothers started sharing their satsangs, I have been wanting to hear from someone who had the same experience as me. But no two darśhans are alike. During my first darśhan, Amma did not hug me. When the darśhan line assistants saw that Amma didn't hug me, didn't look at me, and pretended as though no one was there, they picked me up by my armpits and said, "Next."

In my ignorance, I got up and left the stage where Amma was giving darśhan, thinking that I had breached some protocol, or that I had been impolite or even rude to our most beloved Amma. At that time, my heart was full of stones and I did not know how to cry. I just sat for hours watching Amma hug everyone who came but me.

When I returned the next day and kneeled before Amma, Amma again pretended not to see me. Once again, the assistants asked me to get up and leave to make way for the next visitor. Feeling that something deep inside me was marred and broken, I stood up and walked away. Suddenly, from my eyes that had been dry for years, tears began to fall. It was as if a rain of nectar could finally begin to flow from my heart.

I wept for hours. Knowing absolutely nothing about the Divine Mother Kālī, I sat in front of the sanctum sanctorum in the Kālī Temple with my heart overflowing with pain and tiredness. I strongly felt that God had abandoned me in a loveless and compassionless world. I felt that I was not enough, and unworthy of God's love.

The next day I rejoined the darśhan line, and when I was in front of Amma, she hugged me, kissed me, and rocked me as if I were her baby. At that moment, I let myself fall into her embrace. When she let go of me, Amma was looking into my eyes with a smile as bright as the sun, and a current of warmth and coolness ran through my body. I saw God in front of me and without hesitation, I said, "I love you. Thank you." I left the āśhram that same day knowing that I had found shelter in God and that God was within me.

***

Before I came to live in the āśhram, God gave me ten years of experiences out in the world where I was able to witness Her infinite beauty and grandiosity. It felt as if God was saying, "Go out, serve, and always come back to God."

Like spring had sprung in my chest, the emptiness I had felt in my heart was filled with gratitude — and out of gratitude, joy was born. To be grateful is to flourish. This is what spiritual life is all about to me — to flourish, whatever the circumstances. To flourish is to feel God's joy inside, and from Her joy and love arise our need to serve. So, invitations to serve God began to arrive. Over these years, by Amma's grace and inspiration, I fell in love with humanity and the world.

Amma used me as an instrument to teach yōga and meditation to refugees from Afghanistan, Iraq, Syria, and other countries where terrorism and war are still a threat today. It was her grace that helped me understand that mankind's pain is a reflection of our separation from God. Everyone needs to feel close to Amma always. All we need is to remember her love.

***

Amma's greatest miracle was not saving my life, which she has done several times. The greatest miracle was that someone like me, scared of everything and everyone, fell in love with humanity, and went out to say it out loud.

Empty-handed but with a heart full of Amma, I later traveled to Bidibidi, a refugee camp in Uganda, Africa with a Ugandan children's choir, the "Coro Safari." Driving around the country, with half my body outside the car window, I shouted, "Hello! It's good to see you! I'm happy to be alive and I love you!"

Time flew by. A few months after being in Uganda, I found myself in the Ivory Coast in West-Africa, where a civil war had left many children on the streets with a glue-sniffing addiction. In this place, even today children with AIDS are still thrown away, and many afflicted adults are left to fend for themselves on the roadside without access to treatment.

I know nothing and have nothing to offer except for this God-filled heart. Inside my heart, I felt Amma instructing me to dance with the street children and open a school. She used me as her instrument so that the children could learn music and dance instead of taking drugs on the street. Soon, I was introduced to an organization called "L'Espoir." Here, I taught yōga to children with AIDS. Some of them would cry if I kissed their little hands, feet, or sweaty foreheads. They had not known a mother's love and Amma had planted her love for them in my heart. The source of that love is, as you know, endless. The means God has given us to reach out to others are the same means she has given us to reach God.

In 2019, just before the pandemic, I traveled again to northern Uganda on the border with South Sudan. Many children there don't have a daily meal, access to clean water, toilets, education, or safety at night. The memory of holding a child in my arms who had not eaten for days is something that still weighs on my heart, every time I eat a meal.

At the Bidibidi refugee camp, I was the first woman with white skin that many children had ever seen in their lives. When they saw me coming, they would scream in fear and run to hide. This suddenly changed when I started to act just like them. Every time I saw a child, I shouted, "Aaah! A child!!!

Please, help!!!" and ran to hide. Children started to chase me and wanted to play with "The White."

While I was still there, one morning I woke up shivering with fever, feeling as if I was freezing and with my heart racing so fast I thought I was going to die. Before picking up the phone or any documents to identify me, I went out looking for help. I arrived at a clinic and as soon as I got in, I collapsed. I couldn't see anything, but I could still hear everything around me. I felt some people lift me up and lay me down on a stretcher. A few hours later I opened my eyes and recognized the face of John, a Ugandan friend who had been looking for me. Crying, I said, "Tell my mother that I am here."

As soon as I recovered, I flew straight from Uganda to India. The day after my arrival, I took the microphone during a question and answer session to ask Amma, "As Amma's children, how does Amma want us to behave in the world?" With simplicity and beauty, Amma replied, "There is no such thing as children and non-children of Amma. There is only one humanity, and life has to be lived with coherence."

Then Amma showed us the picture of Mother Kālī that she drew while speaking and said, "Just as leeches were used in ancient times to cleanse blood infections, Mother Kālī cleanses the ego of her children." In Uganda, the doctors said I had suffered from a blood infection. At that very moment I instinctively understood that everything we learn, we learn only from her. I realized that serving God in the form of the satguru is the most holy service one can offer to humanity.

***

A spiritual aspirant has to allow their sādhanā to fully transform their life. This happens when all aspects of life are seen as a form of spiritual practice. Sādhanā is also often a matter of waiting. Learning to wait is the most necessary thing in life, and the most difficult. Let us learn to wait in Amma.

About a year ago, a sister gave me a photo of Amma dressed as Rādhā. On the back of the photo were written three words. "I accept you." I felt as if the flower of my heart, withered with despair in front of a sea of vāsanās (latent tendencies) was blooming again. I wrote a short poem for Amma and kneeling in front of her, I asked, "Renunciation?"

Undaunted by her seemingly playful silence, I asked again. After a third time, Amma looked into the depths of my eyes and took me in her arms. She kissed me and I kissed her soft cheek in return as she hugged me like a baby. She said, "Brahmacharya." A brahmachāriṇī sister later explained to me, "Brahmacharya means you only have God. Lean on God only."

Since I joined the āśhram in Amritapuri, with a service-attitude I've been caring for the organic vegetable garden and watering it with the water of my love and devotion for God. I appreciate the company of butterflies, squirrels, and trees because they dwell in the present. In the silent and solitary contemplation of mother nature, I feel how every second we are embraced by Amma — in the form of the trees, plants, the air and the oceans, the mountains and animals. Even though we don't stop, or do so very little to feel it, every moment is indeed filled with God. She loves us.

Amma, because everything I have including time is yours, I wake up in the morning with enough energy to move mountains for you. How can we not live joyfully and gratefully when we can see in this very life, your delicate and patient love for us all. Everyday, you show us lovingly that it is not about rejecting human love but paying attention and making an effort to revel in God's love. For when we taste a drop of God's love, all worldly love falls off like leaves from the trees.

We are not here to serve you with pride, but to become simple and joyful children who dance your dance with you – to realize that our body is only to enjoy God's play, in God's service. We always look like we are doing something, but in reality we are doing nothing, because God does everything for us.

We should try to carry on, even if life gets difficult at times – to go on being joyful, light as little children or butterflies. If, in the middle of a war someone were to ask, "Where is God?" we should be able to respond without a trace of doubt, "God is within me." Above all, we should try to make them feel that God is within them as well.

One who is at peace in one's own heart is at peace with God. And one who is at peace with God is at peace in one's own heart. Amma says, "The world should know that a lifetime dedicated to love and selfless service is possible." Let us all become her peace instruments.

A few months ago, I sat silently in front of the Kālī shrine in the temple and with tears in my eyes I prayed, "I am only a seed that you have planted in your garden. Divine Mother, do not forsake me. I need to see you to know that you hear me and have not forgotten me. Manifest yourself so that I may know that you are with me always." When I opened my eyes, to my astonishment, Amma was physically there standing right next to me! She immediately started giving darśhan in the temple.

I pray for us all, everywhere, to have mountains of faith. If we are sure of God, we cannot resist the compelling urge to join the dance that overflows in the world and heavens. Then we would dance like Amma dances, in everything that exists. May we all always remember the sweetness of Amma's name in our hearts and lips. May we always choose love. Life always gives us various choices, and one is always love. May we always choose love. May we not become too attached to worldly things, nor become too preoccupied with anything in this life, for that would make us forget Amma. May Amma completely take over our humble existence so that she can act through us. May the thirst for God awaken in all of our hearts.

21

The Strength of That Love

Dr. Sirisha Chakravarthy - India

It was a bright, spring morning in 2017. Traveling by train on my way to work at AIMS Hospital, I stared outside the window as the lush paddy fields, coconut groves, and lotus ponds passed in front of my eyes. Watching the fleeting scenery flash by, I pondered how much I disliked change growing up. I lived and studied in the same school all the way till college, moved out of town only to attend medical school and still have the same friends since the first grade.

Yet here I was, spending my whole day in rapidly changing backdrops, moving between a car, van, train, autorickshaw, hospital and āśhram all in the same day. Amma had asked my husband and me to work at AIMS, which is about a seven-hour round-trip commute to and from the āśhram. Contrary to my personality, which naturally resists change, I embraced these daily transitions willfully and lovingly only because of love and faith towards the one powering and propelling this change — Amma.

Whether one likes it or not, change is inevitable. We all have a tendency to remain within our comfort zones with certain people, objects, and situations, and we dislike it when life forces us out of them. I faced three such events that would change my life forever: my biological mother's death, moving to the U.S., and last but not least, marriage. These events were neither sudden nor forced on me, but they all occurred in a very short period of time, and my mind simply couldn't adjust.

I used to put a 'dislike' label on change because I was attached to, or identified with certain things, and had a fear of facing the unfamiliar. When unfamiliar situations eventually arose, the resistance I had in my mind created a conflict that made them undesirable. However, fear and resistance to undesirable situations help us reflect on the inherent defects in the objects of the world and our thoughts. This understanding can lead us to dispassion.

Lord Kṛiṣhṇa explains what is considered knowledge or jñānam in Chapter 13 of the *Bhagavad Gītā*. Here I would like to focus on verses 9 and 10:

> *indriyārtheṣhu vairāgyam anahaṅkāra ēva cha*
> *janma-mṛityu-jarā-vyādhi-duḥkha-doṣhānudarśhanam*
> *asaktir anabhiṣhvaṅgaḥ putra-dāra-gṛihādiṣhu*
> *nityaṁ cha sama-chittatvam iṣhṭāniṣhṭōpapattiṣhu*

> Dispassion towards sense objects and also absence of egoism; reflection on the pain and evils of birth, death, old age, sickness and disease; absence of attachment and the feeling of mineness to son, wife, home, and the rest, and constant equipoise of mind in both the desirable and the undesirable circumstances.

The experiences of likes and dislikes occur at the level of the mind. We have a pleasurable experience when our mind labels something as a 'like' and a not so pleasurable experience when it labels something as a 'dislike.' Sensory inputs are experienced by the body, but the enjoyment or bhōga is experienced in the mind. Thus, the mind labels things accordingly.

When we wake up, the first thought, 'I' or the ego appears. The 'I' thought instantly becomes identified with the gross body and uses it as an adjunct for experiences. In fact, this is the very reason for our repeated births. This happens naturally, and there is no way to avoid it as long as we are alive and awake.

The stronger the bond between the ego and the body and senses, the stronger the attachment to the world and its objects. This attachment results in the feeling of 'mine.' Though the bond can't be severed, it can be weakened through the discernment between the eternal self and the transient body, mind, intellect, and the world. This is known as nitya-anitya vivēkam.

Slowly, we learn not to label things. Not labeling an object or experience as 'like' does not mean dislike or hate; it means that our mind will not be attached to that experience. We will have dispassion. Sometimes, this happens naturally. Amma gives an example of how when we are sick, we don't get excited to eat our favorite foods such as pāyasam. However, it is not practical to fall sick or have something terrible happen all the time in order for us to develop dispassion.

We may place ourselves in ideal situations that help us develop dispassion. However, vāsanās, the latent tendencies of our minds are like sleeping lions. As long as they are asleep, there's no need to worry. But as soon as a favorable situation arises, they show their prākṛitabuddhi or old conditioned behavior. There is nothing we can do about it because invariably, we will not always have ideal situations for our spiritual practices. Thus, there are times when we experience our discernment and dispassion overpowered by these latent tendencies. Amma reassures us not to get scared when this happens and reminds us to be truthful to ourselves, to accept and face our vāsanās boldly, and keep trudging on our path.

In fact, these predicaments help us develop alertness and strengthen our dispassion by allowing us to see the inherent faults and impending sorrow behind these experiences. We learn not to depend on external things for happiness, and this awakens udāsīnatā or nonattachment of the mind. Discernment gained from knowledge of the śhāstras or scriptures and the guru's teachings is the only way to remove the root cause of sorrow — ignorance. If we don't make any efforts towards this, we may be in a perfect setting for sādhanā such as being in the presence of mahātmā, but our mind will continue to strive to find happiness in objects and experiences.

***

Although I see the sick and dying during my work as a doctor, when my mother passed away, my attachment to her caused me great sorrow. Following this, it was difficult for me to leave a familiar and likable environment, and I resisted adjusting to living in a foreign land. As far as marriage is concerned, little did I know that our Amma had started her work of 'smoothening the edges' by keeping two of her darling rocks (my husband and me) together in a bag, long before we even met her physically.

I diagnosed myself as having adjustment issues, but unknowingly, I was looking for something more stable and unchanging to hold on to in my life. I had a traditional Hindu upbringing, but pūjā and japa were just not cutting it. I needed something more tangible. I started reading spiritual books, including stories of mahātmās. One such book was Shirdi Sai Baba's biography. It made a very profound impression on me, and for the first time in my life, I started praying simply for the sake of prayer itself. The prayer which got very fervent over time, was to show me a guru who would talk, eat, and sing with his or her disciples just as he had done. Baba says, "Like a sparrow drawn with a thread tied to its leg, I draw my people to me." Let me narrate how Amma drew this little sparrow to her.

During my hectic medical training years, I would still manage to visit āśhrams, meditation groups, and retreats on the mountain ranges in the East Coast of the U.S. After my husband and I moved to California, I continued attending such programs.

One day, returning from a party with friends, we stopped at an Indian grocery store where I saw a flier announcing Amma's program. I suddenly remembered meeting a devotee of Amma, Dr. Alka, a couple of months before. Seeing my interest in meeting saints, she showed me a picture of Amma and gave me her biography. My initial thought was, "Yet another mystic! But I've never come across a saint that hugs!" Now, standing in the grocery store, I asked my husband if we could go. I thought that some quiet and peace after partying would be good after all.

So, in 2006 on the eve of our wedding anniversary, we went to Amma's San Ramon āśhram. It was Dēvī Bhāva night! It was nothing like how I had expected an āśhram to be and definitely not quiet. It was a magnificent party! We knew nothing about the program, and did not know anyone there as well. After the ātmā pūjā finished, people were maneuvering excitedly, some arranging chairs, others flower stands, and so on. We were like deer caught in headlights.

In that daze, someone asked us, "Are you here for the first time?" We nodded yes, so they placed tokens in our hands and quickly ushered us to the darśhan line. A volunteer placed a mantra instruction card in my hand, and before I could understand it, we were in front of Amma. Amma had a very big smile, receiving us warmly just like she knew us from before. Then she whispered in Telugu, "Bādha paḍaku!" which means, "Don't worry!" She made us sit next to her, and kept casting her wonderful smiles at us. I received my gift that night — my mantra, the value of which I would appreciate only nine months later.

A week later I found out I was pregnant. I was happy but anxious at the same time, as I had experienced a couple of miscarriages before. However, things went smoothly this time. Amma's words, "Do not worry!" made sense only then. On the day of delivery, as I waited for twenty hours, I remained calm as my mind effortlessly chanted the mantra. Sai was born on the night of Mahā Śhivarātri. However, that night was remarkable in my life for another reason. During times like those I would miss my mother a lot, and I would inwardly blame her for not being around when I needed her the most. That night with our Amma's form in my heart and the gift of my mantra, I let go of that feeling forever!

***

Our lives gradually started to revolve around Amma. During one of her visits, we mentioned to her that we were planning on moving to Hyderabad. Amma said we should move to AIMS in Kochi instead. That was our third time meeting Amma. We were a bit taken aback, and I thought, "We can't speak any Malayalam, so how can we work at AIMS? There must be some misunderstanding." The mind, as Amma says, is like a lawyer that argues only its point of view. All these years I had been yearning for a guru to instruct me directly, but when the instruction came I interpreted it the way that pleased me.

My mind said, "San Ramon is close enough," so we moved there, and I started working in a hospital very close to the āśhram. I was happy with work; the kids were in one of the top schools, and we had satsangs, āśhram sēvā activities, and the excitement of preparing for Amma's visits. It was like I started to reach for the top floor, but feeling very comfortable, decided to settle on the intermediate landing of the stairwell. I was rowing my boat, but it was tethered by a rope.

My husband Chakravarthy stood his ground about moving to work at AIMS. When my elder son Abhi told Amma his worries about adjusting in India, Amma gave the final pull saying, "Join the line of ants going to school from the āśhram." Amma, the embodiment of unconditional love, sensing my hesitation called Dr. Priya and Dr. Krishnanunni and reassuringly told me, "These kids were much younger than your kids when they came to India. Look, now they are doctors."

This time Amma made sure the instruction was loud and clear. Dr. Priya came and told us that Amma wanted us to move as soon as possible. We wrapped up our medical practices and possessions and moved to AIMS the very next month. The rope was cut, and the boat set sail in December, 2013.

When we left the U.S., my colleagues, friends, and family were really surprised. There was one question that everyone would ask, "Why now?" People advised us, "This is not the stage of life to move to India. You are doing so well and could contribute better from here. Go when you retire." All of a sudden everyone became our career coaches, life planners, and investment advisers!

During our initial days in India, Amma was amused by my attempts to speak Malayalam, and she would often mention to others that we had left high-paying jobs to come to India. Hearing those words, along with my beginner's level knowledge of the scriptures, I began to feel that I was only one step away from the ultimate detachment – parāvairāgyam. Little did I know those were words of caution!

Whatever little detachment I had from sensory pleasures was helped and nurtured by favorable conditions, in other words, the fence placed by Amma around this sapling. But dispassion is not complete without mānasika tyāgam, detachment from the subtle ego. Ignoring this in the name of service to the world and God, is a pitfall on this path. If we don't give importance to our goal-directed practices like discernment and dispassion, we can't even save ourselves, let alone perform service to humanity! However, I had my own strong identifications with my profession and family. AIMS was the perfect stage to set me straight, and Amma would pitch in as and when needed.

***

Can we even get rid of the ego? We have seen that the misidentification of the eternal *'I'* with the transient body and mind is unavoidable, and can only be weakened with discernment. Everyone will have a feeling of ego and 'I' in his capabilities, power, and talents. It even sneaks up as, "*I* am a sādhak, *I* am spiritual!" Lord Kṛiṣhṇa says that some of the internal cleansing practices that help in strengthening discernment or vivēkam include amānitva (freedom from pride at a mental level) and adambhitva (freedom from hypocrisy and pride in actions).

This internal cleansing can be very tough and can cause a lot of sadness. I could not help but wonder, "I came to Amma seeing the faults in the world and to get rid of sorrow. Now, this cleansing process is causing even more sadness!" My thoughts were, "I can't even go back to the U.S. Anyhow, there is no comfort there either. Had I not known all this I would have lived comfortably!"

However, when such thoughts overwhelmed me, Amma would find ways to uplift me. During darśhan at the Ernakulam Brahmasthānam festival, Amma called me and asked if I had attended the bhajans. I replied "Yes." Then Amma said, "I sang the Telugu bhajan only for you!" It was *Sāgara Chēpaku*, describing the plight of a fish who feels thirsty even while living in the ocean; just like a seeker lacking spiritual enthusiasm though in the presence of Mother.

No doubt there are many difficulties on this razor-edged path. However, lakṣhya bōdham, our love for the goal propels our sādhanā, and above all, our faith in Amma's words. This faith will give us the strength to face these difficulties and will make the process of internal cleansing and detachment from ego internally effortless!

***

Moving to the āśhram and commuting back and forth to work at AIMS came with many new tests for my attachments! If we are working towards our goal on this spiritual path, we have to introspect sincerely about our attachments and identifications. Renouncing people or objects may not be possible, but what is needed is renouncing the attachment to them. Faith and surrender to the guru will help us rise above the situations we like or dislike and not become overly attached. This helps us move towards equanimity.

Daily train rides back and forth to AIMS were a very important time in my spiritual journey to reflect and address the attachments and identifications I had become conditioned to over many years. We used to leave the āśhram at 6:30 a.m. and be back by 7:45 p.m. – if lucky – just in time for the last bhajan or ārati. Amma used to patiently enquire about our travel timings and delays with train schedules. Those years were direct proof for me that with a mahātmā's saṅkalpa, all of nature aligns – just like fitting together a jigsaw puzzle.

When we started I had so many questions, such as how traveling like this would affect my patients, my work, and my kids. In the beginning, I asked Amma, "What about the kids?" Amma's look implied, "What about them?" Then pointing to the stage and the hall, she said, "They will be here. No problem." Sure enough, they were cared for as needed and mentored by brahmachārīs, brahmachāriṇīs, ammamārs and acchanmārs,[27] to whom I am very thankful.

There have been eventful days, with instances like when the boys wrestled and jumped from the cupolas of the Kālī Temple, ending up needing stitches and casts. These were opportunities for them to go to Amma and have her sort out their disputes with love and diplomacy. Colleagues at the hospital were skeptical about the travel, but patients were unfailingly cared for. Throughout this ordeal, Amma's protective hand was palpable.

However, the best part was traveling by train. We were a small group of doctors commuting together. During our rides we would chant archana and discuss Amma's Q&A sessions that we had missed. When leaving the āśhram in the morning, I would wonder if the kids would be alright that day, and when leaving the hospital in the evening, I would worry about a sick patient or be anxious if I would get a glimpse of Amma that night.

Amma instructed me to visualize my iṣhṭa dēvatā or beloved deity as being all-pervading and riding along with me on the train. While listening to recordings of scripture classes held in the āśhram, I'd reflect on this phrase from the *Upaniṣhads*: 'atra pitā apitā bhavati, mātā amātā, lokā alokā...' — 'this is a state where there is no father, no mother, no world' and I would also add 'putrā aputrā, rōgi arōgi' — 'no kids, no patients' so that finally 'tīrṇō hi tadā sarvāñchōkānhṛidayasya bhavati' — for then one has crossed over all the worries of the heart.'[28]

Thus immersed in my imagination and the swāmī's soothing speech I would really reach that state of no worries — the undivided pure bliss. You may have already guessed the state

---

27 'Ammamārs and acchanmārs' literally means 'mothers and fathers' in Malayalam, referring to the senior residents in the āśhram.

28 Adapted from *Bṛihadāraṇyaka Upaniṣhad*, 4.3.22

I am talking about by now. Suṣhupti — deep sleep! Yes, I would sleep for a good part of my journey. Once, Chakravarthy told Amma that he was feeling very sleepy on the train rides and Amma replied, "You sleep! Go to the upper berth and sleep." I also followed this instruction of Amma's to the 'T.'

Amma's direct instruction to me in my first room darśhan was to study the scriptures. The guru imparts direct teaching to reveal the nature of the self as sat-chit-ānandam, existence-awareness-bliss. Our experience however, is quite contrary. To facilitate comprehension of this truth, nēti-nēti — the method of negation of sensations, feelings, and perceptions — is needed.

During my travels Amma imparted this teaching by negation. Helping me contemplate my false identifications as being a doctor, mother, disciple, she showed me the limitations of the body, mind, and the world with names and forms. Their negation would lead me to the true source — non-negatable pure awareness!

A bird tied to a cage with a thread, flies around throughout the day and then rests in the cage in the evening. Similarly, the high-speed activity I was engaged in during the day at the hospital would automatically come to a pause when I returned home to my nest at the āśhram. All my efforts would cease while I rested in Amma's divine presence.

We usually used to reach home for the last bhajan or ārati, but there were many days when we arrived only after Amma had returned to her room, and the kids had gone to bed. After a couple years, for various reasons Chakravarthy and the other doctors stopped commuting on a daily basis and I was the only one traveling alone. However, soon Amma agreed for me to stay in the āśhram, and her grace helped me receive a project that I could work on from there. My journey from seeing change as unpleasurable to striving to go beyond the unpleasurable and pleasurable experiences could not have happened without my guru, my Amma.

Amma says that mere knowledge of the scriptures is not enough and that people often get deluded. Śhāstra (scripture) is but sound, and knowing the meaning of sound is not going to reveal our true nature. The guru is needed to illuminate the sound. Amma's teachings are śhāstra. We may have the logic and subtle intellect to analyze everything in the śhāstras, but we do not have the ability to assimilate the essence. Only guru kṛipā, the guru's grace, can bestow that!

Amma says the world drags us outside. However, attachment to the guru helps us detach from the world. Higher love gives us the strength to detach from lower forms of love.

May our love not be solely for the external, but for the internal Amma — our real nature! With the deepest gratitude, I pray that we can move forward on the path with the strength of that love.

22

The Essence of Motherhood Is Love

Marieke Engelbregt – Netherlands

Mother, do you remember the first time you made me aware of your all-pervading being and motherhood? For years I was dreaming about the beauty of Mount Shasta in California, and I had a deep desire to go there. After a long time, I went together with my husband and children. The day we arrived we went for a swim at Lake Siskiyou.

I was full of devotion for the lake and the mountain. Although my husband and children jumped in at once, I was standing on the side looking at the beautiful lake and crying. Step-by-step, I went into the lake and lay floating on my back. Then I saw your face! You cradled me and I felt your hands as you held me like a baby while softly speaking to me. Tears fell down my cheeks and I felt your kind, warm, and tender hands wiping them away.

You gave me this clear vision, and I felt so much sorrow when you disappeared. I had no clue who you were. We went to the local health food store, and there I saw your picture hanging on the wall. I started crying again. It was an invitation to the local satsang group, and we decided to go there. It felt like I had found a new home. During the potluck, my husband and children felt the loving grace we received, and they spontaneously became Amma-lovers as well.

A devotee shared with us, "Amma visited Mount Shasta once many years ago during her first U.S. Tour. She saw Lord Śhiva on the mountain and also went to Lake Siskiyou where she blessed the lake." It was in this very same lake that you bestowed your vision upon me.

Mother, your love is ever-revealing, ever-present and shining. With your will and saṅkalpa, you brought me to your path of learning how to be a humble and selfless servant of the world. I admit that it isn't always easy to teach me — but over the years I have learned, and I keep on learning.

Back in the Netherlands, we had our first darśhan and we were overwhelmed by so much love. At first I was a bit scared thinking, "So many people! How do I escape from this crowd?" But you did not let me escape, Mother. I came back again and again to receive your darśhan with friends, my brothers, my mother, and even my mother-in-law. Because of this my life became easier.

I had been ill for a long time and you recognized it. I could barely eat any food and my digestive system was not working well. The very first time I was seated near you, you continuously sent prasād, blessed food, for all the devotees seated on the stage. Prasād and more prasād, and as ignorant as I was, at first I rejected it. A devotee told me that I should really receive it since it had been blessed by your hands. It was amazing to eat pieces of cookies and cake, and incredibly, I had not even the slightest bit of pain in my stomach afterwards.

Once, when you arrived at the venue in the Netherlands, you gave some little cookies to all the devotees. I was not in front and was just waiting, not expecting anything. In a split moment you turned around, took some steps, and looking me in my eyes, gave me a chocolate. I felt so grateful and blessed — it was the first time in years that I ate chocolate. The whole three days of the program, I felt the strength of your blessing from that prasād.

Mother, do you remember the time when I was feeling so desperate and sad? I went out in nature and I cried and cried. At that moment, you appeared to me as a little bird. You came and sat gently on my head. I knew without a doubt that it was you. In that moment you took all my pain and obstacles away, and I happily returned home.

***

For me, sēvā has changed my life more than I could have ever imagined possible. I used to meditate, but I discovered that meditation alone is not enough to cultivate the qualities of universal motherhood.

My first sēvā was to walk around the program with a sign that said, "Are you willing to do sēvā? People needed to do dishes." At first I felt a bit ashamed walking with this sign through the hall. However, at the same time, I could feel a tremendous love flowing through my body. I wondered, "How can this feeling come from only walking around with this sign? I wonder what other sēvās I can do?" So I started to do as many sēvās as possible, and was just so happy to serve anyone during the program.

Your sēvā allowed me to be on my knees, sweating as I prepared your path. You blessed me with the sēvās of cleaning the floor, sewing, vacuuming, cleaning up litter, washing dishes, tidying up shoes, and gathering flowers. I could always perform these tasks with pleasure and ease. This was in contrast to my chores at home, where I often felt so tired due to Lyme disease. However, after these sēvā experiences my desire for life returned.

While doing sēvā, I was always a bit shy and withdrawn, until I went on a spontaneous trip to San Ramon, California. My friend Peter and I flew to the U.S., and we arrived at the āśhram as the program was just about to start. As always, Amma had a plan and we were only puppets.

We were driving our car to the parking lot when we noticed a woman waving her hand. We promptly stopped the car. "Do you already have a sēvā?" she asked us. "No, but we want to do as much sēvā as we can!" we replied, knowing the immense inner strength and love that comes from Amma while serving. "Okay, do you want to coordinate the new bag-check area?" she asked. "Your duty would be to keep the devotee's items safe until they leave the program. The storage tent must be opened at 8 a.m. in the morning till half an hour after Amma leaves the hall at night." We looked at each other and replied, "Okay!"

We had never had a sēvā with so much responsibility, and we really didn't know how to manage it. We spent hours and hours in that tent below the temple, a bit far away from you, Amma. We sat there through the cold nights, but our hearts were full of devotion, and we received all the necessary help we needed. We learned to feel your presence inside our hearts, and to become more independent of our likes and dislikes.

On the last night just before the Dēvī Bhāva program began, it was extremely busy and both halls were super crowded. I thought I would stay in our storage tent and wait until the crowd lessened. However, you found me there, Amma! A couple of minutes before the program started, the woman who gave us the sēvā looked around the corner of the tent and saw me. She insisted that I should be at the pūjā and she had already reserved a chair for me.

The pūjā was amazing, but when I finally got the blessed holy water in my hands, I totally forgot about my sēvā! I was in awe, and I could only think about where to store the holy water to bring it home safely. I brought the holy water to our car which was at least half a mile away. When I returned to my sēvā, only then did I understand how my action had affected the other sevites who were overwhelmed with the busy crowd. It was a lesson for me to remain aware of others' needs.

After a week with very little sleep, I flew home. On the plane, I asked the flight attendant to please not disturb me with food and drinks. She looked at me with compassion, and it felt as if I could see you, Amma, in her eyes. She asked me why I was so tired, and I explained that I had volunteered the entire week. She responded, "Ah, come with me, I will give you another seat." She gave me her own seat where I could recline fully and lie down! I felt so blessed, Amma! I fell asleep and woke up eight hours later as the plane was landing. My husband and children were waiting at the airport, and as I was fully rested, I could happily embrace them and share your loving spirit, Amma!

***

It was about one month later when Peter and I were asked to coordinate the security sēvā for Amma's upcoming program in the Netherlands. We laughed. Why would anyone ask us to do security sēvā? Me, who was always meditating and wandering around in nature, and Peter, the embodiment of innocence himself.

We prayed for help because this task seemed beyond our capabilities. The only way we could survive this huge sēvā was to ask for Amma's help. We first thought, "Amma needs us to do security!" but we soon found out — we need Amma to do security! By her grace, we met exactly the right people at the right times, and it was also amazing that I knew about technical drawings which had to be included for the security and access plan we had to submit for approval to the municipality. I finally understood why I had graduated from Mechanical Engineering and Business Management. I needed to put to use all the skills I had thrown away about twenty years earlier. Amma helped me to see my likes and dislikes shriveling away in my mind. With every step in that sēvā, I felt so much joy and understanding.

Once, we attended the program in Germany, and my two sons joined us for darśhan. When we first arrived, a devotee came to ask my eldest son to do sēvā at the Indian snacks canteen. He immediately joined this sēvā and was so happy. For a year, he had been having such a hard time — he had lost a friend and felt adrift in life. Only two days after returning home, he found a job in a nearby restaurant. Since then, he has worked in restaurants and still works as a cook. Thank you Mother, for being the mother of my children as well.

I have learned so much through sēvā and I realize that I could never have done this without your love, support, and inspiration. Mother, it is you who inspired me to start a foundation to plant trees and clean up litter in nature. The idea for it came after fires had destroyed more than 270 acres of healthy trees in the dunes near my village. Although I often felt your hands on my shoulders in setting up this foundation, it took years before we would actually be able to plant any trees.

When I asked you about the obstacles we were facing, you said, "What is within you is the same as what you see in the world outside." I needed to contemplate this for a long time, until I finally understood at least a spark of the inner meaning of this advice. With hundreds of children and adults we planted 1,800 trees, and since then we continue to plant. Mother, my wish is that we, as your children, may plant thousands of trees in the future.

***

One day during your tour in Germany, I had a question and you gave me the answer, "Satsang, satsang, bhajans, bhajans,

bhajans. Satsang at your home." I was a bit astonished and took a step backwards, but a brahmachāriṇī said, "Amma is waiting for your answer." So I replied, "Yes, Mother, I will do that for you."

So, I started a satsang group at my house to meet and sing bhajans. It took some time to build up the courage, but with the help of my Amma friends in the Netherlands and at Mount Shasta, I was able to start. I often sang Amma's new Dutch bhajan, *Liefde voor God* ('Love for God'):

Love for God, our true nature,
infinite awareness, a heart so pure
Thoughts obstruct, as a cloud before the sun,
The radiant light, the inner Source.

Amma, help me to trust that the 'I' will dissolve
So the path opens to the eternal All.

How much longer the struggle between head and heart,
Bend and watch until the mind has untangled.
Let silence speak and see who you are,
The task in life, to know the Self.

Only with God's grace, the unity will return,
On the path to Truth, you are the bridge.

Amma, Amma, Amma, Amma.

About two years ago, I felt that I should really come to visit Amritapuri. I had never had that wish before and was a bit doubtful. I had been worrying if my nerves were strong enough for such a long trip to India. While my husband encouraged me to go, I denied Amma's inner call, and decided to postpone my visit. I made a mistake, because some weeks later the Covid lockdown started. I became ill again due to all the stress, and

I did not feel my strength and deeper focus for months. It was a difficult period.

I prayed and meditated to deepen and feel my connection with Amma. While I was longing to come to Amritapuri, I often listened to the recording of Amma's sweet loving voice saying, "My darling children, my darling children, please be very careful. It is a bad time for the world, but this will pass by. Never lose confidence and courage! Amma prays for all her children."

Finally, my time to come to Amritapuri arrived, and I was filled with so much gratitude. I immediately felt the pure vibrations, and saw the loving, kind smiles on everyone's faces. It's a place on Earth that truly resembles paradise.

For my sēvā, I was supposed to bring lunch and prepare hydration drinks for an āśhram resident named Purnima. On my first Tuesday, the day Amma serves everyone a blessed prasād meal, I forgot to help Purnima. Later I thought, "Purnima will also be having a prasād meal from Amma, so I don't have to hurry."

I wrote Purnima a short message, "Should I help you today? I might have forgotten, please call me if you need anything!" But as soon as I had written the message, I went on the stage to be with Amma and stayed there for hours. Only when I left the stage, I remembered my message to Purnima. I looked at my phone and saw that she had not answered. "Well, she is probably fine," I thought.

I went to sleep, but there was a little voice inside saying, "I did something wrong. Purnima is in a wheelchair and what if she didn't have something to drink?" I fell asleep feeling guilty. In the middle of the night, I awoke feeling nervous. I thought, "There is only one thing to do — I should go take a look." I put on my clothes and went down the stairs.

I knocked on her door very softly and immediately heard her voice, "Marieke, is it you?" I opened the door and she looked at me in surprise and asked, "Are you a nightwalker?" "No, no!" I replied and kneeled in front of her bed, "Purnima, I am so happy that you are alive!"

"Have you come to tell me that? Now? What time is it, Marieke?" "It is 2 a.m. Purnima. I am so sorry I did not make your drinks today... I thought I better take a look." Purnima laughed and said, "Don't worry, I have someone else to help me on Tuesdays." She had also been doing sēvā, so she had seen my message only later. Purnima took my hand and we could not stop laughing together.

Mother, I feel so grateful that you allowed me to come to Amritapuri, to your abode of love and light. Gratitude for all the insights, for the peaceful stillness of my mind and for deepening the essence of compassion and motherhood within me. The way you teach us, and the essence of what you teach, Amma, is motherhood. For you, love is the very breath of life.

This world needs Your loving kindness, your warmth, your inner strength, compassion, and pure wisdom more than ever before. There are so many who are longing to see you. As your children in this world, there might not be much that we can offer. But you have told us, "When many small streams come together, they form a great river, and the river will return to the infinite ocean." Mother, let us realize that no matter how long it will take, we will each return to you — and merge in your infinite being.

23

Sākṣhī – The Witness

Dr. Chakravarthy - India

Amma came to Mangalore for a two-day program in January 2016. At that time, I was doing sēvā at AIMS Hospital Kochi, serving as an internal medicine consultant. I saw an opportunity to be with Amma in Mangalore and therefore volunteered to attend a conference in nearby Bangalore. Though the conference was scheduled for a Monday, I left early to participate in Amma's program on Saturday and Sunday.

On the first night of the program just before I went to the stage, my wife Sirisha called and told me that my boss was unhappy with me for leaving early. So the whole time I was on stage, I was completely preoccupied with thoughts of justifying my actions, that too with "Amma's teachings." If I were to share all that went on in my mind this satsang would never end.

The next day, Swami Ramakrishnananda saw me and mentioned, "Go spend some time with Amma on stage." This triggered one thought, "Why did I come this far? To be in the presence of Amma or to be caught in the quagmire of my mind?" I went to the stage and started watching my mind. After some time, my mind became completely silent, and I simply sat, watching that silence.

Amma the All-knowing, who never bothered to look at me the first day, suddenly looked at me and called me to her – at that very moment when I was a witness to myself. It was then that Amma gave me the most beautiful gift of my life – the entry ticket to stay in the āśhram. It was one of my most memorable experiences with Amma.

A long time ago, Sirisha told Amma, "I am having too many thoughts." Amma asked her, "Do you know your thoughts?" Sirisha replied, "Yes." Amma then responded, "Then it's okay. As long as you are watching your thoughts, you are fine."

So who is the one who witnesses the thoughts? The Vēdāntic approach to discovering this is somewhat similar to modern research or a scientific inquiry:

1. Pramāṇam — What do the experts in the field say about this? Here, the experts are our ancient ṛiṣhis whose words form the scriptures, as well as the teachings of our own guru, Amma.
2. Yukti (or logic) — Here, logic does not refer to vain arguments, but rather an introverted contemplation based on pramāṇam, the truths expounded by the masters.
3. Sva-anubhavam — Our own personal experience.

To go deeper into the topic, let us consider this potent verse from the *Kēna Upaniṣhad:*

> *śhrōtasya śhrōtaṁ manasō manō yad*
> *vāchō ha vāchaṁ sa u prāṇasya prāṇaḥ*
> *chakṣhuṣhaśhchakṣhuratimuchya dhīrāḥ*
> *prētyāsmāllōkādamṛitā bhavanti*
>
> It is the ear of the ear, the mind of the mind, the speech of the speech, the life of the life, and the eye of the eye. Knowing this, the wise, having relinquished all false identifications of the self with the senses, become immortal. (1.2)

This is a very profound śhlōka that expounds about sākṣhī (the witness), the qualification of the disciple, and the fruit of the recognition, all packed into one.

We all know that sensations and perceptions constantly change; similarly, the feelings and emotions of the mind are in constant flux. However, there is a constant awareness that is conscious of all these changes. Amma simply puts it as the unmoving stage on which all the drama is enacted.

Because we have been conditioned by the world since birth and have grown up in the clutches of material science, we tend to objectify even ātmā (the pure consciousness) or sākṣhī (the witness consciousness). In the above śhlōka it is shown that sākṣhī is different from the ear, eye, speech, prāṇa, and mind. It does not mean that there is another ear for the ear. It is expressed in this way so that the questioner does not identify this sākṣhī within the body-mind complex, or as some light inside the heart, or with a superhuman figure. Another question might arise — isn't it the mind that is watching the mind? Yes, sometimes it is and that's what we call introspection. This doubt can be cleared by asking whether there can be two thoughts at the same time. However, this is impossible. If you think "I am witnessing," that itself becomes another thought. This tells us that the sākṣhī is beyond the mind, that is why it is referred to as 'the mind of the mind.' In other words, witnessing occurs in the state even before you utter the words "I am."

Avidyā is ignorance of our true nature as the Witness Consciousness which is pūrṇatvam — ever-full and inherently blissful. This ignorance gives rise to desires and consequently, the actions based on them. The karma phalam or results of these actions lead to the repeated cycle of birth and death.

Amma once asked me to explain the meaning of kāmākṣhī, karmasākṣhī, mīnākṣhī, and sarvasākṣhī.

Kāmākṣhī is the witness of all our desires, and karmasākṣhī is the witness of all actions. Understanding that our true nature is kāmākṣhī and karmasākṣhī reveals that we are separate from desires and actions. For sākṣhī, there are no desires and actions, dispelling the misconception of our claims of doership and enjoyership.

A similar teaching was given by Sage Aṣhṭāvakra to King Janaka:

> *na tvaṃ dēhō na tē dēhō bhōktā kartā na vā bhavān*
> *chidrūpō'si sadā sākṣhī nirapēkṣhaḥ sukhaṃ chara*
>
> Neither are you this body, nor is this body yours; you are not the doer of actions or the one who bears their results. You are consciousness, the eternal witness, and without desires — so remain blissful.

Aṣhṭāvakra Gītā, 15.4

Mīnākṣhī refers to eyes that are like fish eyes. The eyes of fish have no eyelids, they are always open. This signifies that the sākṣhī is ever present in all three states of consciousness: waking, dreaming, and sleeping. It infers that the sākṣhī is timeless, existing before birth and persisting after death, serving as a witness to the apparent cycle of birth and death. Just as a fish's eyes remain unaffected by the saltwater of the ocean, the sākṣhī remains untouched by the joys and sorrows of the vast sea of saṁsāra.

Sarvasākṣhī is the witness that sees everything. Sarvasākṣhī is said to remove the misconception that there is a different witness in each individual jīva, and to point out that the sākṣhī in you is the sākṣhī in all.

***

Now we come to the second part of the verse from the *Kēna Upaniṣhad* which speaks about the qualification for experiencing sākṣhī and the fruit of this recognition. We shall discuss each phrase.

prētya asmāt lōkāt — withdraw from this world by leaving behind the ideas of 'I' and 'mine'.

Renunciation was a foreign concept to me when I first met Amma. Even though the darśhan hall resonated with the chants of the senior swāmīs — "tyāgēnaikē amṛitatvamānaśhuḥ" — the significance, "by renunciation alone, one gains immortality," took time to resonate within me.

I was still married to my profession, possessions, family, body, mind, and ego, and lacked the basic qualifications needed for embarking on a spiritual path. However, nothing is impossible with Amma's love and compassion.

Each darśhan, Amma's satsangs, the *Awaken Children* books, talks by senior swāmīs, and the satsangs by Swami Paramatmananda Puri that took over my car stereo during my long commutes to work, slowly instilled dispassion in me and a thirst for something higher. Allow me to briefly share some of the key insights Amma has revealed to me that have reshaped my outlook on life since meeting her.

Before we met Amma, we were devotees of Sri Shirdi Sai Baba, and we associated with the only Sai Baba temple in the U.S. during that time. Unknowingly, Amma was sowing the seeds of devotion and a longing for a guru. I first physically met Amma in June 2006 in San Ramon, a few years after I started my medical practice in internal medicine. It was a Dēvī Bhāva day, and before I came to my senses I was in Amma's embrace and had received my mantra. I would not put it as love at first sight. However, with each of Amma's darśhans, love slowly started stirring within me. I would like to share some of the qualities that this love has awakened in me.

Non-complaining. Even though I was making a decent six-figure salary, I would often complain if there were a few more patients added to my list at the end of the day. After seeing Amma calling for more people at the end of every long darśhan, and making sure that no one would leave without receiving her embrace, I stopped some of my complaining.

Compassion towards repeat offenders. Unfortunately, a lot of people become ill due to addictions to substances such as tobacco, alcohol or drugs, or even to unhealthy diet and exercise habits. Generally, physicians tend to get upset or start ignoring such people when they keep returning to the hospital for readmissions. I was no exception. However, after experiencing how Amma showers me with her unconditional love without vexation, despite me returning to her without practicing any of her teachings, I tried to emulate a small part of that attitude towards my patients. I slowly noticed that compassion flows when we don't have preconceived notions and accept people and things as they are. That is when we can appreciate the one underlying substratum.

Childlike innocence. Once, I asked Amma which charitable program to donate to. At that time Amma answered, "Amma doesn't need your money. Amma only wants your childlike innocence." This happened to be my very first conversation with Amma. This answer got etched into my mind. Since then I have been searching for the meaning of childlike innocence. As Amma's words always come true, my childlike love and longing for Amma kept increasing. Gradually I started feeling choked in my material comforts after Amma's visit to the U.S.

Contentment. Finally, I learnt that there is no limit to filling "my begging bowl made of a human skull"[29] — I slowly

---

[29] Amma tells the story of a beggar who goes to the king with his bowl and asks him to fill it. The bowl remains empty even after the king

started making plans to be with Amma. We started by moving near the San Ramon āśhram in California and downsizing to a small condo. We only lasted there for a year before we moved to Amritapuri, and ever since then we have been content with a simple life in service of humanity.

***

Now let us return to the analysis of the *Kēna Upaniṣhad* verse used for contemplation. The first step in developing dispassion is to observe the nature of the world and to ask ourselves, "Is there any such thing as permanent happiness in this world?" Before moving to India, a number of experiences and life lessons started to awaken dispassion in me.

One morning, upon arriving at the office, I discovered that I, along with a few colleagues, was involved in a lawsuit. It wasn't easy for me to digest this news, especially considering I was just starting out in my career and the team had only acted in the best interest of the patient. I was upset, resentful, and angry with the petitioners. However, with Amma's grace, I learned valuable lessons that ultimately helped me develop dispassion.

I began contemplating who determines the results of our actions and how. As physicians, we get ample opportunities to reflect on this deeply. For instance, the patient whom we thought would not make it out of the hospital, goes home completely recovered. In contrast, at times we learn that the patient we had planned to discharge the next day, passed away the night before. Often we see chain smokers and heavy alcoholics get away with mild illnesses, while others succumb to untreatable chronic diseases or cancer. We witness some

---

empties his entire treasury into it. Finally, the beggar reveals that his begging bowl is a human skull and its desires are insatiable.

children born with congenital malformations whereas others are born as prodigies.

Contemplating all this, I slowly started realizing that we only have the power to act but no control over the result. This understanding helped me attenuate the notions of doership and enjoyership. I also started to think about how to get out of this vicious cycle of karma, the cycle of cause and effect.

These contemplations increased my awareness and I also started practicing seeing Amma in all the patients that I treated. My work provided an opportunity to develop surrender to the guru and love for Amma, essential qualities needed for a disciple.

By Amma's grace, the case was settled without any impact on my professional or financial growth. Amma who is 'bhukti-mukti-pradāyinī,' the bestower of both material and spiritual wealth, continued to bless me with exponential growth in my professional and financial career, along with helping me cultivate dispassion for the same. Amma was teaching me the transient nature of power and money, and that there is no permanent happiness in the world.

Amma once said to all the householder devotees, "Don't think you are the ones taking care of your children. Amma is the one who is taking care of all the children." Once, when I was traveling alone with our two kids on a U.S. tour, Amma beautifully demonstrated this with a simple and loving gesture. A cold drizzle had started during a chai stop along the road, and Amma personally took the time to dry our son Sai's hair with her sari, and safely brought him to the tour bus. Yet, despite all this the mind quickly returns to its strong attachments.

After our entry ticket to the āśhram, my wife and I would commute daily to AIMS for sēvā. We went early in the morning and returned almost by the end of bhajans to get a glimpse of

Amma. One darśhan night after returning from AIMS, I was standing behind Amma. She suddenly turned towards me and said in a concerned tone, “You don’t need to travel daily; you can stay back at AIMS some days.” I responded, “Amma, the kids are by themselves here.” Amma replied in a serious tone, “Then take the kids also and stay only at AIMS.” Luckily, I saved myself by replying, “I actually come back to see Amma every day.” I had forgotten for a moment that Amma is the one who is always taking care of the children.

atimuchya – giving up identification with the body, mind and senses.

In one of Amma’s satsangs, she pointed out that in reality there are no sinners. If at all there is any sin, it is the attitude of considering ourselves as this body, mind, and intellect. Amma always says we continue to carry the load on our head even after getting on a train. The load that Amma is pointing to is the illusory idea that, “I am this body, mind, and intellect.” On identification with this illusion, we carry out all activities and experience transient happiness and suffering from the results of our actions. We continue in this vicious cycle until a guru compassionately tells us to unburden this load. This unburdening happens when the illusion of superimposition is recognized, and we remain established in our true self.

I remember an incident when Amma reminded me of this fact. The first time I participated in Amma’s U.S. tour, I was only able to do the first half. Sirisha joined to do the rest of the tour along with the children, and when I was leaving Amma asked me, “Are you sad?” I nodded in agreement. Then Amma sang a beautiful old Malayalam movie song, *Ōriṭattu Jananam Ōriṭattu Maraṇam* (‘Cycle of Birth and Death’):

ōriṭattu jananam ōriṭattu maraṇam
chumalil jīvita bhāram
vazhiyaṛiyātē muṭanti naṭakkum
vidhiyuṭē bali mṛigaṅṅaḷ — nammaḷ

We go through the cycle of birth and death.
We shoulder the responsibilities of life and
blindly walk in an unknown path
thinking it is our fate.

Like the caterpillar, we weave a cocoon around ourselves and are thus unable to see the truth. Amma with her love and patience helps us to break open our own cocoon, awakening us to the truth within. Through her love we are transformed into the beautiful butterfly of a fully liberated soul.

amṛitāḥ bhavanti — one who recognizes his true nature along with the limitation of body, mind, and senses becomes immortal.

Recently I wasn't feeling well, and Sirisha went to inform Amma. Upon further inquiry, Amma explained that I had inherited a health problem from my birth mother, who herself has a similar undiagnosed condition. Contemplating Amma's words I thought, "If I inherited some genes from my parents, what did I inherit from my real mother? I must have inherited amṛitam and ānandam." We are the children of Mātā Amṛitānandamayī — children of immortal bliss — and not this mass of flesh and blood. How wonderful it is to know that we are already that by being Amma's children.

In *Awaken Children Volume 5*, Amma says, "Sākṣhī is like a screen. A screen neither projects the play nor does it enjoy the play. It is simply the underlying ground on which the action of the play takes place. It simply is." Amma further adds, "The sage centered in the self realizes, 'I do nothing at all.' Though seeing, hearing, touching, smelling, eating, walking, emptying, sleeping, holding, opening and closing the eyes, he is assured that only the senses are occupied with their objects."

What words does Amma use to describe the nature of sākṣhī?

silent — *aśhabdam, niśhabdam*
motionless — *achalam, niśhchalam*
innocent — *niṣhkalaṅkam*
all-pervasive — *sarva-vyāpakam*
calm — *praśhāntam*
serene — *suprasannam*
full — *pūrṇam*
divine bliss — *ānandam*
love — *prēmam*
peace — *śhāntam*
contentment — *santuṣhṭi*
pure — *nirañjanam*
empty (devoid of objectivity) — *śhūnyam*
untainted — *nirāmayam*
subtle — *sūkṣmam*
consciousness — *svayam-prakāśham*
the source of breath – inhalation and expiration, and the silence between these two

These words sound familiar, don't they? They are all part of our daily Mā-Ōm Meditation. Amma teaches the highest principles and introduces us to our true nature through this simple meditation technique. As the saying goes, 'yad bhāvayati tad bhavati — you become what you think or imagine.' Since these words are spoken by Amma, a satguru, they will inevitably come true, now or later.

What is the benefit of practicing sākṣhī bhāva? The attitude of being a witness helps us cultivate acceptance toward various situations in life. It enables us to develop equanimity, preventing us from becoming overly elated or depressed as we face the ups and downs of life. Brooding, anguish, guilt, and fear all decrease, and we start to learn how to remain in our inner center, our real home. Acceptance of the situations gives us the ability to stand back and enjoy all the challenges life throws at us.

Once, a disciple came to his guru and told him, "Guruji, I am feeling miserable, and I want to end my life." The guru inquired, "Are you aware of your suffering?" The disciple replied, "Yes, I know I am miserable; I feel it. That's why I have come to you." The guru continued, "If you know you are suffering, you are the knower of it, and thus apart from it." The disciple was convinced and started contemplating what the guru had told him. He met the guru again after a few years and said, "Guruji, now I am very peaceful and happy." The guru quickly responded, "You are not peaceful; you are the knower of peace in your mind."

Amma, our compassionate guru, is also freeing us from suffering by reminding us to become aware of our true nature as sākṣhī — the eternal witness. I pray to Amma that with her blessings we all will be able to become established in sākṣhī, our real home.

24

Love Letter to My Mother

Kuvalaya Nayana - Chile

Sometimes life presents us with an opportunity only once. When Amma gives us a chance to sit by her side and open our hearts, we should not let it pass us by. I sincerely feel that we should have the courage to open our hearts. As Amma always reminds us, "The language we need to learn is the language of love." It is due to this love that I could awaken my courage.

I feel like a beginner on the spiritual path and do not have any deep knowledge of scriptures. For this reason, I do not think that this qualifies as a satsang in the traditional sense, but rather it is a love letter — like the ones which you wrote to your mother when you were a child:

Dear Divine Mother,

Before I met you, I had never bowed down before anyone — only nature. My ignorance did not allow me to worship God in a human form. I was born in a culture which never spoke of God's greatness and various manifestations, and I never studied scriptures or practiced sincere forms of worship. Nature was God for me — and my only refuge. Dear Mother, you revealed yourself to me in the forests I roamed, in the oceans, and through various animals.

Amma, the trees were your arms that would hug me when I needed comfort. When I was little, if I felt anger or sadness I would run outside my house to a big avocado tree which grew in our garden. I would climb as high as I could and stay there, crying and talking to the tree. Now I know, the looks I received from many animals were your looks. You took it upon yourself to look at me and take care of me through your creation.

Amma, as you well know, the sea has given me many beautiful moments. When I am submerged in the ocean, I feel aware that my body is one with the water. Everything is different — colors, textures, and even sounds. It is easier to hear my breathing and the beating of my heart. Many times, I had the sensation of being observed by a presence I could not see. I felt afraid because my mind could not grasp this new experience. In fact, it is much like what I feel when I surrender to you — to God. Many times, I am afraid to dive in and take the plunge. I am afraid of losing control and experiencing something apparently separate from me.

***

In February of 2017, I was in the middle of the Pacific ocean on the volcanic island of Rapa Nui when I received a call from my friends Ramadatt and Akhila from Amritapuri. They were super excited, saying, "You won't believe what just happened!" Akhila had gone for your darśhan, Amma, and had brought her phone to show you a picture for blessing. While Akhila was in your arms, you began to scroll through other pictures on the phone. Suddenly, you found what you were looking for and kept the screen there on one particular photo. After finishing her darśhan a brahmachāriṇī came up to Akhila, gave her the phone and showed her which picture you had found and blessed. To Ramadatt's and Akhila's surprise, the photo that you found was a photo of me!

I had no idea who you were and definitely didn't understand the significance of receiving your darśhan and blessing through the photo. At that moment, I wasn't able to understand the deeper meaning, and how much you would completely change my life. I was oblivious to the truth that their phone call that day would be the beginning of my story with you.

That same year, Ramadatt returned to Chile and gave me an archana book and a rudrākṣha mālā that you blessed. As he put the mālā around my neck, I felt an energy circulating through my whole body. It felt so wonderful that I asked him if he was going back to India because I wanted to meet this saint. That is how in December that year, I traveled 18,000 kilometers from Chile to see you with my very own eyes. I arrived in Amritapuri and was immediately struck by your arrow of love. From that moment onwards, you became the most important thing in my life — you were what I had been searching for in the depths of my being.

In reality, I feel that we are all eternal seekers of the Divine Mother. You have us completely captivated, but we don't know it. Consciously or unconsciously, we live life after life looking for your love. We look for it in different names and forms thinking these will someday bring us inner peace. Living in this way, we ignore that our lives will continue being emotionally empty if we don't seek shelter in God. It is this constant searching that leaves us with the feeling that something is missing within. We all have the great need to feel you, Mother — dancing in our hearts.

How is it possible to long for something or someone unless we have had an experience of it? I feel that, no matter where we have come from, we have all tasted your love before, and that is why we are born with the need to feel that unique, great love again. The love that only you can give us.

Infinite are the blessings that your children receive, and we may not even be conscious of them! Mother, I sometimes wonder why you do not allow us to remember all that we had to undergo in past lives to reach you in this human birth? If we could remember, we could begin to appreciate every second in your holy presence.

Mother, you tell us that when we take one step towards God, God will take one hundred steps towards us. Well my first conscious step in this life was to take three plane rides from one end of the earth to the other to reach you. It was not such a wonder that I made this long journey, since so many of your children will follow you to any corner of the world. What made this moment so magical was that I made the journey without having met you. The strength of that impulse was so great that I never stopped to ponder the fact that I was crossing the entire world just to meet you.

Was it really me who traveled to your arms? Or was it you Amma, who brought me to you? You found my photo and you blessed my mālā. Through these acts, you definitely created the desire in me to meet you. They say that in this Kali Yuga, the guru has to go looking for his devotees and disciples, and not the other way around. Mother, with your divine will you have created the perfect situations for each of us to meet you and have the great blessing to be with you – the Divine Mother incarnate.

I perfectly remember how I felt as I got out of the taxi for the first time. As I stepped on the sacred land on which you were born and which has seen you grow – my main feeling was fear. Fear of what? I have no idea. Maybe my mind was afraid of the great changes and challenges I somehow knew lay ahead, and that everything I had given importance to before would collapse with miraculous ease.

It is only the thought of having lived twenty-five years without knowing you that causes me pain. Only you know the right moment to call us to your arms. I take solace in this thought because I cry when I see early videos of the āśhram and your grand fiftieth and sixtieth birthday celebrations. I don't feel any jealousy towards my brothers and sisters who had the great fortune to be born and grow in your presence. Rather, I really love hearing their experiences with you and I feel them as my own. That is one of the superpowers that a mahātmā has. No matter where your children are, by talking about you and remembering moments by your side, immediately the atmosphere is filled with your presence.

Amma, in 2007 you visited Chile and you never told me! You gave darśhan to thousands of people and I was not one amongst them! Again, I take solace in the faith that only you know what is best for me. You know when and how. I'm here now in your physical presence, and I can only say thank you. I sincerely thank you Amma, because you brought me to your motherly embrace in this lifetime. I thank you for the endless opportunities and your great compassion. I thank you for letting me feel something deeper in my life.

Let me feel
Mother Goddess
let me feel the loving love beat of your heart.
How could I find
that experience of God
which can only be bestowed by your will.
How could I imagine or visualize
something that only through surrender
you make me experience.
Oh beloved Mother!
How could I prolong
something that only you can give me.
How can this daughter of yours look for something
that only with patience you show us.
When all that remains is to contemplate,

give me the ability to love.
To love and forget about myself
to remain in you.

***

Mother, you know I always felt a great love for nature and cared for nature as she cared for me. I liked to imagine living in a jungle, hunting and foraging for fruits in the trees. This same strong feeling also produced the opposite feeling of anger towards humanity for all the destruction we have caused.

I became intolerant and would judge and criticize people. As an adolescent, I observed many injustices in the world around me. I disliked when people told me what to say or do. That rebellious feeling of independence separated me from my inner peace and silence for several years. I began to have problems at school, with my family and friends, and before I knew it my inner world had changed. Amma, how true it is when you say that we see the world based on our mind's thoughts.

During that time, when I was fourteen years old, my father was diagnosed with a very rare disease. Unfortunately this caused me to feel even more disconnected from my own being. I watched my father getting worse every year, even as my mother dedicated many years of her life to caring for him. This should have awakened feelings of compassion in me, but instead I blamed my father for taking so much of my mother's time and energy. Now I seek forgiveness for not being able to understand the situation in the right way — for not opening my heart and giving him more care all those years. Often, I felt guilty that I didn't take care of my father and show him more attention.

In retrospect, I now know that running away from situations will never bring us peace. However, I didn't know this then because I didn't have you to guide me. You know how I escaped my feelings by trying to stimulate my senses to evade pain. Now that I have you beside me, as an example of how to live in service to others, I am able to recognize my birth mother's spiritual qualities. From deep within I feel called to bow before her. Although she never considered herself to be spiritual, she is a woman with many divine qualities. Thank you Amma, for entrusting such a wonderful woman to care for this daughter, and for giving me the discernment to appreciate her qualities. Thank you for giving me the ability to look into the past and understand situations in the light of truth that only your words and presence can give me.

Amma, you constantly repeat how we should never blame others for our circumstances and how we should remove our own weaknesses. You always tell us that when difficulties arise, we should never run away from them in fear. Instead, we should light the lamp of love and faith within and overcome our problems.

For reasons that only you know Amma, I was present at the exact moment when my father died. He was lying on a stretcher in the hospital with very low vital signs and I was standing in front of him. I saw how in an instant, his whole body became rigid. I remember that he tensed all his facial muscles for a few seconds, and then a great silence descended and his whole body relaxed completely. I immediately knew in that precise moment that his soul had departed the body.

This experience was not traumatic for me. On the contrary, it was a great blessing. I was able to see and feel how my father tried to hang on to the last vestiges of his life before dying. This clearly showed me how we are mistakenly identified with the body, and how we fear the moment we have to leave it.

This was one of the many ways in which you, my Divine Mother showed me that you are always with us. We just have to stop and feel how you guide us through different situations, wiping our tears and taking us by the hand. We have to understand that it is only you who teaches us through different people and situations.

It's amazing to see how you prepare us to deal with future situations. During the pandemic you gave us many topics to share our opinions on. Even though I didn't give a talk, I listened to every person's answers on how they applied the scriptures in their daily lives. I listened to how you guided each person and corrected them. This prepared me to respond to questions from loved ones who had no experience of God's presence in their lives.

On my last trip to Chile, my friends and relatives kept asking me what I was doing in India, and who is Amma. I answered each one of them differently. I must say, I did repeat one answer to more than one person. That answer was — love! "Love?" they asked. "Yes, love!" I would reply. "I am living with Amma in India because I am learning how to love — to love in such a way that I will become one with that love."

I don't know if this was the best response, but at least I was happy with it. I have to admit that in those moments, my unspoken response was something more like this: "How could I not be in India when the Divine Mother is there? She has incarnated in human form to reestablish dharma in the world and to elevate all of humanity towards the true goal of life. Where else should I go when all I need is to listen and be guided by my guru who truly knows what is best for me?"

However, we know that someone who is not a devotee might run away hearing these kinds of answers. Amma, you helped us to understand how to explain these ideas to people in ways they can relate to. The purpose of sharing with others the experiences we have lived with you, is so the person is able to feel, even for a second, a connection to something deeper. To awaken a feeling of your presence within them — to help them see a spark of God inside.

***

With your blessings Amma, I have been able to live with you these last three years in Amritapuri. I am taking the first baby steps — learning many things that are new to me. You have said we need to have the innocence of a child. I have found that many things about the āśhram make no logical sense to me. But instead of fighting to understand them, I simply learn to trust that they have some purpose of which I am clearly unaware. It may be months or years before I will understand the meaning of a certain situation I experienced. There are so many daily opportunities to imbibe these lessons, slowly dismantling the mental structures that dictate how I think things should be said or done. These preconceived notions blind my ability to feel your presence and grace in other people.

Amma, you teach me that no matter where we come from or how different we are from each other, we are united in our love for you — for God. I try to remember this daily because it helps me to have more understanding and patience, not only with my brothers and sisters, but also with myself. It helps me remember why I am here, and it is that feeling that invites me to smile and feel grateful. Our day can change completely if we just smile and feel grateful in all situations.

You know that during my first faltering steps on this spiritual path, I can be overtaken by sorrow and anger and forget to smile. That is the naked truth, and I don't have to dress it up in false pretense. You have to show me all the bad tendencies that I have held onto over many lifetimes so that I can surrender them to you.

I am learning to keep quiet and listen to my brothers and sisters who have spent their lives with you in their hearts. As you know Mother, it isn't easy for your children to learn how to listen. Our minds are constantly creating feelings and ideas about people based on our past experiences. But when I make the effort to truly listen, I become aware of all the noise in my head. It is extremely painful to become aware of the crashing waves, or rather tsunamis of our thoughts. It is only by your grace that we can observe them. In that moment of witnessing, we can invite you to calm those thoughts, and then we sink into your presence.

By your infinite compassion, I am slowly learning to go beyond my likes and dislikes. Amma, you know that I never liked to speak publicly. Yet in order to give a satsang in your divine presence, I had to make the effort to go beyond my limitations, my shame, and my fears, which are impediments on the spiritual path.

I am sure that you, our beloved Mother, will always smile and jump with joy when you see the first baby steps that your children take. I imagine you Amma, walking with us and guiding us towards the realization of the source of all love.

Amma, this is your prayer that I would like to share:

> *"May my children's eyes become tender with compassion. May your heads bow in humility. May your hands be ever engaged in selfless service. May your ears be ever willing to listen to the sorrows of the suffering. May your tongue speak words of truth and kindness. May your feet always walk the path of dharma. In this way, may the lives of my children become a blessing for the world."*

Mother, thank you for blessing us with your physical presence. I ask you to continue purifying our minds so that you can reside deep within our hearts. Allow us to behold you and serve you in all of your creation, and find refuge in you always. Bless us so we can happily offer you our entire being — that which belongs only to you.

25

"Everything Will Be Okay Now That You've Come."

Radhika Murali Mohan - USA

Once, there was a householder who lived in her guru's āśhram on top of a hill in a small hut. One day, a great loss occurred when one of the āśhram's beloved sisters passed away. The householder wanted to make an offering to honor the dear soul who had passed. So at the correct time, the householder tilled the land in front of her hut and cast seeds for two kinds of wildflowers. One type of flower was deep blue, which represented the guru. The other wildflower was bright yellow, which represented the departed soul.

The householder harvested the flowers and made a garland of alternating blue and yellow blossoms. With each flower placed in the garland she made a prayer, "May this soul merge into our beloved guru."

The householder placed the garland on her beloved guru's neck with the same prayer and left. The next day, an āśhram sister approached the householder and said, "I do not know what you were thinking when you made that garland, but our guru wore it for a long time, and even after it broke insisted on keeping it."

In this story, the beloved āśhram sister who passed away was our brahmachāriṇī Nirmalāmṛitājī, I am the householder, and indeed as you may have guessed — the guru is our most beloved Amma. This incident remains deeply etched in my mind, serving as a testament to the unfathomable depth of love that Amma has for each and every one of us. The kind of love that takes us to the goal. This was the first loss I experienced after joining the āśhram. For me, it was a poignant reminder of the impermanence of the body.

Amma says, "Worship nature as the visible form of God, and never forget that you too, are a part of the divine that has taken form on this earth." Amma also says, "Trees, plants, rivers, mountains, stars, humans, and animals, are like many multi-colored flowers in an immense divine garden." In this divine garden, Amma's children are her flowers, unfolding into their divine nature.

Amma says that if we try to forcefully open a bud, the whole flower is ruined and the fragrance lost. Whereas, by allowing the flower to open naturally, its fragrance will permeate the air. This can be compared to attuning to Amma's divine grace, which allows our hearts to open naturally like a flower and imbibe the nectar of divine love.

In our daily lives we flit around from one action to another like a bee flying from flower to flower. When the bee flies around the outside of the flower one can hear it humming, but once it lands and enters inside to drink the nectar it becomes still and quiet. Through the daily practice of attuning ourselves within, even during action, we slowly become internally still and quiet just like the bee drinking the flower's nectar. However, we need Amma's grace and continuous guidance to attain that state of stillness and bliss.

ananyāśh chintayantō māṁ yē janāḥ paryupāsatē
tēṣhāṁ nityābhiyuktānāṁ yōga-kṣhēmaṁ vahāmyaham

For those who always think of me, worship me, and are ever absorbed in me, I provide whatever they lack and preserve what they already possess.

Bhagavad Gītā, 9.22

In this śhlōka Kṛiṣhṇa says that the devotee must have one-pointed devotion and be constantly engaged in the worship of the Lord. We as Amma's children, are living in a unique and most fortunate time and place. Amma is giving us both the opportunity and the ability to develop single-pointed devotion, as well as so many experiences that transform our lives into a constant worship of the divine. She is the one who carries our burdens by providing for our needs. Most importantly, she is here to fulfill our ultimate need — the need that ends all needs — to merge in her holy feet!

Through our direct experiences with Amma we slowly attain this one-pointedness. Amma is the embodiment of all doctrines and the essence of all the scriptures. By watching her līlās or divine plays, we are able to gain a level of concentration that would otherwise take us lifetimes to achieve. With this concentration and Amma's grace, every action becomes a worship — an offering of our burdens at Amma's lotus feet. In true worship we offer our whole self to the divine, and through this surrender unfolds. When we surrender ourselves completely, all our needs are fulfilled by our Dēvī, Amma.

Amma says that when we offer each of our actions to the divine without concern for the fruits, these acts become sēvā — acts of selfless service. This state of remembrance in each moment tunes and focuses the mind and its thoughts. The mind starts to turn inward, creating a perfect environment for internal contemplation. Ultimately, our goal is to find Amma inside — to discover the self.

In my own personal journey of self-discovery, I know that Amma has had her work cut out for her, not only as a satguru but also as a mother. Meeting Amma has afforded me not only instruction on the spiritual path, but also the skills I have needed to navigate this external world. Amma has guided me patiently through trials and tribulations, counseled me, and given me unconditional love. She is holding my hand through this journey, and it is to her that I owe my life in its entirety.

***

I would like to share an experience which was a pivotal point in my acceptance of Amma as my guru. Here, Amma manifested the three qualities of a satguru — omniscience, omnipotence, and omnipresence — thus removing any doubt in my mind of her true nature.

This experience took place in Amritapuri in 1989. At that time, a small ferry boat was used to bring water to the āśhram in several fifty-gallon drums. Upon the boat's arrival, we would make an assembly line, and bucket by bucket, fill the āśhram tank. The small ferry boat made many trips back and forth and the process could take all night. We would all catch a few winks of sleep in between boat trips, and would awaken to what became my first two Malayalam words, "Vellam vannu!" — Water has come!

On one such night, it was close to dawn when we finished, and Amma served us all chai in a circle on the backwaters. I had a habit of always sitting directly behind Amma, and at this time, Amma began to rock back and forth leaning into my lap and asking, "Why do you always sit behind me?" I thought to myself, "Because I want to have you inside Amma, not just outside." Amma proceeded to tell a story about Rādhā and Kṛiṣhṇa, and after some time she stood up and left. Papettachan, an older āśhram resident, asked me if I understood Amma's story and proceeded to translate it to me.

One day, Rādhā had traveled to Dvārakā to visit Kṛiṣhṇa. Upon entering the palace inner chambers, Rādhā saw Kṛiṣhṇa and Rukmiṇī reclining on a palanquin. Kṛiṣhṇa, upon seeing Rādhā, very nonchalantly waved from his reclining position for Rādhā to enter. Rādhā, instantly heart-broken by Kṛiṣhṇa's casual attitude, left the palace at once. She decided to go to the forest to do penance. In the forest, Rādhā practiced intense sādhanā, such as standing on one foot. Finally, one day Kṛiṣhṇa appeared in front of Rādhā in the forest. Rādhā, seeing Kṛiṣhṇa, told him she was no longer fooled by his external form. Rādhā now understood his true nature existed within her. Rādhā had merged with Kṛiṣhṇa.

With this story, Amma let me know she is aware of our thoughts, wishes, and deepest desires. That experience still stands out in my mind today. Amma had transformed that dawn by the backwaters into an auspicious, intimate scene. One felt as if the backwaters were indeed the sacred river Yamuna, and the divine līlās of Kṛiṣhṇa and Rādhā became a tangible experience.

Amma had confirmed for me not to rely on her external form alone, but to strive for the internal experience of God. Amma's omniscience, omnipotence, and omnipresence blazed forth in my mind and heart. This deepened my love and faith in Amma as my guru. In fact, it is through these very divine qualities that Amma allowed me to reach her lotus feet in this lifetime.

***

I did not have an easy childhood. I struggled at home with various challenges and had to overcome many obstacles in order to move forward in life. Amma's grace was with me then as well, helping me through all the hardships I faced. Amma works in our lives, walking beside us even before we physically meet her in this life.

I struggled emotionally throughout my childhood, unable to cope with the intensity of my life's experiences. I became angry, sad, and withdrawn. Only by Amma's grace, I was able to graduate school and attend university. In my third year of university, my quest for external gratification had reached a pinnacle. I found myself often crying alone in my room, thinking, "Doesn't anyone truly love us?" It was then that I experienced the foreshadowing of Amma's arrival into my life.

A few months later in 1988, already physically, emotionally, and mentally worn out I left university and returned to New York City. Shortly thereafter, just before my twenty-first birthday, I met Amma. I was invited to a house in Spring Valley, New York where Amma was staying. When I got to the house, there were about fifteen people sitting quietly on the floor with their eyes closed. I joined and sat as well. After a short while, Amma came down the stairs as if she was floating, her figure glowing in her white dress. Suddenly, I was struck by the profundity of the moment and overcome with an inexplicable feeling.

We joined Amma outside in the backyard for meditation. I watched Amma intently until I closed my eyes. I began to shed tears spontaneously, thinking, "Why is life so complicated? Why can't we all live as brothers and sisters?"

Shortly after this, I had my first hug from Amma. I cried uncontrollably in her lap. Amma took a tissue, wiped my eyes and said, "Everything will be ok now that you've come." I fell deeply in love with Amma that day. Although I did not know anything about Amma, where she lived, or how to find her again, a door had been opened for me.

The next summer when Amma returned to the U.S., the first program of the tour was in the Hawaiian Islands where I had been living for the last several months. I felt Amma had found me once again and I joined Amma's tour that summer. After the

U.S. tour was over I felt left behind and desperate to see Amma again. I did not have money to travel to India, so I dejectedly turned to the local Brooklyn Kṛiṣhṇa temple. In just a few short weeks I found myself living on the temple premises.

Within a week of my arrival there I was asked if I would like to make the garland every morning for the Rādhā-Gōvinda mūrti. Thrilled, I did this sēvā every day and would pray ardently to Kṛiṣhṇa, "If Amma is a true master and my guru, please give me a sign."

A few weeks went by, and during a call with my grandfather he said, "I've decided to give you money to go to India." I was in shock! Only one month previously he had emphatically told me he refused to give me money for a trip to India. I also never asked him to finance me, but had only shared my desire to go. Anyway, I played it off very casually and thanked him. But when I put down the receiver, I did a little dance and thanked Kṛiṣhṇa over and over for "the sign" and the reassurance that Amma was a true master and my guru.

So in 1989, just after my twenty-second birthday, I reached the sacred soil of India. When I arrived at Amritapuri I made my way to the darśhan hut. As I stepped over the threshold Amma looked up, smiling happily and said, "You've come!" I had to look around, first over my left shoulder, and then over my right to realize that Amma was actually speaking to me! Amma had remembered me from among the thousands of people she had met. In her infinite grace, Amma welcomed me with open arms.

I had been safely keeping a box with a gift for Amma. When I approached Amma for darśhan, she opened the gift box and took out a hand-fan made of peacock feathers. Then much to my dismay, she began to fan me! Later, Amma helped me to understand that this was an expression of her equal vision, in which she sees us all as an extension of herself.

Being in India and the āśhram was a completely new world for me. The āśhram's appearance was very different then. The only tall building was the Kālī Temple and it was still being built. Most of the accommodations consisted of thatched huts, many of them situated where the main hall is today. There were daily opportunities for sand and brick sēvā, since all around the āśhram there were small lakes that surrounded the premises. Together, we would fill those lakes with sand in order to build the structures we see today. The beach opposite the āśhram was wide and expansive, conducive for meditations with Amma and solo japa walks.

I had the fortune to experience bhajans in the small Kaḷari before they moved to the main Kālī Temple. One of my favorite meditation pictures is of Amma leaning against the Kaḷari wall singing bhajans. I feel that it was such an immense grace to have caught this precious time period.

Three days a week Amma held Dēvī Bhāva in the Kālī temple. This is where for the first time, I saw Amma lick and apply her spittal to the small wounds on Dattan, a man who had suffered from an extreme case of leprosy. Dattan's old wounds appeared mostly healed from numerous darśhans with Amma. It was a deeply moving scene to witness. The way Amma gently held his head in her hands and looked into his eyes. Amma's eyes were glistening pools of unconditional love and acceptance. I had never seen a more intimate expression of divinity in my life. To me, this was a visceral, first-hand experience of Amma's unconditional love and compassion in action. To this day my limited mind and intellect cannot grasp that event fully.

During my stay I was also blessed to travel with Amma and experienced several līlās that further bonded my heart to her and deepened my inner reflection upon her divine nature.

During one Brahmasthānam program, a pūjā was performed during which devotees made symbolic offerings to the deity in clay pots. After the pūjā was completed, the devotees delivered their offerings to the inner sanctum of the temple. Amma stood in the inner sanctum, her eyes closed, and as she swayed in bliss, she poured the contents of each pot over the deity as a final offering.

After hours of Amma offering the pots in this manner, she emerged from the inner sanctum staggering in a divine, otherworldly bliss. Amma was standing just in front of me in her sari with a prayer shawl folded around her waist and tied at the neck. Suddenly, Amma removed the wet shawl she was wearing, tossed it onto me, and spontaneously sat down to give darśhan. It landed over my shoulder, and I was instantly soaked in immense bliss. I could only sit there next to Amma oblivious to everything.

After some time, I once again become aware of my surroundings, the immense, crushing crowd, and being wet and uncomfortable. Unlike Amma, who was unperturbed by her wet clothes and countless people falling into her arms one after the other. I on the other hand, could not ignore the agitation and discomfort I now felt and got up to leave. However, Amma has the ability to ignore all her own needs for the service of each one of us and the world. The example Amma sets is her greatest teaching tool.

Another experience took place while we were traveling through Tamil Nadu farmland. Amma asked the driver to stop the bus. Amma got down and walked straight into a field toward a large water pipe suspended in the air about two meters above the ground. Amma, standing in the water that flowed out from the pipe, cupped her palms and blessed each one of us by pouring water over our heads. After Amma's divine bath,

I bowed at her feet which were submerged in a few inches of water. As I knelt at her feet, a profound thought crossed my mind, "I'd like to pass from this body kneeling and kissing the Divine Mother's feet."

When I returned to the West, I struggled to keep my spiritual practices alive. I had once again fallen prey to the distractions of the world. Finally, I asked Amma how I could contribute to her world service. I felt the question itself was given to me by Amma from within. Instantaneously, Amma turned to me and said, "Because Amma is building so many hospitals and hospices, it would be good if you became a nurse." I was ecstatic and felt I finally had a divine direction in life.

In 1993 after starting my nursing prerequisites, I moved into Amma's San Ramon āśhram in California. Since then I have been fortunate to live and serve in Amma's San Ramon āśhram, AIMS Hospital, and Amritapuri for the last twenty-nine years. As someone who has struggled with learning disabilities throughout my life, becoming a nurse was not an easy task. It is in fact, a miraculous example of Amma's grace. Amma showers us with the necessary knowledge for us to succeed on this path and in this lifetime.

Time and again when I have expressed my fears about situations in life, Amma has reassured me. Once, on a Europe tour I told Amma about some negative thoughts that I had been harboring for a long time. I shared with her that sometimes I felt as if I may one day lose my mental balance. Amma lovingly replied, "This will never happen. You have Amma, the āśhram, all your āśhram sisters and brothers, and the hospital." I was so moved by Amma's love and gentle strokes on my face and arm as she spoke. Amma's words sank deeply into me, healing my heart. As Amma said the last word 'hospital,' I laughed out loud, because for a brief moment I thought Amma was implying that if things ever got really bad, I could at least be admitted to the hospital. Then I realized, "Oh wait, Amma meant that my nursing sēvā at the hospital would support me as well."

In the beginning of āśhram life I struggled a lot with my vāsanās and desires to experience worldly life. Daily I did my sādhanā and sēvā, but my mind was immersed in worldly thoughts. One day, I shared this struggle with Amma. Amma told me, "In life, like in a car, you travel along thinking you are on the highway, unaware that you have actually exited onto the side road." This advice helped me reflect on the ways I had gone off-track in my inner focus. Through Amma's supportive examples, she is able to guide us back to the superhighway. All we need to do is to hold on to her feet as tightly as we can.

Another time when speaking with Amma about the wrestling match going on in my mind, Amma said, "We enter the river to take a bath, but we don't stay in the water after we are done. In this way, we need to live in the world but not indulge in the world. We need to use discrimination in our thoughts, words and actions." I reflected upon what Amma said and came to the conclusion that I had no idea what real discrimination meant. I am still contemplating and refining this teaching within myself.

Yet another time while speaking to Amma, I asked for vivēka and vairāgya. Amma said, "You have the wrong idea of renunciation. Real renunciation is an offering of each breath, in every moment, to the divine." I pray that we can each develop this true spirit of renunciation.

Amma, you are the eminence from which all things come. May we forever be surrendered to your divine lotus feet. May we offer our every thought, word, and action unto thee. Help us to strive for enlightenment and teach us the true meaning of renunciation.

Glossary

abhiṣhēka: ceremonial bath, usually given to deities in a temple.

achanmār: plural form of *achan*, meaning 'fathers' in Malayalam.

Ādi Śhaṅkarāchārya: saint revered as a Guru and chief proponent of the *advaita* (non-dual) philosophy.

advaita: 'not two;' non-dual philosophy that holds that the *jīva* (individual soul) and *jagat* (universe) are essentially one with *brahman*, the supreme reality.

advaitic: pertaining to *advaita*.

AIMS Hospital: Amrita Institute of Medical Sciences, a super-specialty hospital in Kochi, Kerala.

amma: Malayalam word for 'mother.'

ammamār: Malayalam word for 'mothers.'

Amrita Yoga: holistic approach to *yōga* developed under the guidance of Amma emphasizing integration of physical, mental, and spiritual aspects of wellbeing.

Amritanandamayi: the name by which Amma is universally known. *Amṛitānandamayī* means 'full of immortal bliss.'

Amritapuri: the international headquarters of Mata Amritanandamayi Math, located at Amma's birthplace in Kerala, India.

Aṅgulimāla: 'finger garland.' The epithet of a brigand who cut off fingers from his victims and strung them in a garland that he wore. He underwent a transformation upon meeting the Buddha.

ārati: a traditional ritual involving the waving of a lighted lamp to the Guru or deity usually done towards the end of *pūjā* or worship. At some of Amma's programs, multiple devotees take turns waving the lighted lamp to Amma as she showers them with flower petals and the ārati song is sung.

archana: chanting of the 108 or 1,000 names of a particular deity (e.g. *'Lalitā Sahasranāma'*).

Arjuna: great archer and one of the heroes of the *Mahābhārata*. It is Arjuna whom Kṛiṣhṇa addresses in the *Bhagavad Gītā*.

āśhram: 'place of striving.' A place where spiritual seekers and aspirants live or visit, in order to lead a spiritual life. It is usually the home of a spiritual master, saint or ascetic, who guides the aspirants.

asura: demon, often (though not always) depicted as evil and antagonistic towards the *dēvas* (gods).

ātmā pūjā: ceremonial worship (*pūjā*) created by Amma honoring our true self, the *ātman*.

ātmā (ātman): the true self. The essential nature of our real existence. One of the fundamental tenets of *Sanātana Dharma* is that we are not the physical body, feelings, mind, intellect, or personality. We are the eternal, pure, unblemished self.

avidyā: ignorance that is the root cause of all sorrows.

Bhagavad Gītā: 'Song of the Lord,' it consists of eighteen chapters of verses in which Lord Kṛiṣhṇa advises Arjuna. The advice is given on the battlefield of Kurukṣhētra, just before the righteous Pāṇḍavas fight the unrighteous Kauravas. It is a practical guide to overcoming crises in one's personal or social life and is the essence of Vēdic wisdom.

Bhāgavata Purāṇa: also known as *Bhāgavatam*, one of the eighteen *Purāṇas*, a devotional Sanskrit composition narrating the life, pastimes, and teachings of various incarnations of Viṣhṇu, chiefly that of Lord Kṛiṣhṇa.

bhagavatī sēvā: worship of the Goddess. One of the regular *pūjās* conducted in the *Kaḷari.*

Bhaja Gōvindam: a devotional work in Sanskrit composed by Ādi Śhaṅkarāchārya.

bhajan: devotional song or hymn in praise of God.

bhakti: devotion for God.

bhēda-buddhi: a perspective focused on differences and separation.

bhikkhu: monk, typically in Buddhist context.

bhōga: pleasure, usually sensual pleasure.

Brahma Sūtras: a central philosophic text synthesizing the teachings of the *Upaniṣhads*, also known as the *Vēdānta Sūtras.*

brahmachārī (brahmachari): celibate male disciple who practices spiritual disciplines under a guru's guidance; '*brahmachāriṇī*' is the female equivalent.

brahmacharya: celibacy. *Brahma* also means *Vēda*. So, *brahmacharya* is the stage of life in which one pursues the study of the *Vēdas* with self-discipline under the guidance of a qualified teacher.

brahman: the absolute reality, supreme being; the whole; that which encompasses and pervades everything, and is one and indivisible.

Brahmasthānam: 'abode of *brahman*.' The name of the temples Amma consecrated in various parts of India and in Mauritius. The temple shrine features a unique four-faced idol that symbolizes the unity behind the diversity of divine forms.

brahmin: also known as *brāhmaṇa*, a member of the priestly caste whose duty it is to study and teach the *Vēdas.*

Buddha: from 'budh,' meaning 'to wake up;' also, a reference to Sage Gautama Buddha, a spiritual master whose teachings form the foundation of Buddhism.

dāna: gift or offering.

darśhan: audience with a holy person or a vision of the divine. Amma's signature *darśhan* is a hug.

darśhan token: 'token' = a numbered ticket given out to devotees wanting to receive Amma's *darśhan.*

dēva: deity or god; divine being; celestial being. *Dēva* is the masculine form. The feminine equivalent is *dēvī.*

Dēvī: goddess; Divine Mother.

Dēvī Bhāva: 'the divine mood of Dēvī;' occasion when Amma reveals her oneness with the Divine Mother.

dharma: 'that which upholds (creation).' Generally refers to the harmony of the universe; a righteous code of conduct; sacred duty; or the eternal law.

dharmic: in accordance with *dharma.*

dīkṣhā: initiation. Transfer of spiritual power from the *Guru* to the disciple.

Durgā: a fierce manifestation of the Divine Mother, often depicted as wielding a number of weapons and riding a lion or tiger.

Gaṇapati Hōma: a traditional fire ritual to propitiate Lord Gaṇēśha; typically performed before beginning any new endeavor.

Gaṇeśh Chaturthī: festival honoring Lord Gaṇēśha.

Gaṇēśha: deity with an elephant head and human body, son of Lord Śhiva and Goddess Pārvatī.

Gaṅgā: most sacred river in India. Known as the Ganges river in English.

gōpī: milk maiden from Vṛindāvan. The *gōpīs* were known for their ardent devotion to Lord Kṛiṣhṇa. Their devotion exemplifies the most intense love for God.

guru: spiritual teacher.

guru bhāva: attitude of *guru* to an aspirant who expresses sincerity and yearning for spiritual instruction.

Guru Gītā: a sacred scripture consisting of the dialogue between Lord Śhiva and his consort Pārvatī on the significance of the *guru* on one's spiritual journey.

Guru Pūrṇimā: the full moon ('*pūrṇimā*') day in the Hindu month of Āṣhāḍha (June – July) in which disciples honor the guru; also, the birthday of Sage Vyāsa, compiler of the *Vēdas*, and author of the *Purāṇas, Brahma Sūtras, Mahābhārata* and the *Śhrīmad Bhāgavatam*.

Hanumān: the devoted monkey disciple and companion of Rāma and one of the key characters in the *Rāmāyaṇa*.

hōma: ancient Vēdic fire ritual in which oblations are offered to the gods by offering ghee into a consecrated fire.

IAM: Integrated Amrita Meditation Technique® is a meditation practice formulated by Amma that integrates gentle relaxation stretches with an effective and easy-to-practice breathing and concentration technique. It is based on traditional methods and designed for the time constraints of modern life.

iṣhṭa dēvatā: preferred form of divinity.

japa: repeated chanting of a *mantra*.

-ji: an honorific suffixed to names or titles to show respect.

jīvanmukta: one who is spiritually liberated while alive.

jīvātmā (jīvātman): individual soul or self. Sometimes referred to as just '*jīva*.'

Kailash (Kailāsa): Mount Kailaśh is a sacred peak in the Himālayas; abode of Śhiva and Pārvatī.

kaivalya: detachment of the soul from matter (*prakṛiti*), identification with the supreme spirit (*puruṣha*). A term denoting liberation that originates from Sāṅkhya philosophy.

Kaḷari: original small temple where Amma used to hold *Kṛiṣhṇa Bhāva* and *Dēvī Bhāva darśhans.*

Kālī: the Goddess of fearsome aspect; depicted as dark, wearing a garland of skulls, and a girdle of human hands; feminine of *kāla* (time).

Kālī Bhāva: divine mood of Kālī.

Kāḷī Temple: main temple in Amritapuri dedicated to Kāḷī.

Kali Yuga: the present dark age of materialism and ignorance (see *yuga*).

kāma: lust, or desire in general.

karma: action; mental, verbal, and physical activity; chain of effects produced by our actions.

Kollam: a town in Kerala, near the Amritapuri āśhram.

Kṛiṣhṇa: from *'kṛiṣh,'* meaning 'to draw to oneself' or 'to remove sin;' principal incarnation of Lord Viṣhṇu. He was born into a royal family but raised by foster parents, and lived as a cowherd boy in Vṛindāvan, where he was loved and worshiped by his devoted companions, the *gōpīs* (milkmaids) and *gōpas* (cowherd boys). Kṛiṣhṇa later established the city of Dvāraka. He was a friend and advisor to his cousins, the Pāṇḍavas, especially Arjuna, whom he served as charioteer during the *Mahābhārata War,* and to whom he revealed his teachings as the *Bhagavad Gītā.*

Kṛiṣhṇa Bhāva: 'the divine mood of Kṛiṣhṇa,' occasion when Amma revealed her oneness with Lord Kṛiṣhṇa.

Kṛiṣhṇa Jayantī: festival celebrating the birth of Lord Kṛiṣhṇa, also known as *Janmaṣhṭamī.*

Kumbha Mēla: a major Hindu festival occurring every three years in one of four sacred riverbank pilgrimage places in North India.

kumkum: reddish-orange powder made from turmeric and other natural substances, often applied as a dot called a 'bindi' on the forehead.

Lakṣhmaṇa: brother of Lord Rāma.

lakṣhya bōdham: focus on the goal (of liberation).

Lalitā Sahasranāma: thousand names of Śhrī Lalitā Dēvī, a form of the Goddess.

līlā: divine play.

lōkāḥ samastāḥ sukhinō bhavantu: 'May all beings in all the worlds be happy.' A prayer for universal peace and wellbeing.

Ma-Om Meditation: a meditation technique formulated by Amma, one that involves synchronizing the silent intonation of the syllables 'Mā' and 'Ōm' with the inhalation and exhalation.

Mahābhārata: ancient Indian epic that Sage Vyāsa composed, depicting the war between the righteous Pāṇḍavas and the unrighteous Kauravas.

mahātmā: 'great soul;' term used to describe one who has attained spiritual realization.

Mahiṣhāsura Mardini Stōtram: hymn in praise of the Divine Mother who slayed the buffalo demon Mahiṣhāsura.

mālā: garland; rosary, usually made of *rudrākṣha* seeds, *tulasī* wood or sandalwood beads.

Malayalam: language spoken in the Indian state of Kerala.

manōbhāva: mental attitude.

mantra: a sound, syllable, word or words of spiritual content. According to Vēdic commentators, *mantras* are revelations of *ṛiṣhis* arising from deep contemplation.

Matruvani: 'Voice of the Mother.' The *āśhram's* flagship publication dedicated to disseminating Amma's teachings and chronicling her divine mission. It is currently published in seventeen languages (including nine Indian languages).

māyā: cosmic delusion, personified as a temptress; illusion; appearance, as contrasted with reality; the creative power of the Lord.

mōkṣha: spiritual liberation, i.e. release from the cycle of births and deaths.

mūrti: image or statue representing a deity used for worship.

(Ōm) Namaḥ Śhivāya: 'Salutations to Śhiva, the auspicious one, the inner self,' a famous *mantra*; greeting used in Amma's *āśhrams.*

Nārada: wandering sage ever engaged in singing the praises of Viṣhṇu. He composed the *Nārada Bhakti Sūtras*, aphorisms on devotion.

Nārāyaṇa: another name of Viṣhṇu.

Navarātri: 'nine nights' of worship of the three aspects of the Divine Mother, as Durgā, Lakṣhmī, and Saraswatī.

nēti nēti: an Advaitic methodology of discerning between the real and the unreal by negation. Lit. 'not this, not this.'

nirvāṇa: from 'nir' ('out') and 'vāṇa' ('to blow'); complete extinction of self-will and separateness; realization of the unity of all life.

Ōm: primordial sound of the universe; the seed of creation. The cosmic sound, which can be heard in deep meditation; the

Holy Word, taught in the *Upanishads*, which signifies *Brahman*, the divine ground of existence.

Ōṇam: Kerala's biggest festival, occurring in the month of Chiṅṅam (August – September).

pāda pūjā: ceremonial washing of the feet as a form of worship.

pādukā: traditional Indian footwear like sandals that may be used in worship symbolically representing the guru's auspicious feet.

Pāṇḍavas: five sons of King Pāṇḍu, and cousins of Kṛishṇa, who are the main protagonists in the great *Mahābhārata* epic.

papadam: thin, disc-shaped, fried flatbreads made from seasoned black gram or lentil flour, usually used as accompaniment to a meal.

payasam: sweet pudding.

pīṭham: small platform; seat for the Guru; also: a center of learning and power.

poori: deep-fried flatbreads made of whole-wheat flour.

pradakṣhiṇa: circumambulating a sacred object or person, usually in a clockwise direction, as a sign of reverence and spiritual connection.

prāṇa: vital force.

prāṇāyāma: regulated breathing, breath control.

prārabdha: also known as *prārabdha karma*, the results of past actions to be experienced in this life.

prasād: blessed offering or gift from a holy person or temple, often in the form of food.

pūjā: ritualistic or ceremonial worship.

pūjārī: one who performs ritualistic or ceremonial worship. *Pūjāriṇī* is the female equivalent.

puṇya: spiritual merit.

Purāṇas: compendium of stories, including the biographies and stories of gods, saints, kings, and great people; allegories and chronicles of great historical events that aim to make the teachings of the *Vēdas* simple and available to all.

Rādhā: eternal companion of Lord Kṛiṣhṇa, *gōpī* who exemplifies the highest form of devotion.

Rāma: divine hero of the *Rāmāyaṇa*. An incarnation of Lord Viṣhṇu, he is considered the ideal man of *dharma* and virtue. 'Ram' means 'to revel;' one who revels in himself; the principle of joy within; one who gladdens the hearts of others.

Ramakrishna Paramahamsa: spiritual master (1836 – 1886) from West Bengal, hailed as the apostle of religious harmony. He generated a spiritual renaissance that continues to touch the lives of millions.

Ramana Maharshi: spiritual master (1879 – 1950) who lived in Tiruvannamalai, Tamil Nadu. He recommended self-inquiry as the path to Liberation, though he approved of a variety of paths and spiritual practices.

Rāmāyaṇa: 24,000-verse epic poem on the life and times of Lord Rāma.

Rāvaṇa: powerful demon. Viṣhṇu incarnated as Lord Rāma to kill him and thereby restore harmony to the world.

ṛiṣhi: seer to whom mantras are revealed in deep meditation. Also the authors of many scriptural texts.

rudrākṣha: a sacred seed (bead) having spiritual and medicinal value.

sādhak (sādhaka): spiritual aspirant or seeker, one dedicated to attaining the spiritual goal, one who practices *sādhanā*.

sādhanā: regimen of disciplined and dedicated spiritual practice that leads to the supreme goal of self-realization.

sādhu: a religious ascetic, mendicant (monk) or any holy person in Hinduism and Jainism who has renounced worldly life.

sākṣhī: witness, referring to the inner observer of experiences and thoughts.

samādhi: oneness with God; a state of deep, one-pointed concentration, in which all thoughts subside. The mind enters into a state of complete stillness in which only pure consciousness remains as one abides in the *ātman* or self.

saṁsāra: the cycle of birth and death; the world of plurality.

saṁskāra: imprints or impressions left on the mind as a result of past experiences, actions, and thoughts (in this birth and also in prior births). The ritualistic ceremonies performed at significant stages of life, such as birth, marriage, and death, are also called *saṁskāras.*

Sanātana Dharma: 'Eternal Way of Life,' the original and traditional name of Hinduism.

saṅgha: association; community, any number of people living together for a certain purpose (usually spiritual evolution).

saṅkalpa: divine resolve, usually used in association with *mahātmās.*

sannyāsa: a formal vow of renunciation.

sannyāsin: a person who has renounced the material world, including family, career, and other attachments, to pursue a life devoted to spiritual practice and the pursuit of enlightenment or liberation (*mōkṣha*).

Sanskrit: language of the oldest sacred text, the *Ṛig Vēda*, and the other three *Vēdas*; the language of most ancient Hindu scriptures.

saptaṛiṣhi: the famous seven sages of ancient India.

Saraswatī: goddess of learning and the arts. Also the name of a sacred river.

sari: traditional outer garment of Indian women consisting of a long, unstitched piece of cloth wrapped around the body.

sat-chit-ānanda: lit. 'existence-consciousness-bliss,' a description of the subjective experience of the Supreme.

satguru: 'true master.' All *satgurus* are *mahātmās*, but not all *mahātmās* are *satgurus*. The *satguru* is one who, while still experiencing the bliss of the self, chooses to come down to the level of ordinary people in order to help them grow spiritually.

satsang: 'communion with the supreme truth.' Also, being in the company of *mahātmās*, studying the scriptures, and listening to the enlightening talks of a mahātmā; a meeting of people to listen to and/or discuss spiritual matters; a spiritual discourse.

sēvā: selfless service, the results of which are dedicated to God.

sevite: person who performs *sēvā* (plural: *sevites*).

Sharada Devi: spiritual master (1853 – 1920) and consort of Sri Ramakrishna Paramahamsa whom devotees of Sri Ramakrishna reverentially addressed as the Holy Mother.

śhāstra: science; authoritative scriptural texts.

Śhiva: the static aspect of *Brahman* as the male principle. Worshiped as the first in the lineage of Gurus, and as the formless substratum of the universe in relationship to the creative principle, Śhakti. He is the Lord of destruction in the trinity of Brahmā (Lord of creation), Viṣhṇu (Lord of preservation), and Śhiva. Usually depicted as a monk, with his body covered in ash, snakes in his hair, wearing only a loincloth; he carries a begging bowl and a trident in his hands.

Śhivarātri: annual festival also known as *Mahā Śhivarātri*, 'the great night of Lord Shiva.'

śhlōka: scriptural verse.

Sītā: Rāma's consort. In India, she is considered to be the ideal of womanhood.

śhrī (sri): a title of respect originally meaning 'divine,' 'holy,' or 'auspicious.' In modern India, simply a respectful form of address, similar to 'Mr.' The feminine version of this modern usage is *śhrīmatī*, equivalent to 'Mrs.' or 'Ms.'

suṣhupti: deep-sleep state; one of the three states of consciousness.

sūtra: aphorism.

svarūpa: one's own form or true nature.

swāmī (swami): title of one who has taken the vow of *sannyāsa* (see *sannyāsin*); *swāminī* is the female equivalent.

tapas (tapasya): austerities, penance.

Trivēni Saṅgam: the meeting point of three sacred rivers. The most popular site is in Prayagraj (formerly known as Allahabad) where the sacred rivers Gaṅgā, Yamunā, and Saraswatī meet.

udāsīnatā: non-attachment of mind; indifference.

upanayanam: traditional sacred thread ceremony to initiate a child into Vēdic studies.

Upaniṣhad: portions of the *Vēdas* dealing with self-knowledge.

vairāgya: dispassion.

Vālmīki: sage and author of the *Rāmāyaṇa*.

Vāmana: avatar of Lord Viṣhṇu depicted as a dwarf brahmin.

vāsanā: latent tendency or subtle desire that manifests as thought, motive and action; subconscious impression gained from experience.

Vēdānta: 'end of *Vēda*.' The philosophy of the *Upaniṣhads*, the concluding part of the *Vēdas*, which holds the ultimate truth to be "one without a second." A *Vēdāntin* is a follower or practitioner of *Vēdānta*.

Vēdāntic: pertaining to *Vēdānta*.

Vēdas: the most ancient of all scriptures. Originating from God, the *Vēdas* were not composed by any human author but were 'revealed' in deep meditation to the ancient seers. These revelations came to be known as the *Vēdas*, of which there are four: *Ṛig*, *Yajur*, *Sāma* and *Atharva*.

vibhūti: holy ash; can also mean splendor or prosperity.

vidyārambham: a child's first writing ceremony. One of the rites regularly performed by Amma.

Viṣhṇu: 'all-pervader,' Lord of sustenance in the trinity of Brahmā (Lord of creation), Viṣhṇu, and Śhiva (Lord of destruction).

viśhvarūpa: divine and cosmic form of Lord Viṣhṇu.

vivēka: discrimination, especially discrimination between the permanent and the impermanent.

Vivēkachūḍāmaṇi: A Vēdantic work by Ādi Śhaṇkarāchārya.

Vyāsa: lit. 'compiler.' The name given to Sage Kṛiṣhṇa Dvaipāyana, who compiled the *Vēdas*, and therefore is often referred to as 'Vēdavyāsa.' He is also the chronicler of the *Mahābhārata* and a character in it, and author of the eighteen *Purāṇas* and the *Brahma Sūtras*.

yajña: sacred acts of worship performed with the intent of offering something to the divine. Traditionally, a *yajña* consists of oblations offered into a fire according to scriptural injunctions accompanied by the chanting of sacred *mantras*. In a broader sense, a *yajña* can also comprise an act of selflessness performed with the intention of offering something for the welfare of others.

Yama: the god of death and justice.

yōga: 'to unite.' Union with the Supreme Being. A broad term, it also refers to the various methods of practices through which one can attain oneness with the Divine. A path that leads to self-realization.

yōgī: a practitioner or an adept of *yōga*; *yoginī* is the female equivalent.

yuga: according to the Hindu worldview, the universe (from origin to dissolution) passes through a cycle made up of four *yugas* or ages. The first is *Kṛita* or *Satya Yuga*, during which *dharma* reigns in society. Each succeeding age sees the progressive decline of dharma. The second age is known as *Trēta Yuga*, the third is *Dvāpara Yuga*, and the fourth and present epoch is known as *Kali Yuga*.

Pronunciation Guide

Vowels can be short or long:

a – as 'u' in 'but' **ā** – as 'a' in 'far'

e – as 'a' in 'may' **ē** – as 'a' in 'name'

i – as 'i' in 'pin' **ī** – as 'ee' in 'meet'

o – as in 'oh' **ō** – as 'o' in 'mole'

u – as 'u' in 'push' **ū** – as 'oo' in 'hoot'

ṛi – as 'ri' in 'rim' **ṛu** – as 'ru' in Spanish 'Peru'

ḥ – pronounce: **aḥ** like 'aha,' **iḥ** like 'ihi,' **uḥ** like 'uhu,' **ēḥ** like 'ēhē,' and **ōḥ** like 'ōhō.'

Some consonants are aspirated (e.g. kh); others are not (e.g. k):

k – as 'k' in 'kite' **kh** – as 'ckh' in 'Eckhart'

g – as 'g' in 'give' **gh** – as 'g-h' in 'dig-hard'

ch – as 'ch' in 'chat' **chh** – as 'ch-h' in 'staunch-heart'

j – as 'j' in 'joy' **jh** – as 'dgeh' in 'hedgehog'

p – as 'p' in 'pine' **ph** – as 'ph' in 'up-hill'

b – as 'b' in 'bird' **bh** – as 'bh' in 'rub-hard'

Pronounced with the tip of the tongue against the teeth:

t – as 't' in 'teach' **th** – as 'th' in 'anthill'

d – as 'd' in 'door' **dh** – as 'dh' in 'madhouse'

n – as 'n' in 'night'

Retroflex sounds are produced by rolling the tongue back with the tip touching the roof of the mouth. The following examples can be used for practice:

ṭ – as 't' in 'tub'

ṭh – as 'th' in 'lighthouse'

ḍ – as 'd' in 'dove'

ḍh – as 'dh' in 'red-hot'

ṇ – as 'n' in 'naught'

ḷ – as 'l' in 'revelry'

ṣh – as 'sh' in 'shine'

zh – 'rr' in 'hurray' *(in Malayalam and Tamil)*

Other consonants:

y – as 'y' in 'yes'

r – as 'R' in Italian 'Roma'

l – as 'l' in 'like'

v – as 'v' in 'void'

śh – as 'sh' in 'shepherd'

s – as 's' in 'sun'

m – as 'm' in 'mother'

h – as 'h' in 'hot'

ṅ – as 'ng' in 'sing'

ñ – as 'ny' in 'canyon'

Double consonants:

chch – as 'tc' in 'hot chip'

jj – as 'dj' in 'red jet'

Acknowledgements

This book was prepared in the spirit of offering. Behind the scenes Barath Mani, Anita Raghavan, Rajani Menon, Veena Erickson, James Conquest, and Ramana Erickson have provided invaluable editorial support. Once again Jagannath Maas has prepared the layout with great care and Arun Raj has designed a mesmerizing cover. Swami Vidyamritananda was instrumental in crafting the extensive glossary. The unwavering guidance of Swami Jnanamritananda has been our backbone. My heartfelt gratitude to you all.

Julius Heyne

www.ingramcontent.com/pod-product-compliance
Lightning Source LLC
Chambersburg PA
CBHW071206090426
42736CB00014B/2731
* 9 7 8 1 6 8 0 3 7 9 1 3 6 *